Medieval Academy Reprints for Teaching 21

Medieval Academy Reprints for Teaching

Brian Tierney

THE CRISIS OF CHURCH AND STATE 1050–1300

published by University of Toronto Press
Toronto   Buffalo   London
in association with the Medieval Academy of America

© Medieval Academy of America 1988

ISBN 0-8020-6701-8
Reprinted 1989, 1990, 1992, 1996, 1999

First published by Prentice-Hall Inc, in 1964, in the series
Sources of Civilization in the West, Robert Lee Wolff and Crane
Brinton, General Editors, and reprinted from the 1980 paperback
reprinting with the permission of Simon and Schuster Inc.

Printed on acid-free paper

Canadian Cataloguing in Publication Data

Tierney, Brian.
  The crisis of church and state, 1050–1300

  (Medieval Academy reprints for teaching; 21)
  Reprint. First published: Englewood Cliffs, N.J.:
  Prentice-Hall, 1964.
  Includes bibliographical references.
  ISBN 0-8020-6701-8

  1. Church and state – History. 2. Popes – Temporal
  power – History. I. Medieval Academy of America.
  II. Title. III. Series.

  BV630.2.T5 1988   322′.1′0902   C89-002907-5

FOREWORD

In the mid-1960s the student of human affairs finds himself impelled to inquire into the origins of our present political and ecclesiastical arrangements. He soon discovers that the two-and-a-half centuries between the mid-eleventh and the early fourteenth saw a continuing conflict between western church and state in the field of practical politics, and heard a continuing debate between the spokesmen of the two sides, as each strove to find theoretical arguments to justify its policies or to lay claim to authority. The struggle was so momentous that one may almost view it as synonymous with the history of the period. At any rate, without an understanding of the shifting positions in the debate and of the relationship between political theory and what was actually going on, the student soon comes to feel he understands nothing.

Yet he finds the subject complicated, the centuries long, the shifts in argument and in power so subtle that they are hard to pinpoint, and many books on the subject biased or confused. He would like to consult the men of the time, to read what they said, to learn how they felt, to understand them as they tried to justify each new position, to appreciate the real arguments that often underlay the debate, to relate the debate to practical politics. But their works are hard of access even in the original Latin, the few existing translations are inadequate, the references obscure, the minds of the debaters very remote from his own.

It is to this problem that Professor Tierney so skillfully addresses himself in this book. He brings together in clearly-translated prose the key passages from the key original documents. He provides a guide to the thinking of the men of the period between 1050 and 1300 by a brief introductory review of the major arguments of the millennium before their time; so that the reader will find himself able to understand the precedents that loomed as so important for the debaters. Mr. Tierney has also written brief introductions to each series of selections, and has explained all references that seem obscure. Though unobtrusive, these introductory passages are both scholarly and objective.

Robert Lee Wolff
Professor of History
Harvard University

ACKNOWLEDGMENTS

The author wishes to thank the following for permission to quote copyrighted material:

G. Bell and Sons Ltd., for E. F. Henderson, *Select Historical Documents* (London, 1892), pp. 329-333, 365-366, 405-408, 424-425.

Burns, Oates and Washbourne Ltd., for S. Z. Ehler and J. B. Morrall, *Church and State Through the Centuries* (London, 1954), pp. 43-44, 48-49, 63-64, 77, 81, 86; Thomas Aquinas, *Summa Theologica*, trans. by Fathers of the English Dominican Province, VII (London, 1915), pp. 9-15.

Cambridge University Press, for C. H. Monro, *The Digest of Justinian*, I (Cambridge, 1904), pp. xxv-xxvi, xxxiii, 22.

Catholic University of America Press, for *Catholic Historical Review*, XXXII (1946), pp. 200-202.

The Clarendon Press, for J. B. Moyle, *The Institutes of Justinian* (3rd ed., Oxford, 1896), pp. 3-5.

Columbia University Press, for *The Correspondence of Pope Gregory VII*, trans. by E. Emerton (New York, 1932), pp. 48-49, 52-53, 87-89, 90-91, 111 113, 149-152, 166-175; *Imperial Lives and Letters of the Eleventh Century*, trans. by T. E. Mommsen and K. F. Morrison (New York, 1962), pp. 150-153; Otto of Freising, *The Deeds of Frederick Barbarossa*, trans. by C. C. Mierow (New York, 1953), pp. 146-148, 181-186, 193, 199-200; Pierre Dubois, *The Recovery of the Holy Land*, trans. by W. I. Brandt (New York, 1956), pp. 167-169, 171-174.

Constable and Co. Ltd., for L. G. Wickham Legg, *English Coronation Records* (Westminster, 1901), p. 24.

Eyre and Spottiswoode Ltd., for D. C. Douglas and G. W. Greenaway, *English Historical Documents* (London, 1953), p. 742.

Farrar, Straus & Company, Inc., for Dante, *De Monarchia*, trans. by D. Nicholl (New York, 1954), pp. 8-11.

Alfred A. Knopf Inc. and Routledge & Kegan Paul Ltd., for E. Lewis, *Medieval Political Ideas* (New York, 1954), pp. 566-574.

Oxford University Press, for H. Bettenson, *Documents of the Christian Church* (New York, 1947), pp. 141-142, 159-161.

Pontifical Institute of Mediaeval Studies, Toronto, for Thomas Aquinas, *On Kingship*, trans. by G. B. Phelan and I. T. Eschmann (Toronto, 1949), pp. 3-7, 23-24.

The Translator for Bernard of Clairvaux, *On Consideration*, trans. by A Priest of Mount Melleray, pp. 11, 17-18, 56-58, 119-121.

Unless otherwise noted, the author is responsible for translations.

ABBREVIATIONS

Ehler and Morrall,
  Church and State

S. Z. Ehler and J. B. Morrall, *Church and State Through the Centuries* (London, 1954).

Emerton, *Correspondence*

The Correspondence of Pope Gregory VII, trans. by E. Emerton (New York, 1932).

Henderson, *Documents*

E. F. Henderson, *Select Historical Documents* (London, 1892).

MGH

Monumenta Germaniae Historica.

Migne, *PL*

J. P. Migne, *Patrologia Latina.*

CONTENTS

Introduction

A study of the relationship between church and state in the Middle Ages is useful for any student who seeks to understand the Western tradition of government as a whole. That tradition is an unusual one. For century after century it has been marked by continuing tensions between religious and secular authorities and, in spite of innumerable vicissitudes and setbacks, by a persistent tendency toward the emergence of constitutional forms of government. Both characteristics were shaped in part by the experience of the medieval West in the sphere of church-state relations, an experience which also seems quite unusual when compared with developments in other civilizations.

During the period from 1050 to 1300 there took place a series of conflicts between kings and popes which merged into one another in such a fashion that we may regard them all as changing aspects of one long, continuing crisis. In the course of these conflicts far-reaching claims were put forward on behalf of both the temporal and the spiritual authorities. The distinctive character of the medieval experience did not, however, lie in the assertion of such extreme claims. We may be disconcerted by the pretensions of popes who tried to depose emperors or of emperors who expected to appoint bishops, but, in fact, a theocratic ordering of society is a very common pattern of human government. To maintain order and unity in groups larger and less homogeneous than extended family systems is a complex and difficult task. Mere force is seldom sufficient in the long run. The most common solution has been to endow the ruler who controls the physical apparatus of state coercion with a sacral role also as head and symbol of the people's religion. Primitive societies commonly attribute magical powers to their chieftains; the Pharaohs of Egypt, the Incas of Peru, the emperors of Japan were all revered as divine beings; the Roman Caesars bore the title *Pontifex Maximus*. In modern totalitarian despotisms, where the party structure provides a travesty of a church, the simultaneous control of party and state is the very essence of a dictator's authority.

We need not be surprised, then, that in the Middle Ages also there were rulers who aspired to supreme spiritual and temporal power. The truly exceptional thing is that in medieval times there were always at least two claimants to the role, each commanding a formidable apparatus

1

of government, and that for century after century neither was able to dominate the other completely, so that the duality persisted, was eventually rationalized in works of political theory and ultimately built into the structure of European society. This situation profoundly influenced the development of Western constitutionalism. The very existence of two power structures competing for men's allegiance instead of only one compelling obedience greatly enhanced the possibilities for human freedom. In practical life over and over again in the Middle Ages men found themselves having to make genuine choices according to conscience or self-interest between conflicting appeals to their loyalty. On the theoretical level, intellectuals were led to formulate detailed arguments about the deposition of tyrannical kings or popes and to define with more and more precision the due limits of their respective powers.

Like most major historical problems, the problems of church and state in the Middle Ages are complicated ones. In the period with which we are concerned, no simple chronological development led from one set of generally accepted positions to another. Extreme royalists and extreme papalists already flourished in 1050, and both points of view (along with a variety of intermediate ones) were still being vigorously asserted in 1300. The change that did take place was a steady growth in the sophistication of the arguments used to support all the different positions. It is hardly proper to speak of a conflict of church and state in the eleventh century at all, for there was then no real idea of the state, of a public authority exercising sovereign powers of legislation and taxation and administering uniform laws according to a rational system of jurisprudence. The only theoretical defense of monarchical power available was a theological one, an assertion that the emperor or pope was a minister of God on earth and so qualified to rule all the affairs of men. Accordingly papalists and imperialists alike based their discussions almost entirely on the deployment of a few selected texts from the Scriptures or the early Fathers of the church. But by 1300 the situation had changed profoundly. During the course of the twelfth century the revived study of Roman jurisprudence opened up a new world of legal thought to theorists of royal and papal power, and, in the thirteenth century, the rediscovery of Aristotle's *Politics* provided a new philosophical basis for reflections on the very nature of the state itself. By the end of our period it had become possible to construct sophisticated theories of state power which rested more on rational argumentation than on biblical exegesis. Indeed, one of the most important developments in the history of church-state relations during the Middle Ages was the re-emergence of the idea of the state itself.

Since the problems involved in understanding this process are complex ones, it is not surprising that they remain matters of controversy. We shall examine specific problems of interpretation that arise from particular documents in the Introductions to those documents in the following pages, but it may be useful to indicate here the broad issues involved in the disputes among modern scholars.

One school of thought maintains that for a thousand years before 1300 the whole thrust of Catholic Christianity as expounded by the popes was toward the establishment of a papal monarchy directing all the spiritual and temporal affairs of Christendom. In this view, the growth of sovereign secular states in the fourteenth century simply reflects a failure of the popes to achieve their traditional objective. The popes failed on the intellectual level, it would be argued, because they were unable to assimilate into the framework of traditional Christian political theory the essentially pagan concepts of the Roman lawyers and of Aristotle. They failed on the level of power politics because in the end they could not match the financial or military or even the propaganda resources of the fourteenth-century national kings.

A second school of historians maintains, in a quite contrary fashion, that the Christian religion from its very beginnings recognized the need for a dualistic organization of society, for a due discrimination between the spheres of church and state, and that medieval popes never lost sight of this principle even in the heat of all their conflicts with emperors and kings. In this view, the emergence of autonomous secular states was entirely in accordance with a time-honored Christian doctrine that the popes themselves had helped to maintain through the centuries.

Yet a third group of scholars would argue that the dualistic theory was indeed more in accordance with the traditional thinking of the church and the papacy, but that certain popes of the Middle Ages abandoned this old tradition and did for a time commit the Roman see to a theory of papal theocracy. Some scholars see this development in the pontificate of Gregory VII (1073-85). Others would place it in the reign of Innocent III (1198-1216), of Innocent IV (1243-54), or of Boniface VIII (1294-1303). In any case, they would argue, the policy failed because by the end of the thirteenth century the popes were upholding a political theory which was essentially an aberration from an older and sounder tradition of the church that still commanded the support of most of the people of Europe.

This book aims to provide a sufficiently adequate selection of documents in translation to permit a student to form his own judgment about such questions. The reader should bear in mind throughout that he cannot come to understand the development of church-state relations in the Middle Ages unless he views this development against the background of a constantly growing and changing conception of the state itself. He should also note that many of the most subtle and interesting ideas provoked by the clashes of ecclesiastical and secular authority were not concerned directly with the relatively simple and straightforward question of whether emperors could depose popes or popes emperors.

Underlying the overt political issues was a constant preoccupation with the essentially theological problem of defining the right relationship between spiritual power and the temporal order as such, understood as the whole of material creation. Christ and the apostles had been poor in material possessions. The medieval church was rich—too rich, many thought. Secular rulers often tried to gain control of the church's wealth in order to use it for their own political ends; among the defenders of the ecclesiastical power there was no simple, agreed response to the threat. Concern over the whole situation stimulated an incessant debate about the right to own and control ecclesiastical property, an issue which eventually came to be of great importance in the growth of medieval political theory.

In the medieval conflicts which were overtly political it is quite clear that some pontiffs put forward extreme claims to temporal power, but it is by no means certain why the popes thought they possessed all the various rights that they asserted, and it is this uncertainty that has given rise to nearly all the modern controversies. The problem is not so much to measure the extent of papal (or royal) claims as to understand the ideologies that lay behind them. The demands that the popes put forward could certainly have been based on a starkly simple theocratic doctrine maintaining that the Roman pontiff, as God's vicar, possessed a direct political authority over all men and all their affairs. The difficulties of interpretation arise from the fact that many—perhaps all—of the papal claims could also have been deduced from a quite different theory, from a doctrine of "indirect" power.

Any religious leader with wide popular support is in a position to exercise some influence on the course of temporal affairs. During the present century we have seen spokesmen for religious groups intervene with more or less success in political controversies involving issues as diverse as Prohibition, education, and civil rights. In the Middle Ages, when virtually all the peoples of Europe were members of one united church and ecclesiastical institutions enjoyed a correspondingly high prestige, the repercussions of such interventions could be dramatic indeed. If a pope excommunicated a king for some scandalously sinful behavior, the king's subjects might well refuse to be ruled by such a man, rise in rebellion against him, and bring about his deposition, all with the pope's approval. The end result would be much the same as if the pope had simply declared that he was the overlord of all temporal rulers and could depose them at will, but the papal intervention would actually have been based on a different principle: on the right and duty of a spiritual pastor to rebuke any erring member of his flock.

There is one final complication. Sometimes a pope could claim direct temporal lordship over a particular territory without relying on any general theory of papal world-monarchy. Over the course of the centuries many kings and dukes—among them the rulers of Sicily, Sardinia, Corsica, Aragon, Hungary, and Dalmatia—found it advantageous to acknowledge the pope as a feudal overlord in return for papal recognition or protection. There was also a generally accepted though erroneous belief that in the fourth century A.D. the Roman emperor Constantine had endowed the papacy with extensive rights of secular government in the territories of the Western empire. The problem, then, for the historian who seeks to understand the ideology of the medieval papacy is not only to determine whether the popes claimed a "direct" or merely an "indirect" power in any particular case but also, if it seems that direct power was asserted, to decide whether the claim was based on a general theory of papal theocracy or on a specific grant made by some secular ruler in the past. Often we shall find that the most important papal documents wove together particular historical precedents with general theoretical principles in a fashion that makes it very difficult to disentangle the two threads of argument.

For a modern student of the Middle Ages it is a fascinating task to analyze this constant interplay of theory and fact. By doing so we can learn to understand how the heritage of the past and the actual circumstances of their own age impelled popes and kings to take up particular theoretical positions, and how the ideas they expounded reacted in turn on the future world of events.

Part I

THE FIRST
THOUSAND YEARS

1. The Church &
the Roman State

Before turning to the great clashes of spiritual and secular power that occurred between 1050 and 1300 we must first consider some of the documents from the early centuries of the church that were most frequently quoted by the writers of the medieval period.

The possibility of a continuing tension between church and state was inherent in the very beginnings of the Christian religion. Most often, as a society grows from primitive tribalism into an ordered civilization, a common religion permeates all its activities and helps to form all its characteristic institutions. The rise of medieval Islam provides a typical example. In such circumstances the creation of political institutions quite separate from the organization of the accepted religion seems hardly conceivable. Christianity, on the other hand, irrupted into an ancient civilization that already had its own established hierarchy of government and its own sophisticated tradition of political thought based on non-Christian concepts. In the early centuries, therefore, the Christian church had to develop its own structure of governing offices, sometimes parallel to but always apart from those of the secular hierarchy, and from the first there was always the possibility of a conflict of loyalties.

Moreover, the distinction between the secular and religious orders of government inherent in this situation found expression in the earliest sacred writings of Christianity, which provided the starting point for all medieval discussions on problems of church and state. There could be little likelihood of a simple, straightforward identification of spiritual with temporal authority in the religion of a Founder who had said:

7

"Render therefore to Caesar the things that are Caesar's: and to God the things that are God's" (Luke 20:25). Christ himself claimed to be a king, but he added that his kingdom was not of this world (John 18:36). Most important of all for the future controversies, he said to his disciple Peter: "I will give to thee the keys of the kingdom of heaven. And whatsoever thou shalt bind upon earth it shall be bound also in heaven" (Matthew 16:19)—without, however, explaining how this apparently unlimited power to "bind and loose" was to be applied to the political activities of secular rulers. It was taken for granted by all the medieval controversialists whom we shall consider that the powers originally conferred on Peter by Christ were transmitted to Peter's successors in the see of Rome. They disagreed profoundly, however, about the extent of those powers and especially about their applicability to the sphere of temporal government. Peter himself said, "Fear God. Honour the king" (1 Peter 2:17), and then again, "We ought to obey God rather than men" (Acts 5:29). St. Paul provided the classical text in favor of submission to civil authority as a Christian duty when he wrote, "There is no power but from God: and those that are, are ordained of God" (Romans 13:1). But he also rebuked for their lack of true wisdom "the princes of this world that come to nought" (1 Corinthians 2:6).

The genuine difficulties of unraveling the political concepts inherent in New Testament terminology (which continue to perplex modern theologians) were complicated for medieval commentators by their habit of seeing political allegories in passages that probably had no such significance when they were first written. The most famous such text is Luke 22:38: "But they said, 'Lord, behold, here are two swords.' And he said to them, 'It is enough.'" From the eleventh century onward it became very usual to regard the "two swords" as symbols of spiritual and temporal power, and a whole inverted pyramid of political fantasy was erected on the slender basis of this one verse of Scripture.

For the first generations of Christians the problem of church and state as later ages would know it could not exist at all, for as long as the Roman empire remained pagan, the church could hope for nothing from the state except, at best, freedom from persecution. The whole situation was transformed, however, by the conversion of the emperor Constantine in the fourth century and the subsequent spread of Christianity as the official religion of the Roman empire. The church had found a new champion. The crucial question that arose at once was whether she had found a new master too. The emperors of the fourth century were men of autocratic disposition, and they expected everyone, including the leaders of the church, to obey them. There were no real precedents for deciding where the bishops' authority began and where the emperor's ended or if, indeed, any limits at all could be set to the imperial power.

The future course of events was profoundly influenced by Constantine's decision to move his imperial capital from Rome to Constantinople

(A.D. 330), for, almost from the first founding of the new city there was a perceptible divergence between the ecclesiastical tradition of this new Rome in the East and that of the old Rome on the Tiber. Overshadowed by the splendor of the imperial court, protected (and if necessary coerced) by the imperial armies, the prelates of Constantinople tended to accept the claims of the emperors to control the church and to decide any disputes that arose in the ecclesiastical sphere. In the West the gradual disintegration of all effective imperial authority made possible the growth of a quite different tradition, and by the end of the fourth century it had already found its first great spokesman in St. Ambrose, bishop of Milan.

To the allegation that everything was subject to the power of the emperor, Ambrose replied that divine things were not so subject and added, "Palaces belong to the emperor, churches to the priesthood." In response to a summons to appear before the imperial council he declared, "Where matters of faith are concerned it is the custom for bishops to judge Christian emperors, not for Emperors to judge bishops," and again, "The emperor is within the Church, not above the church." In 390 Ambrose went so far as to excommunicate the emperor Theodosius himself, and Theodosius eventually acknowledged his faults and performed a public penance in the cathedral at Milan before being readmitted to communion. Medieval popes liked to remember the episode when they found themselves embroiled in controversies with the emperors of a later age.

The most profound theological inquiry into the intrinsic nature of the political order undertaken during the early period of the church was that of Ambrose's great pupil, St. Augustine, who wrote at the beginning of the fifth century during the first great wave of barbarian incursions into the Western empire. He described two societies competing for men's allegiance through the centuries: a City of God and a City of World. The City of God was the community of those who loved God and who would therefore find their final home in heaven; the City of the World was the community of those whose hearts were set solely on worldly things (No. 1). Augustine did not clearly identify the organized church with his City of God or the organized state with his City of the World, though that meaning suggested itself to some later interpreters of his thought. He did maintain that all subjection of man to man had been brought about by human sin and that, accordingly, the very existence of civil governments with coercive powers represented a departure from an earlier ideal order of things. Similarly, he maintained that the whole existing structure of property rights was a mere contrivance of imperial law made necessary by man's wickedness and greed (No. 2). Augustine did not, however, condemn the state. On the contrary: he thought that, precisely because so many men were in fact sinners, because they would rob and rape and murder unless they were restrained, there had to be governments with police power, and that it was in accordance with God's providence for such governments to arise. The members of the City of God might indeed find some advantage in the civil order that worldly government maintained. But the state and its laws could never have the highest claim on the loyalty of a true Christian. He was a pilgrim and wayfarer on this earth, and his only necessary permanent allegiance was to the heavenly city.

St. Augustine's theology (often misunderstood) exercised a pervasive influence on the climate of Christian political thought at least until the end of the thirteenth century. The widespread acceptance of his view that the state was rooted in human sinfulness impeded for centuries the development of any adequate theory of the intrinsic dignity and excellence of the temporal power as an answer to prelates who regarded themselves as the only true spokesmen for the City of God. At the same time, Augustine's argument that all property rights were derived from imperial law was often used on behalf of secular rulers in the course of their conflicts with the church.

At the end of the fifth century Pope Gelasius (492-96) attempted to define more explicitly than Augustine had done the relationship of priestly to royal power. In a letter to the Eastern emperor Anastasius he declared: "Two there are, august emperor, by which this world is chiefly ruled, the sacred authority of the priesthood and the royal power. Of these the responsibility of the priests is more weighty in so far as they will answer for the kings of men themselves at the divine judgement" (*No. 3*). In the controversies of the Middle Ages this pronouncement appears over and over again, both to support papal claims and to oppose them, both to defend royal autonomy and to assert papal superiority. Its interpretation remains a matter of dispute among modern scholars as well. On the face of it the letter provides a clear statement of a balanced dualism, since it postulates the necessity for *two* governing powers in the world, but a closer scrutiny shows that the pope's terminology can lend itself readily enough to other interpretations. The problem is not only that Gelasius attributed a heavier burden of responsibility to the priesthood than to the kingship but also that he chose to designate the role of the priests by the term "authority" (*auctoritas*) and the role of the prince by the term "power" (*potestas*). Erich Caspar has argued that the word *potestas* implied a real sovereign power backed by effective force, the word *auctoritas* a merely moral authority. This reading makes the pope's statement quite consistent with the position of the Byzantine emperors themselves. Other scholars (most recently Walter Ullmann) have pointed out that in the language of Roman law, with which Gelasius was certainly familiar, *auctoritas* could mean an inherent right to rule and *potestas* only a delegated executive power to carry out instructions. On this interpretation Gelasius's letter becomes an early statement of papal theocracy. Still others have held that the words *auc-*

toritas and *potestas* were used as synonyms and that Gelasius's variation of terminology was simply a rhetorical device of no great significance, adopted to avoid an inelegant repetition.[1] It seems unlikely that this question will ever be resolved on merely philological grounds. Technical arguments can be adduced in favor of all the different positions. The reader can therefore best form a judgment on Gelasius's real meaning by considering his much-quoted aphorism in the context of the whole paragraph in which it occurs and also in the light of Gelasius's other major pronouncement on spiritual and temporal power, presented in his treatise *On the Bond of Anathema* (*No.* 4).

Augustine: The Two Cities

1. *The City of God* (413-426), Book XIX, trans. Marcus Dods, *The Works of Augustinus Aurelianus*, I (Edinburgh, 1871), pp. 323-24, 326-28.

Chapter 15. Of the liberty proper to man's nature, and the servitude introduced by sin. . . .

This is prescribed by the order of nature: it is thus that God has created man. For "let them," He says, "have dominion over the fish of the sea, and over the fowl of the air, and over every creeping thing which creepeth on the earth." (Genesis 1:26). He did not intend that His rational creature, who was made in His image, should have dominion over anything but the irrational creation—not man over man, but man over the beasts. And hence the righteous men in primitive times were made shepherds of cattle rather than kings of men, God intending thus to teach us what the relative position of the creatures is, and what the desert of sin; for it is with justice, we believe, that the condition of slavery is the result of sin. . . .

Chapter 17. What produces peace, and what discord, between the heavenly and earthly cities.

But the families which do not live by faith seek their peace in the earthly advantages of this life; while the families which live by faith look for those eternal blessings which are promised, and use as pilgrims such advantages of time and of earth as do not fascinate and divert them from God, but rather aid them to endure with greater ease, and to keep

---

[1] E. Caspar, *Geschichte des Papsttums*, II (Tübingen, 1933), pp. 65-71, 753-55; W. Ullmann, *The Growth of Papal Government* (London, 1955), pp. 14-28. A. K. Ziegler defended the third point of view mentioned above and also reviewed the earlier literature on the subject in his article, "Pope Gelasius I and His Teaching on the Relation of Church and State," *Catholic Historical Review*, XXVII (1942), pp. 412-37.

down the number of those burdens of the corruptible body which weigh upon the soul. Thus the things necessary for this mortal life are used by both kinds of men and families alike, but each has its own peculiar and widely different aim in using them. The earthly city, which does not live by faith, seeks an earthly peace, and the end it proposes, in the well-ordered concord of civic obedience and rule, is the combination of men's wills to attain the things which are helpful to this life. The heavenly city, or rather the part of it which sojourns on earth and lives by faith, makes use of this peace only because it must, until this mortal condition which necessitates it shall pass away. Consequently, so long as it lives like a captive and a stranger in the earthly city, though it has already received the promise of redemption, and the gift of the Spirit as the earnest of it, it makes no scruple to obey the laws of the earthly city, whereby the things necessary for the maintenance of this mortal life are administered; and thus, as this life is common to both cities, so there is a harmony between them in regard to what belongs to it. But, as the earthly city has had some philosophers whose doctrine is condemned by the divine teaching . . . it has come to pass that the two cities could not have common laws of religion, and that the heavenly city has been compelled in this matter to dissent, and to become obnoxious to those who think differently, and to stand the brunt of their anger and hatred and persecutions, except in so far as the minds of their enemies have been alarmed by the multitude of the Christians and quelled by the manifest protection of God accorded to them. This heavenly city, then, while it sojourns on earth, calls citizens out of all nations, and gathers together a society of pilgrims of all languages, not scrupling about diversities in the manners, laws, and institutions whereby earthly peace is secured and maintained, but recognizing that, however various these are, they all tend to one and the same end of earthly peace. It therefore is so far from rescinding and abolishing these diversities, that it even preserves and adopts them, so long only as no hindrance to the worship of the one supreme and true God is thus introduced. Even the heavenly city, therefore, while in its state of pilgrimage, avails itself of the peace of earth, and, so far as it can without injuring faith and godliness, desires and maintains a common agreement among men regarding the acquisition of the necessaries of life, and makes this earthly peace bear upon the peace of heaven; for this alone can be truly called and esteemed the peace of the reasonable creatures, consisting as it does in the perfectly ordered and harmonious enjoyment of God and of one another in God. When we shall have reached that peace, this mortal life shall give place to one that is eternal, and our body shall be no more this animal body which by its corruption weighs down the soul, but a spiritual body feeling no want, and in all its members subjected to the will. In its pilgrim state the heavenly city possesses this peace by faith; and by this faith it lives righteously when it refers to the attainment of that peace every good action towards God and man; for the life of the city is a social life.

2. On property. *In Joannis Evangelium, Tractatus VI* (413), ed. J. P. Migne, *Patrologia Latina* 35 (Paris, 1845) col. 1437. (Hereinafter cited as *PL*.)
(In this passage Augustine was arguing against the leaders of the Donatist sect who had complained about the confiscation of their estates by the emperor.)

Does not any man possess what he possesses by human law? For according to divine law, "The earth is the Lord's and the fulness thereof" (Psalm 23:1). Poor and rich God made from one clay and the one earth supports poor and rich alike. But by human law a man says, "This estate is mine; this house is mine; this slave is mine." By human law and therefore by the law of the emperors. Why? Because God distributed these human laws to the human race through the emperors and kings of the world. Do you want us to read the laws of the emperors and litigate according to them about the estates? If you claim to possess according to human law then let us recite the laws of the emperors. Let us see if they would have heretics possess anything. "But," you say, "what is the emperor to me?" You possess your lands according to his law. But take away the laws of the emperor and who will dare say, "That estate is mine" or "That slave is mine" or "This house is mine."

Gelasius I: Priesthood and Kingship

3. Letter to the emperor Anastasius (494), ed. E. Schwartz, *Publizistische Sammlungen zum Acacianischen Schisma* ("Abhandlungen der Bayerischen Akademie der Wissenschaften, Philosophisch-Historische Abteilung," Neue Folge X; Munich, 1934), pp. 20-21.

. . . Two there are, august emperor, by which this world is chiefly ruled, the sacred authority [*auctoritas*] of the priesthood and the royal power [*potestas*]. Of these the responsibility of the priests is more weighty in so far as they will answer for the kings of men themselves at the divine judgement. You know, most clement son, that, although you take precedence over all mankind in dignity, nevertheless you piously bow the neck to those who have charge of divine affairs and seek from them the means of your salvation, and hence you realize that, in the order of religion, in matters concerning the reception and right administration of the heavenly sacraments, you ought to submit yourself rather than rule, and that in these matters you should depend on their judgement rather than seek to bend them to your will. For if the bishops themselves, recognizing that the imperial office was conferred on you by divine disposition, obey your laws so far as the sphere of public order is concerned lest they seem to obstruct your decrees in mundane matters, with what zeal, I ask you, ought you to obey those who have been charged with administering the sacred mysteries? Moreover, just as no light risk attends pontiffs who keep silent in matters concerning the service of God, so too no little danger threatens those who show scorn—which God forbid—when they ought to obey. And if the hearts of the faithful should be submitted to all priests in general who rightly administer divine things, how much more should assent be given to the bishop of that see which the Most High wished to be pre-eminent over all priests, and which the devotion of the whole church has honored ever since. As Your Piety is certainly well aware, no one can ever raise himself by purely human means to the privilege and place of him whom the voice of Christ has set before all, whom the church has always venerated and held in devotion as its primate. The things which are established by divine judgement can be assailed by human presumption; they cannot be overthrown by anyone's power.

> 4. On the bond of anathema (c. 496), ed. E. Schwartz, *op. cit.*, p. 14.

. . . It happened before the coming of Christ that certain men, though still engaged in carnal activities, were symbolically both kings and priests, and sacred history tells us that Melchisedek was such a one (*cf.* Genesis 14:18). The Devil also imitated this among his own people, for he always strives in a spirit of tyranny to claim for himself what pertains to divine worship, and so pagan emperors were called supreme pontiffs. But when He came who was true king and true priest, the emperor no longer assumed the title of priest, nor did the priest claim the royal dignity—though the members of Him who was true king and true priest, through participation in his nature, may be said to have received both qualities in their sacred nobility so that they constitute a race at once royal and priestly. For Christ, mindful of human frailty, regulated with an excellent disposition what pertained to the salvation of his people. Thus he distinguished between the offices of both powers according to their own proper activities and separate dignities, wanting his people to be saved by healthful humility and not carried away again by human pride, so that Christian emperors would need priests for attaining eternal life and priests would avail themselves of imperial regulations in the conduct of temporal affairs. In this fashion spiritual activity would be set apart from worldly encroachments and the "soldier of God"

(2 Timothy 2:4) would not be involved in secular affairs, while on the other hand he who was involved in secular affairs would not seem to preside over divine matters. Thus the humility of each order would be preserved, neither being exalted by the subservience of the other, and each profession would be especially fitted for its appropriate functions.

Justinian: An Imperial View

4a. Novella VI (535), ed R. Schoell, *Corpus Iuris Civilis, III (Novellae)* (Berlin, 1895). (This decree of the emperor Justinian introduced a body of legislation regulating the conduct of bishops and clergy.)

The greatest gifts given by God to men from his heavenly clemency are priesthood and empire (*sacerdotium et imperium*). The former serves divine things, the latter rules human affairs and has care of them. Both proceed from one and the same source and provide for human life. Therefore nothing shall so preoccupy emperors as the moral wellbeing of priests, since priests pray constantly to God for the emperors themselves. For, if the priesthood is everywhere blameless and filled with faith in God and the imperial authority orders rightly and efficiently the commonwealth committed to it, a good harmonious relationship will exist, providing whatever is useful for the human race. We, therefore, exercise the greatest care concerning the true doctrines of God and the moral wellbeing of priests through which, if they preserve it, the greatest gifts of God shall be bestowed on us and we shall both hold firmly what we have and acquire what we have not yet received. Now all things are conducted well and properly if a foundation is established which is fitting and pleasing to God. This, we believe, will come about if care is taken for the observance of the sacred rules which the venerable and justly praised apostles handed down as witnesses and ministers of the word of God, and the holy fathers preserved and expounded.

2. The Popes &
the Frankish Monarchy

In the centuries after Gelasius the role of the papacy in temporal affairs was profoundly modified by the total breakdown of Roman imperial authority in the West. England fell to the Angles and Saxons, Gaul to the Franks, Spain to the Visigoths. In Italy itself a brief period of imperial reconquest—directed from Constantinople by the emperor Justinian (527-65)—was ended in 568 by the invasion of the Lombards, the last of the Teutonic peoples to ravage Italy. Thereafter the Byzantine emperors retained control only of south Italy, Sicily, and a few coastal strongholds like Ravenna. This situation produced two results of the greatest importance for the future development of church-state relations. First the popes emerged as temporal governors of Rome and the surrounding region. Then they abandoned their old allegiance to the Byzantine emperors and formed a new alliance with the Frankish kings that led eventually to the creation of a new empire in the West under papal auspices.

Papal sovereignty over central Italy came into existence legitimately enough. It was essentially a question of filling a vacuum of power. Already in 451, when the Huns threatened Rome, Pope Leo was among the leaders of the city who rode out to meet them and who negotiated on behalf of the people. By the time of Gregory I (590-604) the pope was clearly *de facto* ruler of the city. However, it never occurred to Gregory I to repudiate the *de iure* sovereignty of the emperor at Constantinople. Not until the middle of the eighth century, when the Eastern emperor had set himself up as patron of a new heresy—iconoclasm—and the Lombards were threatening Rome once more, did the popes contemplate a radical shift of alliances. In 727 Pope Gregory II (715-31) wrote to the emperor Leo III in a new spirit of defiance (*No.* 5). In 742 the great missionary bishop St. Boniface was sent to France as papal legate, and from that time onward more frequent communication between the Frankish monarchy and the Roman see was maintained. A few years later an anomaly peculiar to the Frankish constitution led to a most important rapprochement between the two courts. For several generations the nominal kings of the Franks had been degenerate nonentities, and all real

16

power had passed into the hands of the principal officer of the royal household, known as the mayor of the palace. In 751 the mayor of the palace, Pepin, determined to seize the kingship for himself and to establish a new dynasty. Eager to obtain the highest possible sanction for his action, he sent an embassy to the pope asking for guidance on the moral issue involved. Was it proper, Pepin innocently inquired, for a man who bore none of the responsibilities of kingship to hold the title of king? The pope, certainly well aware of all that was at stake, gave the desired answer that this was indeed not fitting. On receiving the pope's reply Pepin announced the deposition of King Childeric, obtained the approval of the Frankish nobility, and was duly crowned king by St. Boniface (*No.* 6).

Almost at once the papacy had occasion to seek the help of its new ally, for in 753 the Lombards again threatened Rome. Pope Stephen appealed to Pepin; the king agreed to invade Italy and, most important of all, promised to "return" to the Roman see the lands that he proposed to conquer from the Lombards. That promise was duly fulfilled in 756, and from that year we can date the beginning of a formal papal claim to sovereignty in central Italy (*No.* 7). The popes must have known, however, that their title was insecure so long as it was not recognized by the imperial authorities at Constantinople and, moreover, that the emperors there would never willingly acknowledge it. The only real hope of establishing beyond doubt the legitimacy of the papal claim lay in the institution of a new Roman emperor in the West on whom the popes could rely as a friend and protector. It was probably this factor more than any other which led to the dramatic climax of the Frankish-papal alliance: the coronation of Pepin's son Charlemagne as emperor of the Romans in St. Peter's church at Rome on Christmas Day, A.D. 800. Charlemagne, who by then had already proved himself one of the greatest conquerors in Western history, went to Rome in that year to settle the affairs of the city where a dissident faction had attacked the pope, Leo III, and then accused him of various crimes. At a synod held on December 23 the pope was allowed to clear himself of these charges by taking an oath declaring his innocence. On December 25 Charlemagne went to Mass at St. Peter's. As he rose from prayer Pope Leo III placed a crown on his head, and the congregation, evidently well-drilled beforehand, broke into the ritual acclamations that greeted the accession of a new emperor: "To Charles, most pious Augustus . . . life and victory."

Contemporary sources disagree about Charlemagne's attitude to his new dignity. The Annals of Lorsch record that Charles had agreed to accept the imperial title at the synod of December 23 (*No.* 9), but Charlemagne's biographer Einhard declares that the emperor was so displeased after the ceremony that he declared he would never have entered the church even on such a great feast day if he had known beforehand of the pope's intention (*No.* 11). Perhaps Charlemagne had expected to be hailed as emperor but was angered by the pope's interposition of a novel rite of coronation into the ancient ceremony of acclamation. If this was the case, Charlemagne had reason for his displeasure—better reason than he could have known at the time. There was no historical justification for any participation by the pope in the creation of a new emperor; acclamation by the people was the constitutive act. But by one brilliant gesture Pope Leo established the precedent, adhered to throughout the Middle Ages, that papal coronation was essential to the making of an emperor, and thereby implanted the germ of the later idea that the empire itself was a gift to be bestowed by the papacy.

Indeed all the events of the years 750-800 that we have mentioned acquired a heightened significance in the controversies of later centuries. The episode of King Childeric's deposition, for instance, can be traced from the original account in the Frankish Royal Annals (*No.* 6) to a crucial papal letter of the investiture contest (*No.* 36); from there to Gratian's *Decretum*, the greatest canon law collection of the twelfth century (*No.* 62); and from there again to the canonical commentaries of the twelfth and thirteenth centuries, where it became the basis of a whole theory, or rather of two competing theories, concerning the relationship of spiritual to temporal power.

It was also most probably between 750 and 800 that some enterprising cleric of the Roman curia produced the most famous forgery of the early Middle Ages, the so-called Donation of Constantine. Its drafter must have hoped that it would establish beyond all doubt and for all time the legality of the pope's claim to central Italy, for the Donation purported to be a charter of the first Christian emperor, Constantine, bestowing on the contemporary pope, Sylvester, rule over Rome and its possessions in the West on the occasion of the emperor's withdrawal to his new Eastern capital of Constantinople (*No.* 8). The story was not entirely a fabrication of the eighth century. In the days of Pepin and Pope Stephen there was current in Rome a legend telling how Pope Sylvester not only baptized Constantine but also miraculously cured him of leprosy, and how Constantine in gratitude relinquished his rule over Rome to the pope. This legend, which can be traced back to the fifth century, inspired the forged Donation. There is no reason to doubt that by the middle of the eighth century the popes themselves were entirely convinced of their right to rule Rome, and, as we have observed, the papal government had in fact come into existence in a sufficiently legitimate fashion—as much so certainly as that of any other European state. Moreover, the political situation that developed at Rome was not altogether unique. In many cities of the Western empire during the tumult of the Germanic invasions the people turned to their bishop as a governor, judge, and protector, and throughout the Middle Ages there were prince-bishops who exercised both spiritual and temporal authority over their subjects as the pope did over the Romans. The great difference was that the pope's city was the capital of the old Roman empire. Whoever succeeded to its rule might be tempted to claim all the universal authority of the ancient Caesars, and for later popes the temptation was increased by the vague and far-reaching claims embodied in the Donation of Constantine. Indeed, from the eighth century onward the essentially political claim of the popes to be rightful rulers of Rome came to be increasingly confused with an essentially theological claim that they were overlords of all Christian kings by virtue of their supreme spiritual office.

The Breach with Byzantium

5. Gregory II, letter to the emperor Leo III (727), ed. J. D. Mansi, *Sacrorum Conciliorum Nova et Amplissima Collectio*, XII (Florence, 1766), col. 968-73.

. . . You know that the dogmas of holy church are not the concern of emperors but of pontiffs, who ought to teach securely. The pontiffs who preside over the church do not meddle in affairs of state, and likewise the emperors ought not to meddle in ecclesiastical affairs, but to administer the things committed to them. . . .

The Lombards and Sarmatians and others who live in the north have attacked the wretched Decapolis and have occupied the city of Ravenna itself. They have deposed your governors and appointed governors of their own, and they have determined to do the same at other imperial cities in this neighborhood and even at Rome itself, since you are unable to defend us. All this is the result of your imprudence and stupidity. But you wish to strike terror into them and you say, "I will send to Rome and destroy the image of St. Peter and, having overcome Pope Gregory, will carry him off, as Constantine [II] commanded [Pope] Martin to be carried off." You ought rather to know and to hold for certain that the pontiffs who have ruled at Rome preside there in order to maintain peace, like a wall joining East and West, occupying the middle ground between them, and that they are arbitrators and promoters of peace. . . . If you insolently threaten and insult us there is no need for us to descend to fighting with you. The Roman pontiff will withdraw for a few miles into the Campania; then you may go and chase the wind.

. . . Would that I might, by God's gift, tread the same path as Pope Martin [who died in exile]. And yet I wish to survive and to live for the sake of the people, since the whole western world has turned its eyes upon our humility and, although we are unworthy, the people greatly trust in us and in him whose statue you threaten to cast down and destroy, namely St. Peter, whom all the kingdoms of the West regard as an earthly God. If you want to put the matter to the test, the people of the West are ready and they will avenge the injuries you have inflicted on the people of the East. But we beseech you in the Lord to turn aside from these puerile follies. . . . One thing we take badly is this, that while the savage and barbarous people become peaceful your peacefulness turns to savagery and cruelty. The whole of the West faithfully offers its fruits to the holy prince of the apostles. If you do send anyone to cast down the image of St. Peter, we protest to you that we shall be innocent of the blood that will be shed. The responsibility will fall on your head. . . .

Pepin and the Papacy

6. The deposition of Childeric. *Annales Laurissenses* (A.D. 749-750) , ed. G. H. Pertz, *Monumenta Germaniae Historica. Scriptores,* I (Hanover, 1826), pp. 136, 138. (Hereinafter cited as *MGH.*)

749 A.D. Burghard, bishop of Worms, and the chaplain Fulrad were sent to Pope Zachary to ask him about the kings in France, who at that time had no royal power. Was this right or not? Pope Zachary replied to Pepin that it was better for the man who had power to be called king rather than one who remained without royal power, and, to avoid a disturbance of the right order of things, he commanded by apostolic authority that Pepin should become king.

750 A.D. Pepin was elected king according to the Frankish custom and anointed by the hand of Archbishop Boniface of holy memory and raised to the kingship by the Franks in the city of Soissons. Childeric who had been falsely called king was tonsured and sent to a monastery.

7. The Donation of Pepin (756). *Vita Stephani II*, ed. L. Duchesne, *Liber Pontificalis*, I (Paris, 1886), pp. 452-54.

. . . [An imperial messenger] hastened after the aforementioned most Christian king of the Franks. He found him within the Lombard borders, not far from the city of Pavia, and urgently besought him, with the promise of many imperial gifts, to surrender to the imperial authorities the city of Ravenna and the other cities and fortified places of the Exarchate. But he was not able to persuade the steadfast heart of that most Christian and benevolent king, who was faithful to God and loved St. Peter, namely Pepin the king of the Franks, to surrender those cities and places to the imperial authority. That same friend of

God and most benevolent king absolutely refused to alienate those cities from the power of St. Peter and the jurisdiction of the Roman church or from the pontiff of the apostolic see. He affirmed under oath that he had not engaged in war so often to win the favor of any man but for the love of St. Peter and for the remission of his sins, and he declared that no enrichment of his treasury would persuade him to snatch away what he had once offered to St. Peter. . . .

Having acquired all these cities, he issued a document of donation for the perpetual possession of them by St. Peter and the Roman church and all the pontiffs of the apostolic see. This document is still preserved in the archives of our holy church. The most Christian king of the Franks sent his counsellor Fulrad, a venerable abbot and priest, to receive the cities, and he himself at once set out happily with his armies to return to France. The said venerable abbot and priest, Fulrad, came to the region of Ravenna with emissaries of King Aistulf, and, entering all the cities of the Pentapolis and Emilia, he took possession of them and also took hostages from among the leading men of each city and obtained the keys of the city gates. Then he came to Rome, and, placing on the tomb of St. Peter the keys of Ravenna and of the various other cities of the Exarchate together with the aforementioned donation issued by his king concerning them, he handed them over to be owned and controlled for all time by the apostle of God and by his most holy vicar the pope and all his successors in the papacy. . . .

The Donation of Constantine

8. The forged Donation, trans. H. Bettenson, *Documents of the Christian Church* (New York, 1943), pp. 141-42.

. . . To the holy apostles, my lords the most blessed Peter and Paul, and through them also to blessed Silvester, our father, supreme pontiff and universal pope of the city of Rome, and to the pontiffs, his successors, who to the end of the world shall sit in the seat of blessed Peter, we grant and by this present we convey our imperial Lateran palace, which is superior to and excels all palaces in the whole world; and further the diadem, which is the crown of our head; and the miter; as also the superhumeral, that is, the stole which usually surrounds our imperial neck; and the purple cloak and the scarlet tunic and all the imperial robes; also the rank of commanders of the imperial cavalry. . . .

And we decree that those most reverend men, the clergy of various orders serving the same most holy Roman Church, shall have that eminence, distinction, power and precedence, with which our illustrious senate is gloriously adorned; that is, they shall be made patricians and consuls. And we ordain that they shall also be adorned with other imperial dignities. Also we decree that the clergy of the sacred Roman Church shall be adorned as are the imperial officers. . . .

Wherefore that the pontifical crown should not be made of less repute, but rather that the dignity of a more than earthly office and the might of its glory should be yet further adorned—lo, we convey to the oft-mentioned and most blessed Silvester, universal pope, both our palace, as preferment, and likewise all provinces, palaces and districts of the city of Rome and Italy and of the regions of the West; and, bequeathing them to the power and sway of him and the pontiffs, his successors, we do (by means of fixed imperial decision through this our divine, sacred and authoritative sanction) determine and decree that the same be placed at his disposal, and do lawfully grant it as a permanent possession to the holy Roman Church.

Wherefore we have perceived that our empire and the power of our government should be transferred and removed to the regions of the East and that a city should be built in our name in the best place in the province of Byzantium and our empire there established; for it is not right that an earthly emperor should have authority there, where the rule of priests and the head of the Christian religion have been established by the Emperor of heaven. . . .

Given at Rome, March 30th, when our lord Flavius Constantinus Augustus, for the fourth time, and Galliganus, most illustrious men, were consuls.

The Coronation of Charlemagne

9. The Roman council of A.D. 800. *Annales Laureshamenses,* ed. G. H. Pertz, *MGH Scriptores,* I (Hanover, 1826), p. 38.

Since the title of emperor had become extinct among the Greeks and a woman claimed the imperial authority, it seemed to Pope Leo and to all the holy fathers who were present at the council and to the rest of the Christian people that Charles, king of the Franks, ought to be named emperor, for he held Rome itself where the Caesars were always wont to reside and also other cities in Italy, Gaul and Germany. Since almighty God had put all these places in his power it seemed fitting to them that, with the help of God, and in accordance with the request of all the Christian people, he should hold this title. King Charles did not wish to refuse their petition, and, humbly submitting himself to God and to the petition of all the Christian priests and people, he accepted the title of emperor on the day of the nativity of our Lord Jesus Christ and was consecrated by Pope Leo.

10. The coronation ceremony. *Vita Leonis III* (795-816), ed. L. Duchesne, *Liber Pontificalis*, II (Paris, 1892), p. 7.

On the day of the nativity of our Lord Jesus Christ all [who had been present at the council] came together again in the same basilica of blessed Peter the apostle. And then the venerable and holy pontiff, with his own hands, crowned [Charles] with a most precious crown. Then all the faithful Romans, seeing how he loved the holy Roman church and its vicar and how he defended them, cried out with one voice by the will of God and of St. Peter, the key-bearer of the kingdom of heaven, "To Charles, most pious Augustus, crowned by God, great and peace-giving emperor, life and victory." This was said three times before the sacred tomb of blessed Peter the apostle, with the invocation of many saints, and he was instituted by all as emperor of the Romans. Thereupon, on that same day of the nativity of our Lord Jesus Christ, the most holy bishop and pontiff anointed his most excellent son Charles as king with holy oil.

Annales Laurissenses (801), ed. G. H. Pertz, *MGH Scriptores*, I (Hanover, 1826), p. 188.

On the most holy day of the nativity of the Lord when the king rose from praying at Mass before the tomb of blessed Peter the apostle, Pope Leo placed a crown on his head and all the Roman people cried out, "To Charles Augustus, crowned by God, great and peace-giving emperor of the Romans, life and victory." And after the laudation he was adored by the pope in the manner of the ancient princes and, the title of Patrician being set aside, he was called emperor and Augustus.

11. The account of Einhard. *Vita Caroli Magni* (817-830), ed. P. Jaffé and W. Wattenbach (Berlin, 1876), pp. 48-49.

[Charlemagne] came to Rome to restore the condition of the Roman church, which had been very much disturbed, and spent the whole winter there. At that time he received the title of emperor and Augustus, though he was so much opposed to this at first that he said he would not have entered the church that day had he been able to foresee the pope's intention, although it was a great feast day. Nevertheless he endured very patiently the envy of the [Eastern] Roman emperors, who were indignant about his accepting the title, and, by sending many embassies to them and addressing them as brothers in his letters, he overcame their arrogance by his magnanimity, in which he certainly excelled them.

3. Disintegration,
Theocracy & Reform

Charlemagne's empire was short-lived. His grandsons engaged in endless civil wars against one another and, while they busied themselves in this fashion, all of Western Europe was again subjected to savage attacks by invaders from beyond its borders.

Everywhere men rallied to any local lord who could provide some measure of protection. The lords for their part assumed rights over the persons and property of their followers—rights to judge and punish and levy taxes as well as rights to receive rents and services from the land. Virtually all the tasks that we would consider the responsibility of a public authority embodied in a central government were discharged then, if they were discharged at all, by local lords who regarded such functions as private, profit-making perquisites attached to their property rights over land. It was a savage, squalid era, to most people a time of grim struggle for bare survival, to a few an age of unprecedented opportunities for acquiring wealth and power by the exercise of brute force. All previously established institutions suffered, not least the church. In every part of Europe ecclesiastical lands and offices fell under the control of lay lords. The tendency had been there since the first Germanic invasions of the Roman empire, but now it went quite unchecked. A petty lord regarded the village church and its lands as a part of his estates, the priest as an estate servant like one of his stewards, to be appointed at will. A greater noble, greedy for the vast lands of some local abbey, would set himself up as its "protector" and assume the right to appoint its abbot. The complex of estates belonging to the abbey then became just one more fief rendering services to the lord and subject to his rule. Some richly endowed bishoprics went the same way. They were seized by brigand nobles, let out as fiefs to illiterate warriors, bestowed as dowries on favored daughters, or passed on to younger sons. There is one much quoted case of a philoprogenetive noble of Provence who bought the bishopric of Narbonne for his son, then aged 10 (*No.* 13). Few of the men who acquired ecclesiastical positions in this way cared anything for the spiritual duties of their offices. Nor were they likely to feel bound by the old ascetic discipline of the Western church that prescribed a life of celibacy for priests. It became commonplace for priests and abbots to be married or to keep women without being married, and when such men had sons they sought to pass on to them their ecclesiastical offices and episcopal estates. This practice tended to destroy the whole conception of priesthood as a sacred vocation to such a degree that, in the eyes of later reformers, clerical marriage came to be regarded as a most offensive symbol of the general subordination of spiritual office to material ends that characterized this age.

In such circumstances pious churchmen throughout Europe turned to their kings for leadership and protection. It seemed to them that the only hope for the maintenance of any orderly Christian life lay in the emergence of strong monarchs who could maintain an elementary degree of peace and justice in their lands. Moreover, while seizure of episcopal estates by local barons was mere brigandage, control of the episcopate by a royal master could be given a theological justification. Kingship was itself a sacred office—there were several texts of the Old Testament that said so, and they were all pressed into service in the tenth century. Kings were anointed with elaborate religious ceremonies that closely paralleled the consecration of a bishop; they were regarded as ministers of God set over prelates and people alike; they were hailed as vicars of Christ.

From the king's point of view his theocratic role had enormous advantages, quite apart from the added dignity and prestige that it imparted to his royal office. The warrior nobles who, throughout Europe, were the real rulers of their own districts, usually held their lands and jurisdictions from a king in theory, but they held them by hereditary right. The king had no effective choice of the successor to a fief. He could never be sure that it would pass to a vassal who would remain loyal to him. On the other hand, if a bishop was enfeoffed with a great complex of territories and with the rights of government over them, the king could select from the church a trustworthy and capable servant to rule over those lands in the king's name and could be sure that at the bishop's death the lands would again come into his hands to be disposed of as he saw fit. Accordingly, it became the custom throughout Europe for kings to choose bishops, to enrich them with great fiefs, and to invest them with the ring and pastoral staff that symbolized episcopal office. This practice provided a most effective counter to the disintegrative tendencies of early feudalism, but it was also a radical departure from the canonical tradition of the church. For a time, especially under Nicholas I in the mid-ninth century, the papacy protested against the course of events and asserted in most trenchant language its own claim to guide and rule the whole church. But then the popes themselves became puppets of rival factions contending for the lordship of Rome. Many of them lived in scandalous squalor, devoting themselves almost entirely to issues of local power politics. One such pontiff was eventually deposed for sacrilege, simony, drunkenness, incest, arson, and murder (according to a chronicler who was indeed an enemy of the pope). To ecclesiastical reformers in the tenth century it must have seemed that the whole church from top to bottom was stinking with the sins of clerical immorality and simony (the buying and selling of ecclesiastical office).

There were reformers even in that bleak age. The tenth century has its quota of saints, nearly all of them monks, for in such a time the best hope of living a Christian life in ordered peace was to retire to some still-uncorrupted monastery or to found a new one. And to many fine spirits it seemed then that the best way of helping a world gone to ruin was to pray for it. The foundation of the abbey of Cluny in particular is often regarded as a turning point in the religious history of the Dark Ages. The monastery was established in 910, and its charter (*No.* 12) was carefully worded to exclude the practices that were ruining so many religious houses at that time. It explicitly conceded to the monks in perpetuity the right of electing their own abbot and declared that the abbey was to be subject to no external authority except that of the papacy—and even the popes were warned against undue meddling. Under a series of great abbots Cluny became first a model of rigorous Benedictine observance and then the center of a whole ecclesiastical empire with hundreds of daughter houses throughout Europe under its discipline. This growth of the Cluniac congregation was the most striking reform movement of the tenth century, but it was not the only one, and its influence on the reformed papacy of the eleventh century is sometimes exaggerated. An independent movement of monastic reform flourished in England and another, supported by a succession of zealous bishops, in the Rhineland, while in Italy movements of lay piety protested against the worldliness of ecclesiastical rulers and called on them to return to an apostolic life of simplicity and poverty. The reform party that later grew up in Rome itself had many traditions to draw on.

It was only in the papacy that all the scattered strivings toward a renewal of Christian life could find a common center. In spite of the degeneracy of individual popes of this period, all Christendom continued to revere Rome itself as the city of St. Peter and St. Paul, a place hallowed by the blood of innumerable martyrs, a goal of pilgrims from many lands. Moreover, the tradition of papal administration never quite broke down. Even under the worst popes the papal chancery continued to function; most important of all, the papal archives survived. If there should ever emerge a new line of popes worthy of their greatest predecessors, they would find the records of Leo and Gelasius and Gregory the Great to inspire them and to provide canonical support for their own programs of reform.

There is a certain irony in the sequence of events that led up to the revival of the papacy. To the reformers of the next generation it seemed that the control of ecclesiastical offices by lay rulers was the root of all the evil in the church. But in the circumstances of the mid-eleventh century only the control of papal appointments by the emperor made possible the beginning of a reform movement at Rome. It came about like this. Otto I (936-73), who ruled over all the eastern lands of the old Carolingian empire, had resuscitated the tradition of Charlemagne by journeying to Rome to be crowned as emperor by the pope. Nearly a century later, in 1046, his successor, King Henry III of Germany, also went to Rome for his imperial coronation but was disgusted to find there three rival candidates each of whom claimed to be the rightful pope. Henry settled the issue in high-handed fashion. He dismissed all three would-be popes and installed another of his own choosing. It seemed to Henry just as much his right to appoint a bishop for Rome as for any other diocese in his territories, but he was also very conscious of his duty as vicar of God to appoint the best man available to such a great dignity. His first appointee died after a few months in office, and the second lived only a few weeks. Both of them were apparently poisoned by factions at Rome that resented imperial intervention in the affairs of the city.

Henry's third pope reigned for five years and in that time succeeded in transforming the papacy and inaugurating a vast new program of ecclesiastical reform throughout Europe. Leo IX was a close kinsman of the emperor and came from a Rhineland diocese that had been a center of the Northern reform movement. One of his most important new policies was to appoint experienced reformers from north of the Alps as cardinals. This was a radical innovation that changed the whole institutional structure of the Roman church. There had been cardinals at Rome before but their functions were merely ceremonial. Leo transformed the nature of the office by conferring it on the chosen men whom he gathered together to serve as his principal counselors and administrators. Under Pope Leo synods held at Rome promulgated decrees against the abuses that were considered to be the most besetting sins of the church: simony and clerical marriage or concubinage. But Leo was not content to issue well-meaning decrees from Rome. He traveled northward through France and Germany, holding councils of local bishops and clergy at great ecclesiastical centers like Rheims and Mainz (Nos. 15, 16). In these councils the general reform decrees were promulgated afresh, and individual prelates who had offended against the canons of the church were judged and, if necessary, deposed. The effect of the pope's travels appears to have been electrifying. Clergy to whom the Roman pontiff had seemed a remote and shadowy potentate at the other end of the world now saw him laying down the law and settling the affairs of their own churches as a formidable judge and ruler.

After many great successes Leo's pontificate ended with a major set-
back. In 1053 the pope desisted from his apostolic labors to try to curb
the brutal and destructive activities of aggressive bands of Norman
warriors who had been settling in south Italy since the early years of
the century. He collected an army and marched south, but his forces
were routed by the Normans, and the pope himself taken prisoner. He
was held captive for several months and died shortly after his release—
a humiliating end to a great reign.

The Founding of Cluny

12. The foundation charter of Cluny (910), trans. E. F. Henderson, *Select Historical Documents of the Middle Ages* (London,
1892), pp. 329-33. (Hereinafter cited as *Documents*.)

To all right thinkers it is clear that the providence of God
has so provided for certain rich men that, by means of their transitory
possessions, if they use them well, they may be able to merit everlasting
rewards. . . . I, William, count and duke by the grace of God, diligently
pondering this, and desiring to provide for my own safety while I am
still able, have considered it desirable—nay, most necessary, that from
the temporal goods which have been conferred upon me I should give
some little portion for the gain of my soul. . . . I hand over from my
own rule to the holy apostles, Peter, namely, and Paul, the possessions
over which I hold sway, the town of Cluny, namely, with the court and
demesne manor, and the church in honour of St. Mary the mother of
God and of St. Peter the prince of the apostles, together with all the
things pertaining to it, the vills, indeed, the chapels, the serfs of both
sexes, the vines, the fields, the meadows, the woods, the waters and
their outlets, the mills, the incomes and their revenues, what is culti-
vated and what is not, all in their entirety. . . . I give these things,
moreover, with this understanding, that in Cluny a regular monastery
shall be constructed in honour of the holy apostles Peter and Paul, and
that there the monks shall congregate and live according to the rule
of St. Benedict, and that they shall possess, hold, have and order these
same things unto all time. . . . And let the monks themselves, together
with all the aforesaid possessions, be under the power and dominion
of the abbot Berno, who, as long as he shall live, shall preside over them
regularly according to his knowledge and ability. But after his death,
those same monks shall have power and permission to elect any one
of their order whom they please as abbot and rector, following the rule
promulgated by St. Benedict—in such wise that neither by intervention
of our own or of any other power may they be impeded from making a

purely canonical election. Every five years, moreover, the aforesaid monks shall pay to the church of the apostles at Rome ten shillings to supply them with lights; and they shall have the protection of those same apostles and the defence of the Roman pontiff; and those monks may, with their whole heart and soul, according to their ability and knowledge, build up the aforesaid place. . . . And, through God and all his saints, and by the awful day of judgment, I warn and objure that no one of the secular princes, no count, no bishop whatever, not the pontiff of the aforesaid Roman see, shall invade the property of these servants of God, or alienate it, or diminish it, or exchange it, or give it as a benefice to anyone, or constitute any prelate over them against their will. . . . I, William, commanded this act to be made and drawn up, and confirmed it with my own hand.

The Buying of a Bishopric

13. Complaint of Berengar, viscount of Narbonne, against Wifred, archbishop of Narbonne, presented before a church council at Toulouse (1056), ed. J. D. Mansi, *Sacrorum Conciliorum Nova et Amplissima Collectio*, XIX (Venice, 1774), col. 850-51.

. . . I Berengar, consul of the city of Narbonne, declare plainly before all of you this great complaint that I have against your brother, my metropolitan. The archbishopric of Narbonne used to belong to my uncle, Archbishop Ermengaud, and in his day it was one of the best bishoprics between Rome and Spain, richly endowed with manors and castles, with estates and allodial lands. The church, filled with books and adorned with gilded pictures, caskets and crucifixes, was resplendent with golden crowns and precious stones. The voices of many canons were heard at regular hours, prayers were offered, and all good works increased. . . .

But, when the aforementioned archbishop of holy memory died, Count Wifred of Cerdana, to whom my wife was a kinswoman, came to Narbonne and approached both my parents and myself to obtain the archbishopric for his son, our bishop mentioned above, who was only ten years old at the time; and he offered a great gift of a hundred thousand *solidi* to my father and the count of Rodez. But my father and mother would not agree. I, however, moved by regard for his kinship and deceived by his pretence of friendship, broke with my parents over this matter and declared that I would destroy them if they did not give way to me. My father, seeing me so moved and so hostile to him acceded to my wishes and to the requests of Wifred, and, having received a hundred thousand *solidi* for ourselves and the count of Rodez as the price of the bishopric, we gave it to Wifred's son, our bishop. Calling God to witness and swearing an oath, he gave his firm word and pledged his faith that if he was to be our bishop, as he was and is, no injury would be done to us or ours or to the bishopric. I was confident that when he was enthroned in the cathedral and grew in years and honor he would be a protection to me and a shield against the spears of all my enemies, that he would remember his kinship to my wife and how I had helped to place him in a position of such honor, and that, as he had declared, he would help me to have and to hold my honor. But then, arrogant as a devil, he unexpectedly provoked me to anger and harassed me and built castles against me and made cruel war on me with a vast army, so that on account of him almost a thousand men were slaughtered on both sides. Then he snatched away from God and his ministers the castles and manors, estates and possessions of the aforesaid church, together with the revenues and possessions of the canons and what they held in common, and gave them to the devil and his servants. . . .

Royal Theocracy

14. Prayer for the consecration of a king, trans. L. G. Wickham Legg, *English Coronation Records* (Westminster, 1901), p. 24. (This prayer was used at the coronation of King Edgar of England in 973. Similar formulas were used at coronation rites throughout Western Christendom.)

O Almighty and everlasting God, Creator and Governor of heaven and earth, Maker and Ruler of angels and men, King of kings, and Lord of lords, who didst cause thy faithful servant Abraham to triumph over his enemies; didst give many victories to Moses and Joshua, the governors of thy people; didst exalt thy lowly servant David unto the height of a kingdom, and didst save him from the lion's mouth and from the hand of the beast and of Goliath; and didst also deliver him from the evil javelin of Saul and from all his enemies; didst enrich Solomon with the unspeakable gift of wisdom and peace—graciously give ear to our humble prayers, and multiply thy blessings upon thy servant N., whom in lowly devotion we do elect to the kingdom of the Angles or of the Saxons, and ever cover him with thy powerful hand, that he, being strengthened with the faith of Abraham, endued with the mildness of Moses, armed with the fortitude of Joshua, exalted with the humility of David, beautified with the wisdom of Solomon, may please thee in all things, may always walk uprightly in the way of righteousness, may nourish and teach, defend and instruct the church of the whole realm of N. with the peoples committed to his charge, and like a mighty king minister unto them the government of thy power against all enemies, visible and invisible, that the sceptre depart not from the royal throne of the Angles and Saxons, but by thy help may reform their minds to the concord of true faith and peace; that being underpropped with due obedience and honoured with the condign love of this his people, he may through length of years stablish and govern by thy mercy the height of the glory of his fathers; and being defended with the helmet of thy protection, covered with thy invincible shield, and all clad with heavenly armour, he may gloriously triumph, and by his power both terrify infidels and bring joyful peace to those that fight for thee; bestow on him the virtues with which thou hast adorned thy faithful servants, with manifold blessings, and set him on high in the government of his kingdom, and anoint him with the oil of the grace of the Holy Spirit. . . .

Reform Councils of Leo IX

(No official record survives of the canons of the Council of Rheims. The following list was set down by Anselm, a monk of Rheims who was present at the council. The absence of an explicit condemnation of clerical marriage is surprising, but Canon VIII and Canon XI have both been interpreted to imply such a condemnation. The attack on clerical marriage was especially emphasized in Adam of Bremen's brief account of the Council of Mainz.)

15. Decrees of the Council of Rheims (1049). J. D. Mansi, *Sacrorum Conciliorum Nova et Amplissima Collectio*, XIX (Venice, 1774), col. 741-42.

[It was decreed]:

I. That no one should be advanced to the rule of a church without election by clergy and people.

II. That no one should buy or sell sacred orders or ecclesiastical offices or churches; and that if any cleric had bought anything of the sort he was to hand it over to his bishop and do suitable penance.

III. That no layman should hold an ecclesiastical office or a church and that no bishop should consent to this.

IV. That no one except the bishop or his representative should presume to exact dues at the entrances of churches.

V. That no one should demand anything as a burial-fee or for administering baptism or the Eucharist or for visiting the sick.

VI. That no clerics should bear arms or follow worldly occupations.

VII. That no cleric or layman should be a usurer.

VIII. That no monk or cleric should apostatize from his order.

  IX. That no one should dare to assault any persons in holy orders while they were traveling.

   X. That no one should injure poor men by thefts or frauds.

  XI. That no one should participate in an incestuous union.

 XII. That no one should desert his wife and marry another.

> 16. Council of Mainz (1049). Adamus Bremensis, *Gesta Hammaburgensis Ecclesiae Pontificum,* ed. B. Schmeidler, *MGH Scriptores . . . in usum scholarum . . . separatim editae* (Hanover and Leipzig, 1917), pp. 172-73.

At that time there was held a general council at Mainz under the presidency of the apostolic lord and of the emperor Henry. There were present bishops Bardo of Mainz, Eberhard of Trier, Herimann of Cologne, Adalbert of Hamburg, Engelhard of Magdeburg and other priests of the province. In that council a certain bishop of Speyer, Sibico, who was accused of the crime of adultery was cleared by sacrificial ordeal. Moreover many things were decreed there for the good of the church and, above all, simoniacal heresy and the evil of clerical marriage were forever condemned by the signatures of the council. It is proved that when our lord archbishop came home he was not silent about these things. As regards the women he decreed the same judgement that his predecessor, the memorable Alebrand, and Libentius before him had introduced, namely that they be "put out of the synagogue" (John 9:22) and of the city, lest the seductive presence of their enticements should offend the chaste of vision.

Part II

 THE INVESTITURE
CONTEST

1. Peter Damian &
Humbert

The medieval "crisis of church and state" began when the
two most influential powers that had emerged from the anarchy of the
Dark Ages—the German empire and the Roman church—fell into a
fierce conflict with one another.

For so long a time as Pope Leo IX and Emperor Henry III were
working together there was never any chance that the papal reform movement would turn against the imperial authority. But the pope died in
1054 and the emperor in 1056. Moreover, Henry left only an infant son
to succeed him. During the long minority of this young prince the first
signs of a radical change of attitude toward the imperial authority appeared among the group of reformers that Leo had gathered at Rome.
The issue first arose as a by-product of a dispute between two of his
cardinals, Peter Damian and Humbert, concerning the nature and
effects of simony. These two were men of sharply contrasting tempera-
ments. Peter Damian was an impassioned figure, an ascetic and a mystic,
a writer on the spiritual life, a moralist who castigated with burning
zeal all the vices of his age. Humbert was coldly intellectual, a man
more concerned with justice than with charity, more swayed by abstract
argument than by practical considerations of human need. He could
never resist pressing an argument to its logical conclusion and if the
process led to results that were subversive of the whole existing order of
society, to ideas whose implementation might throw the whole world
into chaos, he would rather risk the chaos than reconsider the argument.
His intransigence as papal legate to Constantinople in 1054 helped to
bring about a schism between the Greek and Roman churches that has

33

never been healed. The acceptance of his views on lay investiture by the papacy precipitated fifty years of bitter conflict between emperors and popes in the West.

The dispute between the two cardinals broke out over a technical point of theology. All the reformers at Rome bitterly detested the traffic in ecclesiastical offices so characteristic of their age. But Humbert maintained that the sin of simony was so heinous that a bishop who paid money to obtain his office became incapable of receiving episcopal orders; his consecration, that is to say, did not make him a true bishop, and it followed as a corollary that any priests whom he ordained were not true priests. Peter Damian argued that although a simonist was a bad bishop, still he was a bishop and, accordingly, priests who were ordained by him received valid sacerdotal orders. The difference of temper between the two men is very evident in their treatment of this issue. Damian looked at it from the point of view of the ordinary humble cleric who went to his bishop to be ordained. How could he know the precise circumstances of the bishop's promotion? Why should he be penalized for his bishop's sin? Humbert produced an argument that sounds like a proposition out of Euclid. "In short, unless grace is freely accepted it is not grace. . . . But simonists do not accept freely what they receive. . . . Therefore they do not receive grace . . . but if they do not receive it they do not have it; if they do not have it they cannot give it. . . ." The acceptance of Humbert's argument, incidentally, would have rendered suspect the ordinations of half the priests in Europe—a conclusion that the cardinal seems to have envisaged with total equanimity.

In this matter Peter Damian was defending the position that Catholic theologians have generally accepted as orthodox, and on this particular point Humbert found few followers. The wider significance of the dispute between the two cardinals is that in discussing the nature of simony both of them were led to reflect on the relations between bishops and kings in general and on the current practice of lay investiture in particular. According to the usual procedure, when an episcopal see became vacant the emperor or king selected a candidate whom he considered suitable and appointed him to the bishopric by investing him with a pastoral staff and a ring. In the course of the ceremony the bishop did homage to the lay ruler and entered into possession of the great complex of feudal estates and jurisdictions that were normally attached to an eleventh-century bishopric. He became at the same time a prelate of the church and a vassal of the king. It is not difficult today to see that the two offices are conceptually separable even though they inhered in the same person, but this became apparent to men of the eleventh century only after a generation's indecisive struggle. To the early reformers it seemed just as obvious as it did to the emperors themselves that all the lands, rights, jurisdictions, and duties of a bishopric formed one, indissoluble juridical entity. This way of thinking was altogether consistent with the prevailing ethos of early feudalism in which public office was regarded as an aspect of land tenure. Moreover, the reformers had a reason of their own for adhering to it. Men who had bought bishoprics sometimes put forward the excuse that they were merely paying for a royal grant of land, not for the sacred office itself, and so were not guilty of any sin. This argument would have justified precisely those simoniacal practices that the reformers were determined to abolish. They therefore maintained that in the ceremony of investiture with ring and staff the whole "episcopate" was conferred, an indissoluble union of spiritual office and temporal endowments, and that, accordingly, anyone who offered money in return for investiture was guilty of simony.

Humbert was particularly insistent about this point (*No.* 20), but the dispute between him and Peter Damian arose over a still more fundamental issue. Humbert came to regard lay investiture itself as the very root of all the evils in the church. Peter Damian, on the other hand, could see no great harm in the practice provided that the royal power was not abused. Any hint of simony did indeed arouse his wrath. He rebuked with savage eloquence not only the crude use of money to acquire ecclesiastical office but also every kind of timeserving and sycophancy by which courtiers sought to obtain promotion in the church (*No.* 17). His letter to the boy king Henry IV (*No.* 19) was written at a time when the royal court was supporting a schismatic claimant to the papacy (Cadalus). Damian therefore insisted on the need for cooperation between kingship and priesthood, and he warned the young prince of the awful judgment of God that would fall on an erring ruler. But he praised Henry III as a king who had eradicated the sin of simony by making ecclesiastical appointments without regard for worldly advantage, and even defended the emperor's right to choose bishops for the see of Rome (*No.* 18).

Humbert's attitude was entirely different. He denounced the practice of lay investiture as a usurpation of sacramental functions by an unqualified lay ruler, and he also insisted that a cleric who was elevated to the episcopate without due canonical election could not be regarded as a true bishop at all. Humbert was not objecting simply to the use of sacred symbols by the king but to any effective royal right of appointment to ecclesiastical offices. He ignored the fact that the prelates concerned would become royal officials, rulers of provinces as well as ministers of sacraments. He held that bishops ought not to be subordinate to kings because the priestly office was intrinsically superior to the royal one; "Just as the soul excels the body and commands it, so the priestly dignity excels the royal" (*No.* 21). The analogy became a favorite with later theorists of papal power, and eventually the most extreme conclusions were derived from it.

During the course of the 1050's Humbert's views on lay investiture won general acceptance among the reformers. The brief pontificate of Pope Nicholas II in 1059 saw three new departures in policy which taken together indicate clearly that Humbert's theories had by then been accepted by the papacy as the basis for its future reform program. The most important innovation concerned the conduct of papal elections. According to Humbert all bishops had to be chosen by canonical election, not by royal designation. If the principle was to have any force at all it had to be applied in the first place to the see of Rome itself, but up until this time there had been no precise definition of how the "canonical election" of a pope was to be conducted. A decree of 1059 put the election for the first time in the hands of the cardinals, primarily of the cardinal bishops. It ignored the rights of the emperors that had accumulated since the days of Charlemagne, and reduced the role of the Roman clergy and people to a mere acclamation of the candidate chosen by the sacred college (*No.* 22). It was in effect a declaration of independence by the reformed papacy directed against both the imperial power and the factions of Roman nobility that had often manipulated papal elections in the past.

It was clear to the reformers that if the cardinals were to exercise in practice the right of election that they now claimed in principle, they would probably need military support during the critical period of a papal vacancy. The papacy now sought to ensure such support by entering into an alliance with the Normans. Robert Guiscard, their leader, was eager to legitimize his position in south Italy by obtaining papal recognition of his rule over the lands he had conquered there. In return for this recognition he agreed to hold his lands as a fief of the Roman church and took an oath of vassalage to the pope in which he explicitly bound himself to assist the cardinals in the conduct of future papal elections (*No.* 24). Finally, in a synod held at Rome in 1059 a general prohibition of lay investiture was added for the first time to the usual reforming decrees against simony and immorality (*No.* 23). There was, however, no attempt to enforce the prohibition during the next few years. That development came with the rise to the papacy of Hildebrand, Pope Gregory VII.

Peter Damian

17. Against the promotion of courtiers to ecclesiastical dignities. Letter to the cardinal-bishop Boniface of Albano (1060-1071), ed. J. P. Migne, *PL* 145 (Paris, 1853), col. 463-66.

Peter, monk and sinner, to the most reverend lord bishop Boniface, his service.

. . . Venerable father, while many things displease me about the bishops of our times, I find this quite intolerable that some of them, hotter than the breath of Etna in their pursuit of ecclesiastical honors, give themselves over to the service of rulers with disgusting subservience like captive slaves. They desert the things of the church while they are greedy for churches; they avoid warfare in order to be set above warriors and, since they are not ashamed to exchange the temple of God for the palace, they pass over from the rule of religion to the ranks of the laity. They put aside the arms of virtue, they abandon the army of spiritual service, they flee the camp, they loose the soldier's belt. They are too proud to receive wages as a reward with the others; they are avid only for pre-eminence in commanding and ruling. Most certainly, these men, who do not enter church through the door but by a worldly back-way, become thieves and robbers, not shepherds of sheep, as the Truth testifies, saying, "He that entereth not by the door into the sheepfold is a thief and a robber" (John 10:1).

. . . Those who hand themselves over to the princes of the world for the sake of obtaining honors have to be lavish with money and also have to fawn on their patrons with soothing flatteries. Men who pay court to princes out of ambition for ecclesiastical office cannot deny that they have handed over money. Those who serve out of lust for power and wealth pay over their own selves and their talents. They humble themselves so that later on they may be arrogant with impunity; they act as lackeys in order to become lords; they wear themselves out with labors for the sake of future pleasure; they suffer want so that afterward they may grow fat with feasting at a perpetual wedding banquet and, as if at a money changer's counter, they pay with service to buy office. "They love the first place at feasts and the first chairs in the synagogues. And salutations in the market place and to be called by men, Rabbi" (Matthew 23:6-7). Some may give a sum of inanimate money, they may weigh out a quantity of inert metal, accounts may be reckoned, chased vases assessed. Some, I say, may give money; others offer themselves as a price. For is not sedulous obsequiousness of service a price?

18. A eulogy of the emperor Henry III, *Liber Gratissimus* (1052), ed. L. de Heineman, *MGH Libelli de Lite,* I (Hanover, 1891), p. 71.

Moreover, while we reflect on the acts of the venerable pope, it is reasonable also to turn our attention to considering the distinguished fame of our great king Henry. It was he, after God, who snatched us from the serpent's insatiable maw, he who cut off all the heads of the many-headed Hydra of simoniacal heresy with the sword of divine courage. He indeed can say not unworthily to the glory of Christ, "All others, as many as have come, are thieves and robbers"

(John 10:8). For down to his time the false priesthood of the empire made endless offerings, as I may say, to the Babylonian Belial; but, after he acquired his father's kingdom by God's will, he soon stuffed the mouth of the serpent with a mass of pitch and thus, like another Daniel, slew the monstrous beast (cf. Daniel 14:26). The love of money can be compared not unreasonably with pitch that burns and holds fast. It so burns in the furnace of a greedy heart as to hold it back from the bounty of the overshadowing mercy and the holy compassion. What does it mean then to thrust a mass of pitch into the mouth of the serpent unless evidently to say with Peter, "Keep thy money to thyself, to perish with thee" (Acts 8:20), which words indeed this prince truly pronounced when "he overthrew the chairs of them that sold doves" and expelled the money changers and cast out venal commerce from the temple of God (cf. Matthew 21:12). Again it does not seem inconsistent with this interpretation that Daniel is described as having mixed fat and hair with the pitch. For what do we understand by "fat" but voluptuousness of the flesh. And what is designated by "hair," which is on the outside of animals' bodies, but external wealth. When, therefore, the king mixed pitch with fat and hair and so burst open the serpent, he not only stood firm against avarice but, because he utterly detested the poison of simony, sought no worldly inducements at all or any gain of exterior wealth in distributing ecclesiastical dignities.

. . . And since he rejected the example of former princes in order to obey the commands of the eternal king, divine providence, not unmindful, conferred on him this privilege, which hitherto was not conceded to most of his predecessors, that the Roman church should be ordered according to his will and that no one should elect a priest to the apostolic see without his authority. If David deserved to be united in marriage with the daughter of a king for overthrowing the Philistine Goliath, there is evidently no cause for wonder if this emperor, victor over the simoniacal heresy which reproached the army of the living God, has received the holy church which is undoubtedly the daughter of the supreme king.

19. Priesthood and kingship (1065). Letter to King Henry IV, ed. J. P. Migne, *PL* 144 (Paris, 1853), col. 440-42.

. . . Just as both powers, the royal and the priestly, are joined to one another in the first place in Christ by the special truth of a sacrament, so too they are mutually bound to one another in the Christian people by a kind of covenant. Each in turn needs the services of the other The priesthood is defended by the royal protection while the kingship is sustained by the holiness of the priestly office. The king is girded with a sword so that he may go armed against the enemies of the church.

The priest devotes himself to vigils of prayer so that he may win God's favor for king and people. The former ought to direct earthly affairs under the lance of justice; the latter should give drink to the thirsty from the spring of divine eloquence. The former is established to coerce evil doers and criminals with the punishment of legal sanctions; the latter is ordained for this, to bind some with the zeal of canonical rigor through the keys of the church that he has received and to absolve others through the clemency of the church's compassion. But hear Paul discussing kings and defining the proper role of the royal office. He said, after much else, "For he is God's minister to thee for good. But if thou do that which is evil, fear; for he beareth not the sword in vain. For he is God's minister, an avenger to execute wrath upon him that doth evil" (Romans 13:4). If then you are God's minister, why do you not defend God's church?

. . . A king is to be revered as long as he obeys the Creator. On the other hand, when a king resists the divine commands, it is right that his subjects despise him; for, if anyone is shown to rule as king not for God but for himself, he does not fight for the camp of the church on the day of battle and is too anxious about his own interests to come to the aid of the church when it is in peril. Again, since the Lord says through Isaias "Come and accuse me" (Isaias 1:18), why should a man disdain to be accused by man when all are bound by the same law of mortality? Again, when the civil law carefully provides that a man who does not take vengeance on the murderers of his parents is not to be admitted to the right of hereditary succession, shall not I, who cannot avenge the murder of my mother the Roman church, at least urge on the avengers? Regard me then, oh king, as one who offers faithful counsel, not insolent reproaches, or, if you please, think of me as one mad with grief over the murder of a mother, not as insolently raised up against the excellence of the royal majesty. Yet would that I were adjudged guilty of treason before your tribunal if only you, the arbiter of equity, would also punish the enemies of the apostolic see. Let the executioner's axe fall on my neck if only the Roman church, restored by you, may ascend to the eminence of its proper dignity. Moreover, if you swiftly destroy Cadalus, as Constantine did Arius, and strive to restore peace to the church for which Christ died, God will soon bring it about that you ascend to the height of imperial rule and carry away titles of glory from all your enemies. It will be otherwise if you still play false and refuse to correct an error that imperils the world when you have the power to do so. I restrain my spirit and leave it for my readers to discern the consequences.

Humbert

20. Against lay investiture. *Libri III Adversus Simoniacos* (1054-
1058), ed. F. Thaner, *MGH Libelli de Lite*, I (Hanover, 1891),
pp. 108, 205-6.

. . . According to the decrees of the holy fathers anyone
who is consecrated as a bishop is first to be elected by the clergy, then
requested by the people and finally consecrated by the bishops of the
province with the approval of the metropolitan. A man cannot be held
or called a true, undoubted established bishop unless he has a definite
body of clergy and people to govern and unless he has been consecrated
by the other bishops of the province with the authority of the metropolitan, who has charge of the province on behalf of the apostolic see. Anyone who has been consecrated without conforming to all of these three
rules is not to be regarded as a true, undoubted, established bishop nor
counted among the bishops canonically created and appointed. Rather
he is to be called a pseudo-bishop; for a bishop is called a governor
or supervisor, but what clergy or people can a man govern when no
clergy or people has chosen him to govern them, and when he lacks
the authority of the metropolitan and of the provincial bishops?

. . . Whereas men venerable throughout the world and supreme
pontiffs inspired by the Holy Spirit have decreed that the election of the
clergy should be confirmed by the judgement of the metropolitan, and
the petition of the nobles and people by consent of the prince, now
everything is done in such disorder that the first are last and the last
first, so that the sacred canons are rejected and the whole Christian
religion trampled underfoot. The secular power is first in choosing and
confirming; the consent of nobles, people and clergy and then finally
the decision of the metropolitan come afterwards whether they are willing or not. Hence, as stated above, men promoted in this fashion are
not to be regarded as bishops, for the manner of their appointment
is upside down; what ought to be done first is done last and by men
who should not be concerned in the matter at all. For how does it
pertain to lay persons to distribute ecclesiastical sacraments and episcopal or pastoral grace, that is to say crozier staffs and rings, with which
all episcopal consecration is principally effected and by which it functions and is sustained? Surely the crozier staffs, hooked and bent at the
top to attract and draw forward, pointed and armoured at the bottom
to repel and drive off, symbolize what is conveyed by them, that is,
pastoral care. . . . Again, the ring is a symbol of heavenly mysteries,
warning preachers that, like the Apostle, they should speak and present

the secret wisdom of God among the mature and keep it like a sealed mystery from the immature who are not yet ready for solid food but need only milk; or the ring signifies that, like betrothed lovers, they should unceasingly show forth and praise the pledge of faith of their own bride which is the church.

Anyone, then, who appoints a man with these two symbols undoubtedly claims all rights of pastoral care for himself in so presuming. For, after this institution, what choice concerning such rulers who have already been appointed can be exercised by the clergy, nobles and people or by the metropolitan who is to consecrate them or merely be present, except only to acquiesce? A man so instituted first intrudes on the clergy, nobles and people in order to lord it over them by force instead of being acknowledged, sought after and requested by them. So too he attacks the metropolitan, not submitting to his judgement but rather judging him; he does not require or receive the metropolitan's approval but demands and exhorts the service of prayer and anointing which is all that is left to him, for how can it pertain to the metropolitan or what purpose would it serve to confer again the staff and ring that he already has? . . .

21. Priesthood and kingship (1054-58), *ibid.*, p. 225.

Among the other absurd deceptions with which sycophants, like bird-catchers, snare the unwary for the sake of gain, they exalt the worldly power and especially the imperial and royal power beyond all measure to the open and avid ears of princes, while minimizing the dignity of the church. And since everything under the sun has its vicissitudes, sometimes prospering, sometimes declining, they estimate the merit and power of the priestly dignity according to the outward prosperity or decline of the church's cause, sometimes preferring the secular power to the priestly like sun to moon, sometimes setting them together like two suns, sometimes—but this is very rare—by the one title of son subordinating the secular power like a son to a father.

. . . Hence any prince who seeks to attain felicity on earth and to prepare himself for beatitude in the life to come should take care to pay no heed to such persons, for "a Prince that gladly heareth lying words hath all his servants wicked" (Proverbs 29:12). They should not treat the priests of Christ and the things that pertain to them differently than did the great Constantine and his orthodox successors in the empire.
. . . Anyone then who wishes to compare the priestly and royal dignities in a useful and blameless fashion may say that, in the existing church, the priesthood is analogous to the soul and the kingship to the body, for they cleave to one another and need one another and each in turn demands services and renders them one to another. It follows from this that, just as the soul excels the body and commands it, so too the priestly

dignity excells the royal or, we may say, the heavenly dignity the earthly. Thus, that all things may be in due order and not in disarray the priesthood, like a soul, may advise what is to be done. The kingship in turn, like a head, excels all the members of the body and leads them where they should go; for just as kings should follow churchmen so also layfolk should follow their kings for the good of church and country. And so the people should be taught by one power and ruled by the other, but neither power should heedlessly follow the people. . . .

The Legislation of 1059

22. Decree on papal election (April 1059), ed. E. Friedberg, *Corpus Iuris Canonici*, I (Leipzig, 1879), col. 77-79.

. . . Supported by the authority of our predecessors and the other holy fathers, we decree and order that:

When the pontiff of this universal Roman church dies the cardinal bishops shall first confer together most diligently concerning the election; next they shall summon the other cardinal clergy; and then the rest of the clergy and the people shall approach to give their assent to the new election, the greatest care being taken lest the evil of venality creep in by any way whatsoever. The most eminent churchmen shall be the leaders in carrying out the election of a pope, the others followers. Certainly this order of election will be found right and lawful if anyone examines the rules and acts of the various fathers and also calls to mind the judgment of our holy predecessor Leo. "No reason permits," he says, "that men should be regarded as bishops who have not been chosen by the clergy or requested by the people or consecrated by the bishops of the province with the approval of the metropolitan." But since the apostolic see is superior to all the churches in the world it can have no metropolitan set over it, and so the cardinal bishops who raise the chosen pontiff to the summit of the apostolic dignity undoubtedly act in place of a metropolitan. They shall make their choice from the members of this church if a suitable man is to be found there, but if not they shall take one from another church, saving the honor and reverence due to our beloved son Henry who is now king and who, it is hoped, will in future become emperor with God's grace, according as we have now conceded this to him and to his successors who shall personally obtain this right from the apostolic see.

If, however, the perversity of corrupt and evil men so prevails that a pure, sincere and free election cannot be made in the City, the cardinal bishops, together with the God-fearing clergy and the Catholic laity, even though they are few, may have the right and power of electing a pontiff for the apostolic see in any convenient place.

If, after an election has been made, a time of war or the efforts of any malignant men shall make it impossible for the person elected to be enthroned in the apostolic see according to custom, it is clear that, nonetheless, the person elected shall acquire authority to rule the Roman church and to dispose of all its resources as a true pope, for we know that the blessed Gregory acted thus before his consecration. . . .

> 23. First prohibition of lay investiture (April 1059), ed. L. Weiland, *MGH Constitutiones et Acta*, I (Hanover, 1893), p. 547. (The new prohibition was included as *No.* 6 in the following group of canons, which otherwise were typical of earlier reform legislation.)

Nicholas, bishop, servant of the servants of God, to all Catholic bishops and to all the clergy and people, affectionate greetings and apostolic benediction.

Since we must be diligently solicitous for all men with the vigilance that pertains to our universal rule, taking heed for your salvation, we are carefully sending to you the decrees that were canonically enacted in a synod recently held at Rome in the presence of one hundred and thirteen bishops and, despite our unworthiness, under our presidency; for we desire that you give effect to them for your salvation, and by apostolic authority we command this.

1. Firstly it was enacted in the sight of God that the election of the Roman pontiff should be in the power of the cardinal bishops, so that anyone who is enthroned without their previous agreement and canonical election and without the subsequent consent of the other orders of clergy and of the people shall not be held for a pope and an apostle, but rather for an apostate.
2. That when the bishop of Rome or of any city dies no one shall dare to plunder their possessions, but these shall be preserved intact for their successors.
3. That no one shall hear the mass of a priest who, he knows for certain, keeps a concubine or has a woman living with him. . . .
4. And we firmly decree that those of the above-mentioned orders who, in obedience to our predecessors, have remained chaste shall sleep and eat together near the church to which they have been ordained as is fitting for pious clergy and that they shall hold in common whatever revenues come to them from the church, and we urge them especially that they strive to attain the apostolic way of life, which is a life in common.
5. Further, that tenths and first fruits and gifts of living or dead persons be faithfully handed over to the church by lay folk and that they

be at the disposal of the bishop. Any who keep them back are cut off from the communion of holy church.

6. That no cleric or priest shall receive a church from laymen in any fashion, whether freely or at a price.

7. That no one shall receive the habit of a monk in the hope or with the promise of becoming an abbot.

8. Nor shall any priest hold two churches at the same time.

9. That no one shall be ordained or promoted to any ecclesiastical office by simoniacal heresy. . . .

The Norman Alliance

24. Oath of Robert Guiscard to Pope Nicholas II (August 1059), ed. P. Fabre and L. Duchesne, *Le Liber Censuum de l'église romaine* (Paris, 1910), p. 422.

I, Robert, by the grace of God and St. Peter duke of Apulia and Calabria and, with the help of both, future duke of Sicily, will from this hour forward be faithful to the holy Roman church and the apostolic see and to you, my lord Pope Nicholas. I will not give any counsel or commit any act whereby you would lose life or limb or fall into vile captivity. I will not knowingly disclose so as to injure you any information that you impart to me and forbid me to disclose. So far as lies within my power I will support the holy Roman church in holding and acquiring the temporalities and possessions of St. Peter everywhere and against all men, and I will help you to hold the Roman papacy securely and honorably. I will not invade or seek to acquire or presume to dispoil the lands and principality of St. Peter unless you or your successors who have entered upon the honor of St. Peter give explicit permission, and that in addition to the things which you are now conceding to me and which your successors will concede. I will faithfully ensure that the holy Roman church shall have each year such payment as has been laid down from the lands of St. Peter which I hold or shall hold. Also I will put all churches in my lordship and their possessions under your power and I will defend them as one faithful to the Roman church; and I will not swear fealty to anyone without reserving the fealty owed to the Roman church. Moreover, if you or your successors shall depart this life before me, I will assist in the election and consecration of a pope to the honor of St. Peter according to the advice of the leading cardinals and of the Roman clergy and people. All these things I will observe with due fidelity to the Roman church and to you, and I will observe this fidelity to your successors, consecrated to the honor of St. Peter, who confirm to me the investiture you have conceded. So help me God.

2. The Program of Gregory VII

Hildebrand was the youngest of the reforming cardinals whom Leo IX had gathered together at Rome. By the end of the pontificate of Alexander II (1061-73) he was almost the only survivor of the original group and had emerged as the dominant figure in the Roman curia. At the burial of Alexander a tumult arose among the people. They clamorously demanded that Hildebrand become their pope and, according to his own account, "dragged [him] to the place of apostolic rule." The cardinals were of the same mind as the people, and Hildebrand was duly elected, taking the name of Gregory VII. There is no doubt that the election was canonically valid, but the technical irregularity that the people had expressed their preference before the meeting of the cardinals made it possible later for his enemies to question the legitimacy of his position.

Gregory's reign was filled with conflict, above all with King Henry IV of Germany who had grown to manhood and begun to assume personal control of his kingdom in the years just before the pope's election. The immediate cause of the clash was Gregory's re-enactment of the earlier decree against lay investiture and his determination to enforce the decree in practice. But the apparently technical nature of the dispute should not obscure the fundamental importance of the issues involved. Henry could not give up the right of appointing bishops without abandoning all hope of welding Germany into a united monarchy. Gregory could not acquiesce in the imperial claims, which included a claim to appoint the popes themselves, without jeopardizing the continuance of the entire reform movement, for Henry showed none of his father's spontaneous zeal for the task of revivifying the church. When Henry turned to his bishops for support in resisting the pope's decree, and Gregory in turn appealed to the German princes to assist him in deposing Henry from his kingship, it became clear that the whole leadership of Christian society was at stake in the dispute.

The documents printed below illustrate how the whole substance of Gregory's program, including his specifically political claims, was set out in the first two years of his pontificate, before the open breach with

Henry IV. There is no question here of an extreme policy developing only under the pressure of uncontrollable events. In 1074 Gregory held a council at Rome which promulgated afresh the usual reforming decrees against simony and clerical marriage. This legislation is described in the pope's letter to Bishop Otto of Constance (*No.* 25). In February of 1075 came the crucial decree prohibiting lay investiture. In March of 1075 there was inserted in the pope's official Register the peculiar document known as the *Dictatus Papae* (*No.* 26), which contained the first explicit claim that a pope could depose an emperor. The unusual form of the document has been much discussed, and the most convincing explanation of it is that the *Dictatus* presents chapter headings for a proposed collection of canons which would have supported each proposition with a selection of relevant authorities. In any case there seems to be no doubt that the *Dictatus* presents the considered opinions of Gregory VII at the outset of his reign. Document *No.* 27 illustrates the pope's determination to preserve every shred of temporal power over secular kings that the Roman see had obtained through feudal transactions in preceding generations.

This program of Gregory VII has provoked a variety of conflicting judgments from historians. Some condemn the pope as a worldly-minded prelate obsessed by a selfish ambition to dominate Europe. Others praise him as a selfless servant of the church whose whole life was dedicated to the ideals of religious liberty and ecclesiastical reform. This dispute goes back to the days of Gregory himself, for he was accused of undue ambition by his .own contemporaries. Peter Damian once called him "My holy Satan"—and Satan's sin was the sin of pride. The pope himself was deeply sensitive to this accusation; time and again he found it necessary to deny that he sought worldly power for its own sake. (In the very act of deposing King Henry IV he declared, addressing St. Peter: "Rather would I have chosen to end my life as a pilgrim than to seize upon thy place for earthly glory.") Both views of the pope's character may contain an element of truth. Gregory at any rate was not a dispassionate intellectual or much given to self-analysis, but rather a man of action, filled with tumultuous energy, prone to make impetuous decisions. It is not difficult to see such a man driven by an ineluctable will to power and at the same time utterly convinced in his own heart that all his energies are being poured out in the service of a cause greater than himself.

A related controversy has grown up concerning the central objectives of Gregory's program. Augustin Fliche emphasizes the pope's concern with moral reform and sees the conflict with Henry IV arising out of the young king's obdurate resistance to the reform program in Germany. Even in the matter of lay investiture, Fliche suggests, "with a prince other than Henry IV things could have been arranged." In a quite different spirit Walter Ullmann maintains that the whole point of Gregory's program was to translate abstract theocratic principles into concrete governmental actions.[1] Here the two positions seem mutually exclusive but, again, both express important truths. Gregory VII was deeply preoccupied with moral reform and sometimes seems to have set this objective above all others. For example, he strove to enforce rigorously the decrees on clerical celibacy—which were especially unpopular among the lower clergy of Germany—in the months immediately before his breach with Henry IV, when elementary political prudence would have indicated that he was likely to need every possible source of support in the German church (No. 25). But it is misleading to suggest that Gregory was simply a peace-loving pontiff reluctantly driven into a conflict because Henry IV resisted his reform policy. The prohibition of lay investiture was of the essence of Gregory's program, and it was a demand that no king of that time could have accepted. No king did accept it.

This raises a further question that has also been a matter of much dispute. Was Gregory essentially a conservative or a revolutionary in the objectives he pursued? Both Fliche and Ullmann would argue in their different ways that he was really a traditionalist, continuing a line of papal policy that dated back to the early centuries of the church. Erich Caspar, on the other hand, called Gregory "the great innovator who stood all alone," and Norman Cantor has recently described the eleventh-century reform movement as one of the four great "world-revolutions" of Western history.[2] Here again it seems possible to take a middle position. Gregory certainly thought that he was being a traditionalist. All the reformers can be called conservatives in that they consciously aimed at reviving ancient laws of the church which had fallen out of use in the chaos of preceding centuries. For that reason they devoted a great deal of time and energy to searching through old records in order to produce compilations of canons that would provide authoritative support for their own programs. In a sense the policies they pursued really were traditional ones. It is certainly true that canonical election and clerical celibacy belonged to the early tradition of the Western church and that lay investiture was a fairly recent innovation, unsupported by canonical authority; but it is no very uncommon paradox in Western history that the literal application by would-be reformers of half-understood old texts from a different historical epoch can have revolutionary implications for their own times. The use of medieval precedents by the English parliamentarians of the seventeenth century is a case in point. So too in the 11th century the ancient rules that the reformers wanted to enforce acquired a radically changed significance when they were applied in a

[1] A. Fliche, La réforme grégorienne (Paris, 1946), p. 131; W. Ullmann, Growth of Papal Government (London, 1955), p. 262.

[2] E. Caspar, "Gregor VII in seinen Briefen," Historische Zeitschrift, CXXX (1924), pp. 1-30; N. Cantor, Church, Kingship and Lay Investiture in England (Princeton, 1958), pp. 6-9.

historical context quite different from the one which had originally given rise to them. However conservative the eleventh-century reformers intended to be, the inevitable result of their activities was not to re-establish an old order of things but to bring a new order into existence.

Moral Reform

25. Letter of Gregory to Otto, bishop of Constance (December 1074), trans. E. Emerton, *The Correspondence of Pope Gregory VII* (New York, 1932), pp. 52-53.

Gregory . . . to Otto, bishop of Constance, greeting. . . .
A report has come to us with regard to Your Fraternity, which I have heard with grief and regret—a report which, if it had been made to us of the lowest member of the Christian community, would undoubtedly have called for a severe disciplinary sentence. While we were zealously striving to wipe out the heresy of Simony and to enforce the chastity of the clergy, inspired by apostolic authority and the authentic opinions of holy fathers, we enjoined upon our colleague, the venerable archbishop of Mainz, whose suffragans are numerous and widely scattered, that he should diligently impress this decree upon his whole clergy, in person and through his assistants, and should see that it was carried out without exception.

To you also, who preside over the numerous clergy and the widespread population of the church of Constance, it has, for the same reason, seemed good to us to send a special letter under our own seal. With this as your authority you can more safely and more boldly carry out our orders and expel from the Lord's holy place the heresy of Simony and the foul plague of carnal contagion. The apostolic authority of St. Paul is here of especial force, where, counting in fornicators and adulterers with other vicious persons, he gives this plain decision: "With such a one, no, not to eat."

Furthermore the whole body of the Catholic Church consists of virgins or married persons or those holding themselves in restraint. Whoever, therefore, is outside those three classes is not to be counted among the sons of the Church or within the bounds of the Christian religion. Wherefore we also, if we should know for certain that even the lowest layman was involved in concubinage, would cut him off completely from the body and blood of the Lord until he should perform due penance. How then shall one be the distributor or server of the holy sacraments who cannot in any wise be partaker of them? Further, we are urged to this by the authority of the blessed Pope Leo [I] who deprived subdeacons of the right to marry, a decree to which his successors in the

Holy Roman Church, especially that famous doctor Gregory [I], gave such force of law that henceforth the marriage bond has been absolutely forbidden to the three orders of priests, levites and subdeacons.

But when we, in our pastoral forethought, sent word to you that these orders were to be carried out you, not setting your mind on the things that are above, but on the things that are upon the earth, loosed the reins of lust within the aforesaid orders so that, as we have heard, those who had taken concubines persisted in their crime, while those who had not yet done so had no fear of your prohibitions. Oh, what insolence! Oh, what audacity, that a bishop should despise the decrees of the Apostolic See, should uproot the precepts of holy fathers—nay more, by orders from his high place and his priestly office should impose upon his subjects things contrary and repugnant to the Christian faith.

Wherefore we command you to present yourself before us at the approaching synod in the first week of Lent to give answer according to canon law as well for this disobedience and contempt of the Apostolic See as for all the other offenses charged against you.

Papal Power

26. *The Dictatus Papae* (March 1075), trans. S. Z. Ehler and J. B. Morrall, *Church and State Through the Centuries* (London, 1954), pp. 43-44.

1. That the Roman Church was founded by God alone.
2. That the Roman Pontiff alone is rightly to be called universal.
3. That he alone can depose or reinstate bishops.
4. That his legate, even if of lower grade, takes precedence, in a council, of all bishops and may render a sentence of deposition against them.
5. That the Pope may depose the absent.
6. That, among other things, we also ought not to stay in the same house with those excommunicated by him.
7. That for him alone it is lawful to enact new laws according to the needs of the time, to assemble together new congregations, to make an abbey of a canonry; and, on the other hand, to divide a rich bishopric and unite the poor ones.
8. That he alone may use the imperial insignia.
9. That the Pope is the only one whose feet are to be kissed by all princes.
10. That his name alone is to be recited in churches.
11. That his title is unique in the world.
12. That he may depose Emperors.
13. That he may transfer bishops, if necessary, from one See to another.

14. That he has power to ordain a cleric of any church he may wish.
15. That he who has been ordained by him may rule over another church, but not be under the command of others; and that such a one may not receive a higher grade from any bishop.
16. That no synod may be called a general one without his order.
17. That no chapter or book may be regarded as canonical without his authority.
18. That no sentence of his may be retracted by any one; and that he, alone of all, can retract it.
19. That he himself may be judged by no one.
20. That no one shall dare to condemn a person who appeals to the Apostolic See.
21. That to this See the more important cases of every church should be submitted.
22. That the Roman Church has never erred, nor ever, by the witness of Scripture, shall err to all eternity.
23. That the Roman Pontiff, if canonically ordained, is undoubtedly sanctified by the merits of St. Peter; of this St. Ennodius, Bishop of Pavia, is witness, many Holy Fathers are agreeable and it is contained in the decrees of Pope Symmachus the Saint.
24. That, by his order and with his permission, subordinate persons may bring accusations.
25. That without convening a synod he can depose and reinstate bishops.
26. That he should not be considered as Catholic who is not in conformity with the Roman Church.
27. That the Pope may absolve subjects of unjust men from their fealty.

Feudal Lordship

27. Letter to Solomon, king of Hungary (October 1074), trans. E. Emerton, *Correspondence*, pp. 48-49.

Gregory . . . to Solomon, king of Hungary, greeting. . . .
Your letter to us arrived late owing to delay on the part of your messenger. It would have been more graciously received at our hands had not your ill-considered condition been so grievously offensive to St. Peter. For, as you may learn from the chief men of your country, the kingdom of Hungary was long since offered and devotedly surrendered to St. Peter by King Stephen as the full property of the Holy Roman Church under its complete jurisdiction and control. Furthermore, the emperor Henry [III] of pious memory, after his conquest of that kingdom, in honor of St. Peter sent to his shrine a spear and a crown, and in celebration of

his triumph delivered the insignia of sovereignty to the place where he knew the headship of that power belonged.

This being so you, nevertheless, who in other respects also have widely departed from the character and quality of a king have, as we hear, degraded the right and the honor of St. Peter as far as you could by accepting a kingdom which is his as a fief from the king of the Germans. If this is true, you yourself know how much favor from St. Peter or good will from ourself you can expect. You cannot receive these or hope to reign long without apostolic reproof unless you correct your fault and acknowledge that the scepter of the kingdom which you hold is a fief of the apostolic and not of the royal majesty. For neither fear nor favor nor any respect of persons shall, so far as in us lies, prevent us from claiming with God's help every possible honor due to him whose servant we are.

If you are prepared to correct these wrongs and to order your life as becomes a king, then beyond a doubt you shall enjoy in full measure the affection of the Holy Roman Church as a beloved son of a mother, and also our own friendship in Christ.

Lay Investiture

(Gregory's first prohibition of lay investiture was issued in February 1075. The text of the decree has not survived, but its substance was repeated in the later enactments given below which were promulgated in November 1078 and March 1080 respectively.)
28. Decrees against lay investiture, trans. E. F. Henderson, Documents (London, 1892), pp. 365-66.

Inasmuch as we have learned that, contrary to the establishments of the holy fathers, the investiture with churches is, in many places, performed by lay persons; and that from this cause many disturbances arise in the church by which the Christian religion is trodden under foot: we decree that no one of the clergy shall receive the investiture with a bishopric or abbey or church from the hand of an emperor or king or of any lay person, male or female. But if he shall presume to do so he shall clearly know that such investiture is bereft of apostolic authority, and that he himself shall lie under excommunication until fitting satisfaction shall have been rendered.

Following the statutes of the holy fathers, as, in the former councils which by the mercy of God we have held, we decreed concerning the ordering of ecclesiastical dignities, so also now we decree and confirm:

that, if any one henceforth shall receive a bishopric or abbey from the hand of any lay person, he shall by no means be considered as among the number of the bishops or abbots; nor shall any hearing be granted him as bishop or abbot. Moreover we further deny to him the favour of St. Peter and the entry of the church, until, coming to his senses, he shall desert the place that he has taken by the crime of ambition as well as by that of disobedience—which is the sin of idolatry. In like manner also we decree concerning the inferior ecclesiastical dignities.

Likewise if any emperor, king, duke, margrave, count, or any one at all of the secular powers or persons, shall presume to perform the investiture with bishoprics or with any ecclesiastical dignity—he shall know that he is bound by the bonds of the same condemnation. And, moreover, unless he come to his senses and relinquish to the church her own prerogative, he shall feel, in this present life, the divine displeasure as well with regard to his body as to his other belongings: in order that at the coming of the Lord, his soul may be saved.

The Role of the Laity

(One of Gregory's most radical measures commanded layfolk to reject priests who failed to conform to his reform decrees.) 28a. Letter of Gregory to Otto, bishop of Constance (March 1075). ed. P. Jaffé. *Bibliotheca Rerum Germanicarum*, II (Berlin, 1865), p. 525.

. . Those who obtain churches by the gift of money must forfeit them completely, and no one henceforth shall be permitted to buy or sell them. Also, those who fall into the crime of fornication may not celebrate masses or serve at the altar in minor orders. We have further decreed that, if they disobey our statutes, or rather those of the holy fathers, the people shall in no way accept their ministrations, so that those who are not corrected by the love of God or the honor of their office may be brought to their senses by the shame of the world and the rebuke of the people.

3. The Struggle
with Henry IV

Even before Gregory became pope, two causes of friction between the papacy and the royal government in Germany had arisen. In a disputed election to the great see of Milan Pope Alexander II had supported one candidate, the king another. Also, Alexander had had occasion to rebuke the young king for tolerating simoniacal practices at his court. Later on Henry would prove an intransigent opponent, but at the time of Gregory's election in 1073 his royal power was threatened by a great rebellion in Saxony, and he was in no position to make new enemies. He therefore wrote to Gregory most submissively, acknowledging Gregory as pope even though he had taken no part in Gregory's election and promising to accept papal correction in the affair of Milan. During the course of 1074 Gregory began to complain to the German bishops that his reform decrees were not being enforced effectively (*No. 25*). In February of 1075 came the papal decree forbidding all lay investiture. Henry never had the slightest intention of complying with this decree, and he was able to defy it openly after he won a great victory over the Saxons in June.

It then required only a test case to bring pope and king into open conflict, and the test case was already at hand in the dispute over the episcopal election at Milan. After a riot in the city Henry renewed his support for a royal candidate against the papally approved bishop. In December of 1075 Gregory wrote to him about this matter reproachfully and, for the first time, threateningly, reminding Henry that the pope possessed all the powers of St. Peter and that the king, like all other Christians, was bound by the papal decrees (*No. 29*). Henry responded by summoning a council of German bishops that denounced Gregory as a usurper of the papacy and accused him of perjury, immorality, and gross abuses of papal authority in the dioceses of Germany. In February of 1076 Gregory replied with a decree in which he declared Henry excommunicated and deprived of his royal authority (*No. 31*). At about this time Henry wrote two defenses of his position. One, addressed to the pope, was an outright assertion of divine-right kingship. Its whole tone and substance are epitomized in the salutation, "Henry, King not by usurpation, but by the pious ordination of God, to Hildebrand, now not Pope, but false monk" (*No. 30*). The second, sent to the German bishops, repeated that Henry had been called to the kingship by God, and accused Gregory of seeking to pervert the divine ordering of human affairs by uniting priesthood and kingship in his own person (*No. 32*).

The next few months showed that Henry had greatly overestimated the strength of his position. The turbulent princes of medieval Germany were never willing to submit to the rule of a powerful, centralized monarchy, and Henry, after his triumph over the Saxons, was far too strong for their liking. The announcement of the king's excommunication and deposition was therefore very welcome to many of the nobles. Moreover, the moral effect of the pope's condemnation, with its solemn invocation of the authority of St. Peter, seems to have been very great indeed. Even the bishops who had joined Henry in condemning the pope soon deserted him to seek Gregory's pardon. Henry found himself faced by an overwhelming coalition of nobles and bishops and was compelled to accept humiliating terms of surrender. He agreed that a diet should be held at Augsburg in February of 1077. The pope was to preside in person at this diet, which would consider Henry's behavior and decide whether to permit him to continue reigning as king. It was a most satisfying prospect for Pope Gregory.

In January 1077 the pope, traveling northward to the diet, paused at the castle of Canossa on the Italian side of the Alps. Then came the most dramatic episode of the whole struggle. Henry slipped away from Germany, crossed the Alps with an escort of only a few personal attendants, and presented himself as a humble penitent, barefoot in the depths of winter, at the gates of the pope's castle. Gregory was faced with a difficult choice. As a spiritual pastor faced with a penitent sinner seeking forgiveness, his obvious duty was to give absolution. But as a political leader playing for high stakes, his obvious course was to send Henry packing back to Germany with a reminder that his case was to be considered at the diet of princes in February and not before. Gregory permitted himself the luxury of keeping the king waiting for three days, but he did in the end give the desired absolution and released Henry from his sentence of excommunication, without, however, restoring him to the office of kingship. He then wrote to the German princes giving them an account of his actions (*No. 33*).

The pope behaved with complete propriety on this occasion, but the political effects of his decision were disastrous. Many of Henry's former supporters rallied to his cause again when they heard that he had made his peace with the pope. The princes who continued to oppose Henry thought that Gregory had betrayed them, and without consulting him elected a king of their own, Rudolph of Swabia. Gregory had not foreseen this turn of events and announced that he could not decide which of the two candidates to recognize without carefully considering their merits. He took three years to reach a decision, while a most savage and destructive civil war raged in Germany between the partisans of the two claimants to the throne. At last the pope decided for Rudolph and in 1080 again declared Henry excommunicated and deposed from the kingship (*No.* 35). This second excommunication apparently had little of the moral effect of the first. Gregory was widely blamed in Germany for all the disasters of the civil war, and in any case his decision came too late. Henry had already gained the upper hand in the fighting, and a few months after the second papal sentence against him his rival Rudolph was defeated and killed.

Henry no longer thought of seeking a reconciliation with the pope. He summoned councils of German and Lombard bishops which again declared that Hildebrand was a usurper and no true pontiff. This time, moreover, they elected an antipope who called himself Clement III, and Henry marched on Rome to expel Gregory and to install his own pope there. The city held out against imperial sieges from 1081 to 1084, a most exceptional display of stamina and fortitude on the part of the citizens of medieval Rome. Gregory, more than most popes, commanded their loyalty and affection. But in the end Henry burst into the city and enthroned his antipope in St. Peter's while Gregory took refuge nearby in the impregnable fortress of St. Angelo.

During the siege of Rome Gregory had renewed the papal alliance with the Normans of south Italy. Now at last, too late, Robert Guiscard marched on the city to rescue his nominal overlord. The imperial armies withdrew without giving battle. The Normans, finding Rome at their mercy, fully lived up to their reputation for savage brigandage and looted the whole city, leaving a third of it razed by fire. Then they withdrew to the south, taking the pope with them. Gregory died among the Normans a few months later. His last words, it is said, were a bitter parody of Psalm 44: "I have loved justice and hated iniquity—and so I die in exile."

Two major problems of interpretation arise from the pope's letters concerning Henry IV. The first is to determine with precision just what claims Gregory did put forward in the temporal sphere. The second is to assess the quality of the arguments by which he supported those claims. It would seem clear from the very explicit wording of the decrees of 1076 and 1080 (*Nos.* 31, 35) that he did at least claim the right definitively to depose a king, but even this has been questioned. The main difficulty is that in several letters written after 1076 Gregory continued to use the royal title in mentioning his opponent, referring to him still as "King Henry." Probably no one will ever succeed in constructing an entirely coherent system of thought out of all of Gregory's scattered phrases. He was not an original thinker, still less a tidy-minded systematizer of abstract theories, and there is no consistency of usage in the references to Henry that occur in his letters. Sometimes he remembered to refer to his adversary as a "so-called king" or "tyrant," sometimes not. A recent study has pointed out that Gregory did not consider either of his two decrees against Henry as final and irrevocable.[1] He never lost sight of the possibility that Henry might mend his ways, come to an agreement with the pope, and be reinstated in his kingship by general consent. This fact seems sufficient to account for Gregory's inconsistencies of terminology. The flat assertion of the *Dictatus Papae* that the pope had the power to depose emperors, taken together with the two deposition decrees themselves, seems to establish beyond all doubt that Gregory did claim the right to dethrone secular rulers.

As for the basis of that claim, we are fortunate in having the pope's own letter to Bishop Hermann of Metz in which he set out his views at length (*No.* 36). The letter consists in part of historical examples which, Gregory thought, provided precedents for his treatment of Henry IV, and in part of theological argumentation explaining why the pope possessed a right to depose kings. The historical examples are not very convincing. There was in fact no clear precedent for the outright deposition of a king by a pope. It does not require the apparatus of modern scholarship to discern the fact; some of Gregory's contemporary critics were able to attack him effectively on this point. The theoretical sections of Gregory's letter are more interesting. They rely heavily on the doctrine proclaimed earlier by Cardinal Humbert that secular power was intrinsically inferior to spiritual. St. Ambrose, the pope declared, had held that the priestly office was as superior to the royal as gold to lead (a spurious text this, though Gregory believed it to be genuine). Pope Gelasius too had maintained that the priesthood was entrusted with a higher responsibility than the kingship. Finally, arguing from a kind of perverted Augustinism, Gregory contrasted secular rulers "who raised themselves above their fellows by pride, plunder, treachery, murder" with ecclesiastical ones who were divinely ordained successors to the priesthood of Christ.

There is a flaw in this whole line of argument that was evidently never apparent to Gregory himself. The assertion that ministers of religion have a higher responsibility than secular rulers does not necessarily imply that ecclesiastical officials can depose temporal ones. It is possible to maintain simply that the two structures of offices are separate from one another. Whatever Gelasius meant by his famous pronouncement, he certainly did not maintain that he as pope could depose the emperor Anastasius; nor did it ever occur to St. Ambrose that he could depose Theodosius; nor, we may well suppose, did any such idea ever occur to St. Peter himself in connection with the emperor Nero. Ambrose and Gelasius both took for granted the existence of two separate orders of government, each with its own defined sphere of action. But the pattern familiar to Gregory was that of a unitary church-state. When Gregory

---

[1] Karl F. Morrison, "Canossa: A Revision," *Traditio,* XVIII (1962), pp. 121-48.

read in his old texts of a superiority inherent in the spiritual power, he conceived of it as a superiority within a single, unified system of govern- ment, implying the hierarchical subordination of one power to the other. In this matter he seems to have been completely a captive of the con- ventional presuppositions of his own age.

Gregory did not attempt to work out in detail or to assert either in theory or practice all the logical implications of his belief in the intrinsic superiority of the spiritual power. Indeed, for a full understanding of his position it is as important to notice what he did not claim as what he did. Although he asserted a right to depose Henry he never suggested that the king's authority was in principle delegated to him by the pope; nor did he claim in practice the right to choose anyone he wished as king, but rather acknowledged that the right of election belonged pri- marily to the princes. Least of all did he ever suggest that he could him- self assume the role of a king of Germany and so combine in his own person supreme spiritual and temporal power.

The same kinds of reservations occur also in the king's letters. Henry insisted that his authority came from God alone and that only God could depose him—certainly not the pope. But he also insisted that the two swords of spiritual and temporal government should remain separate from one another and did not claim both for himself. His assertion that Gregory alone was guilty of confusing the two orders of government may seem disingenuous since it was the king's insistence on his right to ap- point bishops that caused the whole dispute. But Henry did not main- tain, at least in principle, that all spiritual and temporal authority be- longed to him as vicar of God. The assertions of both rulers thus fell far short of claims to absolute theocratic power.

The Beginning of the Dispute

29. Letter of Gregory to Henry complaining of the king's mis- treatment of the church (December 1075), trans. E. Emerton, *The Correspondence of Pope Gregory VII* (New York, 1932), pp. 87-89.

Gregory, bishop, servant of God's servants, to King Henry, greeting and the apostolic benediction—but with the understanding that he obeys the Apostolic See as becomes a Christian king. . . .

We marvel exceedingly that you have sent us so many devoted letters and displayed such humility by the spoken words of your legates, calling yourself a son of our Holy Mother Church and subject to us in the faith, singular in affection, a leader in devotion, commending yourself with every expression of gentleness and reverence, and yet in action showing yourself most bitterly hostile to the canons and apostolic decrees in those duties especially required by loyalty to the Church. Not to mention other cases: the way you have observed your promises in the Milan affair, made through your mother and through bishops, our colleagues, whom we sent to you, and what your intentions were in making them is evident to all. And now, heaping wounds upon wounds, you have handed over the sees of Fermo and Spoleto—if indeed a church may be given over by any human power—to persons entirely unknown to us, whereas it is not lawful to consecrate anyone except after probation and with due knowledge.

It would have been becoming to you, since you confess yourself to be a son of the Church, to give more respectful attention to the master of the Church, that is, to Peter, prince of the Apostles. To him, if you are of the Lord's flock, you have been committed for your pasture, since Christ said to him: "Peter, feed my sheep" (John 21:17), and again: "To thee are given the keys of Heaven, and whatsoever thou shalt bind on earth shall be bound in Heaven and whatsoever thou shalt loose on earth shall be loosed in Heaven" (Matthew 16:19). Now, while we, un-worthy sinner that we are, stand in his place of power, still whatever you send to us, whether in writing or by word of mouth, he himself receives, and while we read what is written or hear the voice of those who speak, he discerns with subtle insight from what spirit the message comes. Wherefore Your Highness should beware lest any defect of will toward the Apostolic See be found in your words or in your messages and should pay due reverence, not to us but to Almighty God, in all matters touch-ing the welfare of the Christian faith and the status of the Church. And this we say although our Lord deigned to declare: "He who heareth you heareth me; and he who despiseth you despiseth me" (Luke 10:16). . . .

This edict [against lay investiture], which some who place the honor of men above that of God call an intolerable burden, we, using the right word, call rather a truth and a light necessary for salvation, and we have given judgment that it is to be heartily accepted and obeyed, not only by you and your subjects but by all princes and peoples who confess and worship Christ—though it is our especial wish and would be especially fitting for you, that you should excel others in devotion to Christ as you are their superior in fame, in station and in valor.

Nevertheless, in order that these demands may not seem to you too burdensome or unfair we have sent you word by your own liegemen not to be troubled by this reform of an evil practice but to send us prudent and pious legates from your own people. If these can show in any reason-able way how we can moderate the decision of the holy fathers [at the council] saving the honor of the eternal king and without peril to our own soul, we will condescend to hear their counsel. It would in fact have been the fair thing for you, even if you had not been so graciously admonished, to make reasonable inquiry of us in what respect we had offended you or assailed your honor, before you proceeded to violate the apostolic decrees. But how little you cared for our warnings or for doing right was shown by your later actions.

However, since the long-enduring patience of God summons you to improvement, we hope that with increase of understanding your heart and mind may be turned to obey the commands of God. We warn you with a father's love that you accept the rule of Christ, that you consider the peril of preferring your own honor to him, that you do not hamper by your actions the freedom of that Church which he deigned to bind to himself as a bride by a divine union, but, that she may increase as greatly as possible, you will begin to lend to Almighty God and to St. Peter, by whom also your own glory may merit increase, the aid of your valor by faithful devotion.

> 30. Letter of Henry to Gregory refusing to recognize him as pope (1076), trans. T. E. Mommsen and K. F. Morrison, *Imperial Lives and Letters of the Eleventh Century* (New York, 1962), pp. 150-51.

Henry, King not by usurpation, but by the pious ordination of God, to Hildebrand, now not Pope, but false monk:

You have deserved such a salutation as this because of the confusion you have wrought; for you left untouched no order of the Church which you could make a sharer of confusion instead of honor, of malediction instead of benediction.

For to discuss a few outstanding points among many: Not only have you dared to touch the rectors of the holy Church—the archbishops, the bishops, and the priests, anointed of the Lord as they are—but you have trodden them under foot like slaves who know not what their lord may do. In crushing them you have gained for yourself acclaim from the mouth of the rabble. You have judged that all these know nothing, while you alone know everything. In any case, you have sedulously used this knowledge not for edification, but for destruction, so greatly that we may believe Saint Gregory, whose name you have arrogated to yourself, rightly made this prophesy of you when he said: "From the abundance of his subjects, the mind of the prelate is often exalted, and he thinks that he has more knowledge than anyone else, since he sees that he has more power than anyone else."

And we, indeed, bore with all these abuses, since we were eager to preserve the honor of the Apostolic See. But you construed our humility as fear, and so you were emboldened to rise up even against the royal power itself, granted to us by God. You dared to threaten to take the kingship away from us—as though we had received the kingship from you, as though kingship and empire were in your hand and not in the hand of God.

Our Lord, Jesus Christ, has called us to kingship, but has not called you to the priesthood. For you have risen by these steps: namely, by cunning, which the monastic profession abhors, to money; by money to favor; by favor to the sword. By the sword you have come to the throne of peace, and from the throne of peace you have destroyed the peace. You have armed subjects against their prelates; you who have not been called by God have taught that our bishops who have been called by God are to be spurned; you have usurped for laymen the bishops' ministry over priests, with the result that these laymen depose and condemn the very men whom the laymen themselves received as teachers from the hand of God, through the imposition of the hands of bishops.

You have also touched me, one who, though unworthy, has been anointed to kingship among the anointed. This wrong you have done to me, although as the tradition of the holy Fathers has taught, I am to be judged by God alone and am not to be deposed for any crime unless— may it never happen—I should deviate from the Faith. For the prudence of the holy bishops entrusted the judgment and the deposition even of Julian the Apostate not to themselves, but to God alone. The true pope Saint Peter also exclaims, "Fear God, honor the king" (1 Peter 2:17). You, however, since you do not fear God, dishonor me, ordained of Him.

Wherefore, when Saint Paul gave no quarter to an angel from heaven if the angel should preach heterodoxy, he did not except you who are now teaching heterodoxy throughout the earth. For he says, "If anyone, either I or an angel from heaven, preach any other gospel unto you than that which we have preached unto you, let him be accursed" (Galatians 1:18). Descend, therefore, condemned by this anathema and by the common judgment of all our bishops and of ourself. Relinquish the Apostolic See which you have arrogated. Let another mount the throne of Saint Peter, another who will not cloak violence with religion but who will teach the pure doctrine of Saint Peter.

I, Henry, King by the grace of God, together with all our bishops, say to you: Descend! Descend!

31. Deposition of Henry by Gregory (February 1076), trans. E. Emerton, *Correspondence*, pp. 90-91.

O blessed Peter, prince of the Apostles, mercifully incline thine ear, we pray, and hear me, thy servant, whom thou hast cherished from infancy and hast delivered until now from the hand of the wicked who have hated and still hate me for my loyalty to thee. Thou art my witness, as are also my Lady, the Mother of God, and the blessed Paul, thy brother among all the saints, that thy Holy Roman Church forced me against my will to be its ruler. I had no thought of ascending thy throne as a robber, nay, rather would I have chosen to end my life as a pilgrim than to seize upon thy place for earthly glory and by devices of this world. Therefore, by thy favor, not by any works of mine, I believe that it is and has been thy will, that the Christian people especially committed to thee should render obedience to me thy especially constituted representative. To me is given by thy grace the power of binding and loosing in Heaven and upon earth.

Wherefore, relying upon this commission, and for the honor and defense of thy Church, in the name of Almighty God, Father, Son and Holy Spirit, through thy power and authority, I deprive King Henry, son of the emperor Henry, who has rebelled against thy Church with unheard-of audacity, of the government over the whole kingdom of Germany and Italy, and I release all Christian men from the allegiance which they have sworn or may swear to him, and I forbid anyone to serve him as king. For it is fitting that he who seeks to diminish the glory of thy Church should lose the glory which he seems to have.

And, since he has refused to obey as a Christian should or to return to the God whom he has abandoned by taking part with excommunicated persons, has spurned my warnings which I gave him for his soul's welfare, as thou knowest, and has separated himself from thy Church and tried to rend it asunder, I bind him in the bonds of anathema in thy stead and I bind him thus as commissioned by thee, that the nations may know and be convinced that thou art Peter and that upon thy rock the son of the living God has built his Church and the gates of hell shall not prevail against it.

> 32. Letter of Henry to the German bishops (1076), trans. T. E. Mommsen and K. F. Morrison, *op. cit.*, pp. 152-54.

. . . Let your good will stand by us, therefore, together with your power at this opportune time, the good will for which not only our need is earnestly longing, but also that of all your fellow bishops and brethren, nay rather, that of the whole oppressed Church. Certainly, you are not ignorant of this oppression. Only see to it that you do not withdraw assistance from the oppressed Church, but rather that you give your sympathy to the kingship and to the priesthood. Just as hitherto the Church was exalted by each of these offices, so now, alas, it is laid low, bereft of each; since one man has arrogated both for himself, he has injured both, and he who has neither wanted nor was able to be of benefit in either has been useless in each.

To keep you in suspense no longer as to the name of the man under discussion, learn of whom we speak: it is the monk Hildebrand (a monk indeed in habit), so-called pope who, as you yourself know clearly, presides in the Apostolic See not with the care of a pastor but with the violence of a usurper and from the throne of peace dissolves the bond of the one catholic peace. To cite a few things among many: without God's knowledge he has usurped for himself the kingship and the priesthood. In this deed he held in contempt the pious ordinance of God, which especially commanded these two—namely, the kingship and the priesthood—should remain, not as one entity, but as two. In his Passion, the Savior Himself meant the figurative sufficiency of the two swords to be understood in this way: When it was said to him, "Lord, behold there are two swords here," He answered, "It is enough" (Luke 22:38), signifying by this sufficient duality, that the spiritual and the carnal swords are to be used in the Church and that by them every hurtful thing is to be cut off. That is to say, He was teaching that every man is constrained by the priestly sword to obey the king as the representative of God but by the kingly sword both to repel enemies of Christ outside and to obey the priesthood within. So in charity the province of one extends into the other, as long as neither the kingship is deprived of honor by the priesthood nor the priesthood is deprived of honor by the kingship. You yourself have found out, if you have wanted to discover it, how the Hildebrandine madness has confounded this ordinance of God; for in his judgment, no one may be a priest unless he begs that [honor] from his arrogance. He has also striven to deprive me of the kingship—me whom God has called to the kingship (God, however, has not called him to the priesthood)—since he saw that I wished to hold my royal power from God and not from him and since he himself had not constituted me as king. And further, he threatened to deprive me of kingship and life, neither of which he had bestowed. . . .

Canossa and the Aftermath

33. Letter of Gregory to the German princes giving an account of the incident at Canossa (January 1077), trans. E. Emerton, *Correspondence*, pp. 111-12.

Whereas, for love of justice you have made common cause with us and taken the same risks in the warfare of Christian service, we have taken special care to send you this accurate account of the king's penitential humiliation, his absolution and the course of the whole affair from his entrance into Italy to the present time.

According to the arrangement made with the legates sent to us by you we came to Lombardy about twenty days before the date at which some of your leaders were to meet us at the pass and waited for their arrival to enable us to cross over into that region. But when the time had elapsed and we were told that on account of the troublous times—as indeed we well believe—no escort could be sent to us, [and] having no other way of coming to you, we were in no little anxiety as to what was our best course to take.

Meanwhile we received certain information that the king was on the way to us. Before he entered Italy he sent us word that he would make satisfaction to God and St. Peter and offered to amend his way of life and to continue obedient to us, provided only that he should obtain from us absolution and the apostolic blessing. For a long time we delayed our reply and held long consultations, reproaching him bitterly through messengers back and forth for his outrageous conduct, until finally, of his own accord and without any show of hostility or defiance, he came with a few followers to the fortress of Canossa where we were staying. There, on three successive days, standing before the castle gate, laying aside all royal insignia, barefooted and in coarse attire, he ceased not with many tears to beseech the apostolic help and comfort until all who were present or who had heard the story were so moved by pity and compassion that they pleaded his cause with prayers and tears. All marveled at our unwonted severity, and some even cried out that we were showing, not the seriousness of apostolic authority, but rather the cruelty of a savage tyrant.

At last, overcome by his persistent show of penitence and the urgency of all present, we released him from the bonds of anathema and received him into the grace of Holy Mother Church, accepting from him the guarantees described below. . . . And now that these matters have been arranged, we desire to come over into your country at the first opportunity, that with God's help we may more fully establish all matters pertaining to the peace of the Church and the good order of the land. For we wish you clearly to understand that, as you may see in the written guarantees, the whole negotiation is held in suspense, so that our coming and your unanimous consent are in the highest degree necessary. Strive, therefore, all of you, as you love justice, to hold in good faith the obligations into which you have entered. Remember that we have not bound ourselves to the king in any way except by frank statement—as our custom is— that he may expect our aid for his safety and his honor, whether through justice or through mercy, and without peril to his soul or to our own

34. Henry's oath at Canossa (January 1077), trans. E. Emerton, *Correspondence*, pp. 112-13.

I, Henry, king, within the term which our lord Pope Gregory shall fix, will either give satisfaction according to his decision, in regard to the discontent and discord for which the archbishops, bishops, dukes, counts and other princes of the kingdom of Germany are accusing me, or I will make an agreement according to his advice— unless some positive hindrance shall prevent him or myself—and when this is done I will be prepared to carry it out.

Item: If the same lord Pope Gregory shall desire to go beyond the mountains or elsewhere he shall be safe, so far as I and all whom I can constrain are concerned, from all injury to life or limb and from capture—both he himself and all who are in his company or who are sent out by him or who may come to him from any place whatsoever— in coming, remaining or returning. Nor shall he with my consent suffer any hindrance contrary to his honor; and if anyone shall offer such hindrance, I will come to his assistance with all my power.

> 35. The second deposition of Henry (March 1080), trans. E. Emerton, *Correspondence*, pp. 149-52.

O blessed Peter, chief of the Apostles, and thou, Paul, teacher of the Gentiles, deign, I pray, to incline your ears to me and mercifully to hear my prayer. Ye who are disciples and lovers of the truth, aid me to tell the truth to you, freed from all falsehood so hateful to you, that my brethren may be more united with me and may know and understand that through faith in you, next to God and his mother Mary, ever virgin, I resist the wicked and give aid to those who are loyal to you. For you know that I entered holy orders not of my own pleasure, and that I accompanied the lord Pope Gregory [VI] unwillingly beyond the mountains, but still more unwillingly returned with my master Pope Leo [IX] to your special church, where I have served you as best I could; and then most unwillingly and unworthy as I was, to my great grief and with groans and lamentations I was set upon your throne.

I say this because it is not I that have chosen you, but you that have chosen me and laid upon me the heavy burden of your Church. And because you have commanded me to go up into a high mountain and denounce their crimes to the people of God and their sins to the sons of the Church, those limbs of the Devil have begun to rise up against me and have dared to lay hands upon me even unto blood.

The kings of the earth, and the princes, both secular and clerical, have risen up, courtiers and commons have taken counsel together against the Lord, and against you, his anointed, saying, "Let us burst their chains and throw off their yoke," and they have striven utterly to overwhelm me with death or banishment.

Among these especially Henry, whom they call "king," son of the emperor Henry, has raised his heel against your Church in conspiracy with many bishops, as well ultramontanes as Italians, striving to bring it under his control by overturning me. Your authority withstood his insolence and your power defeated it. In confusion and humiliation he came to me in Lombardy begging for release from his excommunication. And when I had witnessed his humiliation and after he had given many promises to reform his way of life, I restored him to communion only, but did not reinstate him in the royal power from which I had deposed him in a Roman synod. Nor did I order that the allegiance of all who had taken oath to him or should do so in future, from which I had released them all at that same synod, should be renewed. I held this subject in reserve in order that I might do justice as between him and the ultramontane bishops and princes, who in obedience to your Church had stood out against him, and that I might establish peace amongst them, as Henry himself had promised me to do on his oath and by the word of two bishops.

The above-mentioned ultramontane bishops and princes, hearing that he had not kept faith with me, and, as it were, in despair about him, chose Duke Rudolf for their king, without my approval as you will bear witness. Then King Rudolf immediately sent an envoy to me declaring that he had assumed the government of the kingdom under compulsion, but nevertheless was prepared to obey me in every way. And to make this the more acceptable, from that time on he repeatedly sent me the same declaration, adding that he would confirm his promise by sending as hostages his own son and the son of his liegeman Bertaldus [of Zähringen].

Meanwhile Henry was beginning to beg for my help against Rudolf. I replied that I would gladly take action after I had heard both sides in order that I might learn which was the more in accord with what was right. But he, thinking himself strong enough to overcome his opponent, paid no attention to my reply. Later, however, as he saw that he could not do as he had hoped, the two bishops of Verdun and Osnabrück came to Rome on the part of his followers and at a synod requested me in behalf of Henry to do what was right by him. The envoys of Rudolf made the same request. Finally, by divine inspiration as I believe, I decreed at the same synod that a conference should be held beyond the mountains that peace might be restored there, or else that he should be recognized as king whose cause seemed to be the more just. For I, as you, my fathers and my lords, will bear me witness, have never to the present day taken either side except as justice required. And because I reckoned that the wrong side would not be willing to have a conference in which justice was to prevail, I excommunicated and placed under the bonds of anathema all persons, whether of a king or a duke or a bishop or of any vassal, who should try by any device to prevent the holding of a conference. But the aforesaid Henry together with his supporters, not fearing the perils of disobedience— which is the crime of idolatry—incurred excommunication by preventing a conference and bound himself in the bonds of anathema and caused a great multitude of Christians to be delivered to death, churches to be scattered abroad and almost the whole kingdom of the Germans to be desolated.

Wherefore, trusting in the justice and mercy of God and of his most worshipful mother Mary, ever virgin, and relying upon your authority, I place the aforesaid Henry, whom they call "king," and all his supporters under excommunication and bind them with the chains of anathema. And again forbidding him in the name of Almighty God and of yourselves to govern in Germany and Italy, I take from him all royal power and state. I forbid all Christians to obey him as king, and I release all who have made or shall make oath to him as king from the obligation of their oath. May Henry and his supporters never, so long as they may live, be able to win victory in any encounter of arms. But that Rudolf, whom the Germans have chosen for their king in loyalty to you, may rule and protect the kingdom of the Germans, I grant and allow in your name. And relying upon your assurance, I grant also to all his faithful adherents absolution of all their sins and your blessing in this life and the life to come. For as Henry is justly cast down from the royal dignity for his insolence, his disobedience and his deceit, so Rudolf, for his humility, his obedience and his truthfulness is granted the power and the dignity of kingship.

And now, most holy fathers and princes, I pray you to take such action that the whole world may know and understand that if you are able to bind and loose in Heaven, you are able also on earth to grant and to take away from everyone according to his deserts empires, kingdoms, principalities, dukedoms, marquisates, earldoms and the property of all men. You have often taken patriarchates, primacies, archbishoprics and bishoprics away from wicked and unworthy men and have granted them to pious holders. And if you can give judgment in spiritual things, what may we not believe as to your power over secular things? Or, if you can judge the angels who guide all haughty princes, what can you [not] do to their servants? Now let kings and all princes of the earth learn how great is your power, and let them fear to neglect the commands of your Church. And against the aforesaid Henry send forth your judgment so swiftly that all men may know that he falls and is overwhelmed, not by chance but by your power—and would that it were to repentance, that his soul be saved in the day of the Lord!

Gregory's Defense of His Policy

36. Letter of Gregory to Bishop Hermann of Metz (March 1081), trans. E. Emerton, *Correspondence*, pp. 166-75.

. . . You ask us to fortify you against the madness of those who babble with accursed tongues about the authority of the Holy Apostolic See not being able to excommunicate King Henry as one who despises the law of Christ, a destroyer of churches and of the empire, a promoter and partner of heresies, nor to release anyone from his oath of fidelity to him; but it has not seemed necessary to reply to this request, seeing that so many and such convincing proofs are to be found in Holy Scripture. Nor do we believe that those who abuse and contradict the truth to their utter damnation do this as much from ignorance as from wretched and desperate folly. And no wonder! It is ever the way of the wicked to protect their own iniquities by calling upon others like themselves; for they think it of no account to incur the penalty of falsehood.

To cite but a few out of the multitude of proofs: Who does not remember the words of our Lord and Savior Jesus Christ: "Thou art Peter and on this rock I will build my Church, and the gates of hell shall not prevail against it. And I will give thee the keys of the kingdom of heaven and whatsoever thou shalt bind on earth shall be bound in heaven and whatsoever thou shalt loose on earth shall be loosed in heaven" (Matthew 16:19). Are kings excepted here? Or are they not of the sheep which the Son of God committed to St. Peter? Who, I ask, thinks himself excluded from this universal grant of the power of binding and loosing to St. Peter unless, perchance, that unhappy man who, being unwilling to bear the yoke of the Lord, subjects himself to the burden of the Devil and refuses to be numbered in the flock of Christ? His wretched liberty shall profit him nothing; for if he shakes off from his proud neck the power divinely granted to Peter, so much the heavier shall it be for him in the day of judgment. . . .

Thus Pope Gelasius, writing to the emperor Anastasius, gave him these instructions as to the right theory of the principate of the Holy and Apostolic See, based upon divine authority: "Although it is fitting that all the faithful should submit themselves to all priests who perform their sacred functions properly, how much the more should they accept the judgment of that prelate who has been appointed by the supreme divine ruler to be superior to all priests and whom the loyalty of the whole later Church has recognized as such. Your Wisdom sees plainly that no human capacity whatsoever can equal that of him whom the word of Christ raised above all others and whom the reverend Church has always confessed and still devotedly holds as its Head."

So also Pope Julius, writing to the eastern bishops in regard to the powers of the same Holy and Apostolic See, says: "You ought, my brethren, to have spoken carefully and not ironically of the Holy Roman and Apostolic Church, seeing that our Lord Jesus Christ addressed her respectfully, saying, 'Thou art Peter and upon this rock I will build my church, and the gates of hell shall not prevail against it; and I will give thee the keys of the kingdom of heaven.' For it has the power, granted by a unique privilege, of opening and shutting the gates of the celestial kingdom to whom it will." To whom, then, the power of opening and closing Heaven is given, shall he not be able to judge the earth? God forbid! Do you remember what the most blessed Apostle Paul says: "Know ye not that we shall judge angels? How much more things that pertain to this life?" (1 Corinthians 6:3).

So Pope Gregory declared that kings who dared to disobey the orders of the Apostolic See should forfeit their office. He wrote to a certain senator and abbot in these words: "If any king, priest, judge or secular person shall disregard this decree of ours and act contrary to it, he shall be deprived of his power and his office and shall learn that he stands condemned at the bar of God for the wrong that he has done. And unless he shall restore what he has wrongfully taken and shall have done fitting penance for his unlawful acts he shall be excluded from the sacred body and blood of our Lord and Savior Jesus Christ and at the last judgment shall receive condign punishment." Now then, if the blessed Gregory, most gentle of doctors, decreed that kings who should disobey his orders about a hospital for strangers should be not only deposed but excommunicated and condemned in the last judgment, how can anyone blame us for deposing and excommunicating Henry, who not only disregards apostolic judgments, but so far as in him lies tramples upon his mother the Church, basely plunders the whole kingdom and destroys its churches—unless indeed it were one who is a man of his own kind?

As we know also through the teaching of St. Peter in his letter touching the ordination of Clement, where he says: "If any one were friend to those with whom he [Clement] is not on speaking terms, that man is among those who would like to destroy the Church of God and, while he seems to be with us in the body, he is against us in mind and heart, and he is a far worse enemy than those who are without and are openly hostile. For he, under the forms of friendship, acts as an enemy and scatters and lays waste the Church." Consider then, my best beloved, if he passes so severe a judgment upon him who associates himself with those whom the pope opposes on account of their actions, with what severity he condemns the man himself to whom the pope is thus opposed.

But now, to return to our point: Is not a sovereignty invented by men of this world who were ignorant of God subject to that which the providence of Almighty God established for his own glory and graciously bestowed upon the world? The Son of God we believe to be God and man, sitting at the right hand of the Father as High Priest, head of all priests and ever making intercession for us. He despised the kingdom of this world wherein the sons of this world puff themselves up and offered himself as a sacrifice upon the cross.

Who does not know that kings and princes derive their origin from men ignorant of God who raised themselves above their fellows by pride, plunder, treachery, murder—in short, by every kind of crime—at the instigation of the Devil, the prince of this world, men blind with greed and intolerable in their audacity? If, then, they strive to bend the priests of God to their will, to whom may they more properly be compared than to him who is chief over all the sons of pride? For he, tempting our High Priest, head of all priests, son of the Most High, offering him all the kingdoms of this world, said: "All these will I give thee if thou wilt fall down and worship me." (Matthew 4:9).

Does anyone doubt that the priests of Christ are to be considered as fathers and masters of kings and princes and of all believers? Would it not be regarded as pitiable madness if a son should try to rule his father or a pupil his master and to bind with unjust obligations the one through whom he expects to be bound or loosed, not only on earth but also in heaven? Evidently recognizing this, the emperor Constantine the Great, lord over all kings and princes throughout almost the entire earth, as St. Gregory relates in his letter to the emperor Mauritius, at the holy synod of Nicaea took his place below all the bishops and did not venture to pass any judgment upon them but, even addressing them as gods, felt that they ought not to be subject to his judgment but that he ought to be bound by their decisions.

Pope Gelasius, urging upon the emperor Anastasius not to feel himself wronged by the truth that was called to his attention said: "There are two powers, O august Emperor, by which the world is governed, the sacred authority of the priesthood and the power of kings. Of these the priestly is by so much the greater as they will have to answer for kings themselves in the day of divine judgment"; and a little further: "Know that you are subject to their judgment, not that they are to be subjected to your will."

In reliance upon such declarations and such authorities, many prelates have excommunicated kings or emperors. If you ask for illustrations: Pope Innocent excommunicated the emperor Arcadius because he consented to the expulsion of St. John Chrysostom from his office. Another Roman pontiff [Zachary] deposed a king of the Franks [Childeric], not so much on account of his evil deeds as because he was not equal to so great an office, and set in his place Pippin, father of the emperor Charles the Great, releasing all the Franks from the oath of fealty which they had sworn to him. And this is often done by Holy Church when it absolves fighting men from their oaths to bishops who have been deposed by apostolic authority. So St. Ambrose, a holy man but not bishop of the whole Church, excommunicated the emperor Theodosius the Great for a fault which did not seem to other prelates so very grave and excluded him from the Church. He also shows in his writings that the priestly office is as much superior to royal power as gold is more precious than lead. He says: "The honor and dignity of bishops admit of no comparison. If you liken them to the splendor of kings and the diadem of princes, these are as lead compared to the glitter of gold. You see the necks of kings and princes bowed to the knees of priests, and by the kissing of hands they believe that they share the benefit of their prayers." And again: "Know that we have said all this in order to show that there is nothing in this world more excellent than a priest or more lofty than a bishop."

Your Fraternity should remember also that greater power is granted to an exorcist when he is made a spiritual emperor for the casting out of devils, than can be conferred upon any layman for the purpose of earthly dominion. All kings and princes of this earth who live not piously and in their deeds show not a becoming fear of God are ruled by demons and are sunk in miserable slavery. Such men desire to rule, not guided by the love of God, as priests are, for the glory of God and the profit of human souls, but to display their intolerable pride and to satisfy the lusts of their mind. Of these St. Augustine says in the first book of his Christian doctrine: "He who tries to rule over men— who are by nature equal to him—acts with intolerable pride." Now if exorcists have power over demons, as we have said, how much more over those who are subject to demons and are limbs of demons! And if exorcists are superior to these, how much more are priests superior to them!

Furthermore, every Christian king when he approaches his end asks the aid of a priest as a miserable suppliant that he may escape the prison of hell, may pass from darkness into light and may appear at the judgment seat of God freed from the bonds of sin. But who, layman or priest, in his last moments has ever asked the help of any earthly king for the safety of his soul? And what king or emperor has power through his office to snatch any Christian from the might of the Devil by the sacred rite of baptism, to confirm him among the sons of God and to fortify him by the holy chrism? Or—and this is the greatest thing in the Christian religion—who among them is able by his own word to create the body and blood of the Lord? or to whom among them is given the power to bind and loose in Heaven and upon earth? From this it is apparent how greatly superior in power is the priestly dignity.

Or who of them is able to ordain any clergyman in the Holy Church —much less to depose him for any fault? For bishops, while they may ordain other bishops, may in no wise depose them except by authority of the Apostolic See. How, then, can even the most slightly informed person doubt that priests are higher than kings? But if kings are to be judged by priests for their sins, by whom can they more properly be judged than by the Roman pontiff?

In short, all good Christians, whosoever they may be, are more properly to be called kings than are evil princes; for the former, seeking the glory of God, rule themselves rigorously; but the latter, seeking their own rather than the things that are of God, being enemies to

themselves, oppress others tyrannically. The former are the body of the
true Christ; the latter, the body of the Devil. The former rule themselves that they may reign forever with the supreme ruler. The power
of the latter brings it to pass that they perish in eternal damnation with
the prince of darkness who is king over all the sons of pride. . . .

Let kings and princes fear lest the higher they are raised above their
fellows in this life, the deeper they may be plunged in everlasting fire.
Wherefore it is written: "The mighty shall suffer mighty torments"
(Wisdom 6:7). They shall render unto God an account for all men subject to their rule. But if it is no small labor for the pious individual
to guard his own soul, what a task is laid upon princes in the care of
so many thousands of souls! And if Holy Church imposes a heavy
penalty upon him who takes a single human life, what shall be done
to those who send many thousands to death for the glory of this world?
These, although they say with their lips, *mea culpa,* for the slaughter
of many, yet in their hearts they rejoice at the increase of their glory
and neither repent of what they have done nor regret that they have
sent their brothers into the world below. So that, since they do not
repent with all their hearts and will not restore what they have gained
by human bloodshed, their penitence before God remains without the
fruits of a true repentance.

Wherefore they ought greatly to fear, and they should frequently be
reminded that, as we have said, since the beginning of the world and
throughout the kingdoms of the earth very few kings of saintly life can
be found out of an innumerable multitude, whereas in one single chair
of successive bishops—the Roman—from the time of the blessed Apostle
Peter nearly a hundred are counted among the holiest of men. How
can this be, except because the kings and princes of the earth, seduced by
empty glory, prefer their own interests to the things of the Spirit,
whereas pious pontiffs, despising vainglory, set the things of God above
the things of the flesh. The former readily punish offenses against themselves but are not troubled by offenses against God; the latter quickly
forgive those who sin against them but do not easily pardon offenders
against God. The former, far too much given to worldly affairs, think
little of spiritual things; the latter, dwelling eagerly upon heavenly subjects, despise the things of this world.

All Christians, therefore, who desire to reign with Christ are to be
warned not to reign through ambition for worldly power. They are to
keep in mind the admonition of that most holy pope Gregory in his
book on the pastoral office: "Of all these things what is to be followed,
what held fast, except that the man strong in virtue shall come to his
office under compulsion? Let him who is without virtue not come to
it even though he be urged thereto." If, then, men who fear God come
under compulsion with fear and trembling to the Apostolic See where

those who are properly ordained become stronger through the merits of the blessed Apostle Peter, with what awe and hesitation should men like Saul and David become worse! What we have said above is thus stated in the decrees of the blessed pope Symmachus—though we have learned it by experience: "He, that is St. Peter, transmitted to his successors an unfailing endowment of merit together with an inheritance of innocence"; and again: "For who can doubt that he is holy who is raised to the height of such an office, in which if he is lacking in virtue acquired by his own merits, that which is handed down from his predecessor is sufficient. For either he [Peter] raises men of distinction to bear this burden or he glorifies them after they are raised up."

Wherefore let those whom Holy Church, of its own will and with deliberate judgment, not for fleeting glory but for the welfare of multitudes, has called to royal or imperial rule—let them be obedient and ever mindful of the blessed Gregory's declaration in that same pastoral treatise: "When a man disdains to be the equal of his fellow men, he becomes like an apostate angel. Thus Saul, after his period of humility, swollen with pride, ran into excess of power. He was raised in humility, but rejected in his pride, as God bore witness, saying: 'Though thou wast little in thine own sight, wast thou not made the head of the tribes of Israel?' " (1 Kings 15:17) and again: "I marvel how, when he was little to himself he was great before God, but when he seemed great to himself he was little before God." Let them watch and remember what God says in the Gospel: "I seek not my own glory," (John 8:50), and, "He who would be first among you, let him be the servant of all" (Mark 10:44). Let them ever place the honor of God above their own; let them embrace justice and maintain it by preserving to everyone his right; let them not enter into the counsels of the ungodly, but cling to those of religion with all their hearts. Let them not seek to make Holy Church their maidservant or their subject, but recognizing priests, the eyes of God, as their masters and fathers, strive to do them becoming honor.

If we are commanded to honor our fathers and mothers in the flesh, how much more our spiritual parents! If he that curseth his father or his mother shall be put to death, what does he deserve who curses his spiritual father or mother? Let not princes, led astray by carnal affection, set their own sons over that flock for whom Christ shed his blood if a better and more suitable man can be found. By thus loving their own son more than God they bring the greatest evils upon the Church. For it is evident that he who fails to provide to the best of his ability so great and necessary an advantage for our holy mother, the Church, does not love God and his neighbor as befits a Christian man. If this one virtue of charity be wanting, then whatever of good the man may do will lack all saving grace.

But if they do these things in humility, keeping their love for God and their neighbor as they ought, they may count upon the mercy of him who said: "Learn of me, for I am meek and lowly of heart" (Matthew 11:29). If they humbly imitate him, they shall pass from their servile and transient reign into the kingdom of eternal liberty.

(In the last year of his life Gregory was still protesting that he had sought only to defend the Church.)

36a. Letter of Gregory to all the faithful (1084), ed. E. Caspar. *MGH Epistolae Selectae* II (1920-23), p. 575.

. . . Ever since by divine providence Mother Church raised me, all unworthy and God knows unwilling, to the apostolic throne, I have been concerned above all that Holy Church, the bride of God, our lady and mother, should return to her own proper dignity and remain free, chaste, and catholic. But because these things were greatly displeasing to the ancient enemy, he armed his members against us to defeat them. Thus he has achieved more against us — or rather against the Apostolic See — than he has been able to achieve since the time of the emperor Constantine the Great. And no wonder! for the nearer the time of Antichrist approaches the more he strives to destroy the Christian faith.

So now, my dearly beloved brothers, listen carefully to what I say. Throughout the whole world all who bear the name of Christian and truly understand the Christian faith know and believe that blessed Peter, prince of the Apostles, is the father of all Christians and their chief pastor after Christ, and that the Holy Roman Church is mother and mistress of all the churches. If therefore you believe this and hold it without a doubt I, as your brother and unworthy master, ask and command you by Almighty God to help and succor these your father and mother if you wish to gain through them absolution of all your sins, and blessing and grace in this world and the world to come. May Almighty God, from whom all good things proceed, enlighten your minds and make them grow in love of God and of your neighbor, so that you may deserve by your steady devotion to have your father and mother become your debtors, and enter without shame into their fellowship.

4. The War
of Propaganda

The conflict between Gregory VII and Henry IV stimulated an unprecedented outburst of polemical pamphleteering, a new departure in the medieval tradition of political thought.

The initial exchanges between Gregory and Henry had confused rather than clarified the issues between them. From the reformers' point of view the real need was to discriminate between the spheres of spiritual and temporal authority so clearly as to end the practice of kings arbitrarily appointing bishops and bestowing on them the symbols of their spiritual office. But Gregory found it impossible to conceive of any effective separation between church and state and by his claim to depose a king laid himself open to the charge of seeking supreme temporal and spiritual power for himself. The essential interest of the king was to retain an effective voice in the selection of bishops, since these officials played a vital role in the civil government of his kingdom. His right to make such appointments had formerly been based on the theocratic assumption that the royal office was itself an ecclesiastical dignity, that the king was head of the church, but Henry had largely abandoned this ground when he insisted on a separation of priesthood and kingship in the course of his argument against Gregory. There was a great need then for intellectuals to reconsider the theoretical issues that lay behind the open strife of pope and king.

A striking feature of the whole debate is that hardly any of the major participants propounded really extreme doctrines of papal or royal theocracy. The one who came closest to doing so was the anonymous royalist author of the so-called York Tractates (No. 37), who wrote in England about 1100, and even he started out from the Gelasian doctrine that sacerdotal authority and royal power were both necessary for the governance of the Christian people. Having stated the principle, however, he certainly succeeded in developing it in a way that very thoroughly subordinated the priestly office to the royal one. It is often pointed out that the "Anonymous of York" held a theory of "sacral kingship" that was already somewhat archaic in his own day, and it is true that for the rest of the Middle Ages kings chose to defend their authority with arguments that were more legalistic and less theological.

But it must also be remembered that a belief in the supernatural authority of kings remained widespread throughout Europe for centuries after 1100, and, indeed, the existence of such a trend of thought contributed significantly to the eventual defeat of the more extreme political claims of the papacy. The doctrine of royal theocracy cannot be dismissed as an aberration of the Dark Ages but was rather a continuing element in European political theory.

More typical examples of eleventh-century polemical writers are Manegold of Lautenbach (*No.* 38), a vehement supporter of Gregory VII, and the author of the *Liber de Unitate Ecclesiae Conservanda* (*No.* 39), an adherent of the imperial party. Both addressed themselves with particular care to the question whether a pope could depose a king. Manegold built up an impressive picture of the supreme jurisdiction that inhered in the Roman church as the see of St. Peter and gave a wholly approving account of the proceedings in Rome when Pope Gregory deprived Henry IV of his royal office. But he did not conclude his argument with an assertion that the pope possessed a superior temporal jurisdiction which empowered him to depose a king. Instead his thought moved off in a quite different direction and he propounded a primitive but quite explicit theory of social contract. The king's power was derived from the people, he argued, and they chose him with the understanding that he would rule justly. If a king became a tyrant, he broke the contract that bound him to the people and so by his own action relinquished the royal dignity and released the people from all obligations of obedience to him. Manegold did not suggest at all that the king's power was derived from the pope and, indeed, the whole argument implied that any sentence pronounced by the pope could only be a declaratory one.

The imperialist argument in the *Liber de Unitate Ecclesiae Conservanda* was even more explicitly dualistic. The author not only quoted Gelasius but insisted that the pope's teaching required a real division of authority between spiritual and temporal rulers. The special interest of his work is that he took up all the historical arguments that Gregory had advanced in his letter to Hermann of Metz and refuted them one by one in a very effective rebuttal of a large part of Gregory's case.

Although the problem of Henry's deposition was obviously of the highest importance, the most valuable contribution that 11th century intellectuals could make to the resolution of the whole conflict was something other than this scoring of debating points about the licitness or otherwise of the pope's action. There was also an urgent need for a new analysis of the whole act of royal investiture which would start out from the premise that spiritual office and temporal jurisdiction were two different things, conceptually separable from one another. Ivo of Chartres, a French canonist of massive learning, took a major step in this direction in a pungent and penetrating letter (1097) to Archbishop Hugh of Lyons, the papal legate in France (*No.* 40). Ivo was writing to defend one Daimbert, archbishop of Sens, who had been attacked by Hugh for accepting investiture from the king. Ivo was himself a supporter of the reform movement, but he suggested that Hugh and the other papal reformers were losing sight of the essential goal of their own program. "You strain at a gnat and swallow a camel," he wrote tartly. The one really important thing according to Ivo was that bishops should be chosen by canonical election and without simony. The king obviously could not bestow spiritual office; on the other hand, he did have a right to bestow the temporal possessions of the bishopric on the chosen candidate. It was of no great significance, Ivo thought, whether the king performed this legitimate function by conferring an episcopal staff or by some other symbolic ceremony.

It is not quite true—as has sometimes been maintained—that Ivo was the first to suggest the solution to the investiture contest that eventually came to be accepted in practice. His distinction between the spiritual office and the temporal possessions of a bishop was indeed all-important, but the episcopal staff was too widely regarded as a symbol of spiritual office for the reformers ever to acquiesce in its continued use by secular rulers. A solution more acceptable to them was put forward by Hugh of Fleury, a moderate royalist who wrote a few years after Ivo (*No.* 41). The king, he suggested, had the right to assent to an episcopal election on behalf of the layfolk, whose acceptance of a newly elected bishop was part of the established canonical procedure, and a right to invest the new bishop with the temporal lands and jurisdictions pertaining to his see. But he ought not to use the disputed symbols of staff and ring in doing so. The staff and ring were rather to be bestowed by the consecrating archbishop, since they symbolized the "care of souls." The temporalities of the see were to be conferred by the king in some other fashion. In this way, Hugh concluded, the command of Christ would be fulfilled to "render to Caesar the things that are Caesar's and to God the things that are God's."

The "Anonymous of York"

37. *Tractatus Eboracenses* (c. 1100), ed. H. Boehmer, *MGH Libelli de Lite*, III (Hanover, 1897), pp. 663, 667, 679.

By divine authority and by institution of the holy fathers kings are ordained in the church of God and are consecrated at the altar with sacred unction and benediction, that they may have the power of ruling the people of the Lord, the Christian people, which is the holy church of God—a chosen race, a holy race, a purchased people (cf. 1 Peter 2:9). What else indeed is the church but the congregation of faithful Christians living together in the house of Christ in charity and in the one faith? Therefore kings receive in their consecration the power to rule this church, that they may rule it and strengthen it in judgement and justice and administer it in accordance with the discipline of the Christian law; for they reign in the church, which is the kingdom of God, and reign together with Christ, in order that they may rule, protect and defend it. To reign is to rule the subjects well and to serve God with fear. The episcopal order too is instituted and consecrated with sacred unction and benediction, that it also may rule the holy church according to the form of doctrine given to it by God Accordingly the blessed pope Gelasius speaks thus, "Two there are by which this world is chiefly ruled, the priestly authority and the royal power." By "this world" he means the holy church, which is a sojourner in this world. In this world, then, the priestly authority and the royal power hold the principate of sacred government. Some seek to divide the principate in this fashion, saying that the priesthood has the principate of ruling souls, the king that of ruling bodies, as if souls could be ruled without bodies and bodies without souls, which cannot be done by any means. For if bodies are well ruled it is necessary that souls are well ruled too and vice versa, since both are ruled for this purpose, that at the resurrection they may both be saved together.

Christ, God and man, is the true and highest king and priest. But he is king from the eternity of his divinity, not made, not created, not below or separate from the Father, but equal to and one with the Father. He is priest from his assumption of humanity, made and created according to the order of Melchisedech and so less than the Father. As king he created all things and rules and preserves all things, governing both men and angels. As priest he only redeemed men that they might reign with him. This is the sole reason why he was made priest, to offer himself as a sacrifice so that men might be made sharers of his kingdom and of his royal power. For everywhere in the Scriptures he promised the kingdom of heaven to the faithful but nowhere the priesthood. It is clear, therefore, that in Christ the royal power is greater and higher than the priestly in proportion as his divinity is greater and higher than his humanity. Hence some hold that among men likewise the royal power is greater and higher than the priestly and the king greater and higher than the priest, as being an imitation and emulation of the better and higher nature or power of Christ. And so it is not contrary to the justice of God, they say, if the sacerdotal dignity is instituted by the royal or subjected to it, for so it was done in Christ; he was made a priest by his royal power and was subjected to the Father in his priestly power while he was equal to him in his royal power. . . . But now let us see what the king confers on a man who is to be created bishop by the prerogative of the pastoral staff. I think that he does not confer the order or right of priesthood, but what pertains to his own right and to the rule of worldly things, namely the lordship and guardianship of the things of the church, and the power of ruling the people of God, which is the temple of the living God, and the holy church, the bride of Christ our Lord. That a bishop has lordship over earthly things, that is, possession of estates, by the law of kings is stated by Augustine at the end of his sixth treatise on John where he says "Each man possesses all he does possess by human law for, by divine law, 'the Lord's is the earth and the fullness thereof'. . . . By human law and therefore by the law of emperors. . . ."

No one should take precedence by right over [the king], who is blessed with so many and such great blessings, who is consecrated and made like unto God with so many and such great sacraments, for no one is consecrated and made like God with more or greater sacraments than he is, nor indeed with equivalent ones, and so no one is co-equal with him. Therefore he is not to be called a layman, for he is the anointed of the Lord, a God through grace, the supreme ruler, supreme shepherd, master, defender and instructor of holy church, lord over his brothers, worthy to be adored by all men, chief and highest prelate. It is not to be said that he is inferior to the bishop because the bishop consecrates him, for it often happens that lesser men consecrate a greater, inferiors their superior, as when the cardinals consecrate a pope or suffragan bishops a metropolitan. This can be so because they are not the authors of the consecration but ministers. God makes the sacrament efficacious; they administer it.

Manegold of Lautenbach

38. *Manegoldi ad Gebehardum Liber* (1080-85), ed. K. Francke, *MGH Libelli de Lite,* I (Hanover, 1892), pp. 325, 358, 365, 391-92.

. . . Since then it is evident from the aforementioned opinions of the holy fathers and from others, so numerous that it is irksome to include them, that the Roman church is distinguished with such great authority and indeed excels all the principalities and powers of this world in its singular and incomparable dignity, and since, according to the harmonious witness of the holy fathers, no one is permitted to judge its judgements or reverse its sentences and no one may rightfully have the will or power to disobey its decrees, anyone who has not remained in communion with it is a stranger and a sinner and an enemy of God, and whatever is done against its discipline can in no wise be held lawful. Let our conspirators see then, let them see, these men who publicly and contumaciously forsake the holy faith and the Catholic religion, how guilty they are of sacrilege, how inextricably they are bound by the knot of their innumerable wickednesses, these men who day by day destroy the souls of those whom they lead to despise the Roman see, who subject to the torment of eternal fire along with themselves as many as they seduce from its unity by their rash examples of sacrilege and their pestiferous arguments.

. . . As for the king himself, the author and fomenter of so much evil, the holy council decreed that the apostolic sword be unsheathed to cut him off from the body of the whole church and that, bound by the bond of anathema, he be deprived of the royal dignity. It absolved from their oaths all those who had sworn oaths to him and forbade anyone to serve him as king, for it was fitting that he who had presumed to annul and trample under foot the honor divinely conferred on St. Peter by special privilege should himself lose the honor that he seemed to possess, and that he who disdained to obey as a Christian should be judged unworthy to rule over Christians. . . .

Just as the royal dignity and power surpasses all earthly powers, so too the man appointed to exercise it should not be base and infamous but should excel others in wisdom, justice and piety as he does in place and dignity. It is necessary, therefore, that the one who is to have charge of all and govern all should display greater virtue than others and should be careful to exercise the power committed to him with a fine balance of equity; for the people do not exalt him above themselves so as to concede to him an unlimited power of tyrannizing over them, but rather to defend them against the tyranny and wickedness of others. However, when he who is chosen to repress evil-doers and defend the just begins to cherish evil in himself, to oppress good men, to exercise over his subjects the cruel tyranny that he ought to ward off from them, is it not clear that he deservedly falls from the dignity conceded to him and that the people are free from his lordship and from subjection to him since it is evident that he first broke the compact by virtue of which he was appointed? Nor can anyone justly or reasonably accuse the people of perfidy when it is evident that he first broke faith with them. To take an example from a meaner sphere, if a man hired someone for a fair wage to look after his swine and then found that he was not caring for them but stealing, killing and destroying them, would not the man withhold the promised wage from him and remove him ignominiously from his task of caring for the swine? Now, if this is observed in base things, that a man who does not care for his swine but destroys them shall not be kept as a swineherd, are there not just and reasonable grounds for maintaining that, in proportion as humans differ from swine, so too it is more fitting that anyone who does not strive to rule his subjects but rather to lead them into error should be deprived of the power and authority over men that he has received? Why should we be surprised if this rule is observed under the Christian religion when the ancient Romans in the days of the illustrious Collatinus and Brutus, refusing to endure the pride of Tarquin because of the shameful deed which his son, not he himself, had perpetrated against the noble matron Lucretia, expelled him and his son from the country and from the kingship, and created a government by two consuls holding office for a year to prevent anyone growing haughty through long exercise of authority. . . .

The nature of man excels that of all other living creatures in this, that, being capable of treating by reason whatever has not fallen out by fortuitous hazard, it inquires into the causes of things with rational judgement and considers not only what is done but why it is done. Since then no one can make himself an emperor or king, the people raise some man above themselves for these reasons, to rule and govern them by virtue of his just authority, to apportion to each his own, to protect the good, to repress the wicked and to deal out justice to all. If, however, he breaks the compact by which he was elected and ruins and confounds what he was established to order correctly, reason justly considers that he has absolved the people from their duty of submission to him since he himself first broke the bond of mutual fidelity by which he was bound to them and they to him.

De Unitate Ecclesiae Conservanda

39. *De Unitate Ecclesiae Conservanda* (1090-93), ed. W. Schwenkenbecher, *MGH Libelli de Lite*, II (Hanover, 1892), pp. 185-87, 194-96.

. . . [Pippin], when he was head of the household in the Frankish kingdom, that is, prefect of the palace, and all the royal power and dignity belonged to him, was the first of the prefects of the palace to be chosen king. He was consecrated with the blessing of the holy Boniface, Archbishop of Mainz, the judgement of Pope Zacharias having been obtained beforehand since the consent and authority of the Roman pontiff seemed necessary for this matter. Burchard of Wurzburg, a bishop of holy life, with other messengers fit for this mission, was sent to him by command of the princes to consult the oracle of his opinion and receive his response concerning this question, how they might reform the realm of the Franks and bring it to the state of its former dignity. For a long time it had lacked the prerogative of royal honor, since the one who was called king possessed nothing but the shadow of an empty name. Neither the wealth nor the power of the kingdom nor any ordering of its affairs rested with him but rather with the head of the household who controlled the palace. Therefore it seemed to them just and fitting that hereditary succession to the whole royal dignity and power be taken away from Hilderic [Childeric] and that the royal title be transferred to Pippin, at that time prefect of the palace, who was worthy of it by virtue of his nobility and courage. Seeing that he vigorously carried on the government of the household and of the armies of the realm it would be appropriate for him to receive the title of king along with the labors and the duties of the office. When Pope Zacharias had considered this proposal and deemed it just and expedient he gave his consent to it and afterwards Pope Stephen confirmed this judgement. Pippin was made king by common consent of the princes, and Hilderic received the tonsured crown and the habit of monastic life in place of the empty name of king. Now if this is so, or rather because this is so, it seems that the above-mentioned Pope Gregory, also called Hildebrand, unjustly imputed to Zacharias and Stephen, holy pontiffs of the Roman church, the acts of deposing Hilderic from the kingship solely by their own authority and of absolving the Franks from the oaths of fidelity that they had sworn to him, when perchance the princes of the realm would have considered it unworthy to swear an oath to a man of the sort described above. He wrote this, along with much else, to Hermann, Bishop of Metz, in order to convince his party that they might safely abandon their king, as if this example proved that he had power to depose him. . . .

If [his] words had been tempered with the charity that edifies, the breach with the rulers of the world that now exists would not have arisen since, as the holy Pope Leo writes, "There can be no general security unless the things that pertain to the profession of religion are defended by royal and priestly authority." So too Pope Gelasius declared, "Christ, mindful of human frailty, regulated with an excellent disposition what pertained to the salvation of his people. Thus he distinguished between the offices of both powers according to their own proper activities and separate dignities. . . ." Since God himself has thus arranged things and has instituted these two, the royal power and the sacred authority of priests, by which this world is chiefly ruled, who can attempt to go against this except one who resists the ordinance of God? . . .

. . . The above-mentioned Pope Hildebrand cites St. Ambrose in his letter in order to strengthen and confirm his party in schism, saying that Ambrose excommunicated the emperor Theodosius for a certain sin. But St. Ambrose, who corrected with ecclesiastical discipline the emperor

Theodosius when he was incited by the clamor of some of his supporters to avenge the grave crime of the Thessalonians, did not divide the church; rather he taught that we should render to Caesar the things that are Caesar's and to God the things that are God's. . . . It is this excommunication, which was profitable to the church and the emperor Theodosius alike, that is now cited in the letter with which we are dealing as a precedent for propagating a schism by which princes and nobles of the realm are separated from the companionship and service of their emperor. Ambrose, that strong tower and wall of the church, attempted nothing of the sort. . . . It is written indeed that Pope Innocent excommunicated the emperor Arcadius because he consented to the deposition of the holy bishop John. Where this is taken from is still unknown to us but we know for certain that it is not found in the *Gesta Romanorum Pontificum* or in the *Liber Decretorum* or in the *Historia Tripertita,* where we find more about that sentence of deposition than anywhere else. . . .

Ivo of Chartres

40. *Epistola ad Hugonem Archiepiscopum Lugdunensem* (1097), ed. E. Sackur, *MGH Libelli de Lite,* II (Hanover, 1892), pp. 644-46.

. . . You write that the chosen candidate [Daimbert] received episcopal investiture from the hand of the king, but we have not been informed of this by anyone who saw it. In any case, even if he did, we cannot see how the inclusion or omission of this investiture injured the faith or holy religion since it does not have the force of a sacrament in the making of a bishop. Again, it does not seem that kings are prohibited by apostolic authority from installing in bishoprics after canonical election has been held, for we read that supreme pontiffs of holy memory have sometimes interceded with kings on behalf of men elected to churches in order that the bishoprics to which they were elected might be granted to them by those same kings, and we read that others have delayed consecrations because royal installation did not follow the election. . . . Why should it matter whether this installation is accomplished by hand or by gesture, by word or by staff, when the kings do not intend to bestow anything spiritual but only to add their assent to the petition of the people, or to confer on the persons elected the ecclesiastical estates and other worldly goods which the churches receive through the munificence of kings. Thus Augustine writes in his sixth treatise on the Gospel of John, in the first part, "Does not a man possess whatever he possesses by human law? For by divine law 'the Lord's is the earth and the fulness thereof.' By human law we say, 'This estate is mine, this house is mine, this slave is mine.' Take away the laws of the emperors and who will dare say, 'This estate is mine, that slave is mine, that house is mine'. . . ."

If these things [*i.e.*, rules against lay investiture] were established by eternal law it would not lie within the power of rulers sometimes to judge strictly according to them, sometimes to relax them out of mercy so that men remain in dignities received in a fashion contrary to what they prescribe. But since in fact what they forbid is illicit essentially because it has been prohibited by rulers, so too the remission of them by rulers according to their own judgement is licit. We see no one or almost no one condemned for this kind of transgression but we see many disquieted, many churches despoiled, many scandals arisen, and a division between the kingship and the priesthood without whose harmonious cooperation there can be no sound and secure conduct of human affairs. . . . I do not say this as one who wants to set himself up against the apostolic see or resist its salutary decrees or cast doubt on the decisions of his superiors in so far as they are supported by cogent reasons and by the evident authority of the ancient fathers; but I do wish, together with many other devout persons, that the ministers of the Roman church, like experienced doctors, would concern themselves with curing the most grievous sicknesses and not have to hear their mockers saying, "You strain at a gnat and swallow a camel. You pay tithes on mint and anise and cummin but leave undone the weightier matters of the law" (*cf.* Matthew 23:23-24). . . .

Hugh of Fleury

41. *Tractatus de Regia Potestate* (1102-04). ed. E. Sackur, *MGH Libelli de Lite*, II (Hanover, 1892), p. 472.

I think that a king, inspired by the Holy Spirit, can appoint a pious cleric to the honor of prelacy. The archbishop indeed ought to commit to him the care of souls. The most Christian kings and princes promoted holy men in the church according to this prudent custom down to our own times. . . . If, indeed, a bishop has been elected by clergy and people reasonably and according to ecclesiastical custom the king ought not to use force against the electors tyrannically or harass them but rather should lawfully give his consent to the ordination. But if the one elected is found to be reprehensible, not only the king but the people of the province ought to withhold their assent and approval from his election and, moreover, they ought to expose publicly the crimes that mark him with detestable infamy so that by this reproach the audacity of the electors may be restrained. After the election the elected bishop ought to receive from the king's hand, not the ring and staff but the investiture of secular things, and he ought to receive from the archbishop, among his orders, the care of souls through the ring or staff, so that this kind of business may be carried through without dispute and the privilege of his authority may be maintained by both earthly and spiritual powers. If this is regularly observed, what our Savior commanded in the Gospel will be fulfilled—"Render to Caesar the things that are Caesar's and to God the things that are God's" (Luke 20:25). A procedure firmly and properly established will not be in doubt, and holy church will be freed from a host of tribulations. For the king, as was set out above, bears the likeness of God the Father, and the bishop of Christ. Although the Lord Jesus Christ himself seems to say in the Gospel to his disciples and their followers, ". . I appoint you to a kingdom as my Father has appointed me" (Luke 22.27). This was a kingdom of holy souls, not a kingdom of this world, as Christ witnessed at the time of his passion when he said to Pilate, "My kingdom is not of this world" (John 18.36). For, as the apostle Paul wrote to Timothy, "No one serving as God's soldier entangles himself in worldly affairs" (2 Timothy 2.4.).

5. The End of
the Contest

The struggle over investiture continued after Gregory VII's death and spread also to France and England. Ivo of Chartres and Hugh of Fleury had pointed the way to a possible solution of the dispute by drawing a distinction between the spiritual and temporal offices of a bishop, but their ideas made slow headway against the established opinion of the reformers that a bishopric—office and lands together—was a single juridical entity. A compromise was indeed reached in England as early as 1107 by which the king gave up the practice of investing bishops with ring and staff while retaining the right to receive feudal homage for the lands attached to their churches, but the pope of the time, Paschal II, regarded this as only a temporary concession, not as a permanent settlement of the investiture question.

Paschal is famous for another, far more radical solution that he proposed in his dealings with the emperor Henry V (son and successor to Henry IV). In 1111 Henry V occupied Rome with a German army, hoping to be crowned as emperor and to achieve a final settlement of the dispute with the papacy. The issue was now clearer than ever before. The king would not give up his right to appoint bishops because they were feudal lords exercising secular jurisdiction over lands that they held from the king. The pope would not acknowledge this royal right of appointment because bishops were ministers of God wielding a spiritual authority that was not derived from any lay ruler. Paschal's proposal for ending the impasse was a simple one—one of those simplicities that would have turned the world upside down. He suggested that the German churches renounce and return to the king all the vast lands and jurisdictions with which they had been endowed over the course of the centuries. The bishops would become once more simple pastors of souls, living on the tithes and free gifts of the faithful without any responsibilities for temporal government. The king would no longer have any reason for meddling in their appointments on political grounds (No. 42). Henry V accepted this proposal, and the new agreement was announced during the coronation service for the emperor-to-be in St. Peter's. At once a tumult broke out. The cardinals denounced the agreement, and the German bishops in the emperor's entourage refused to be bound by it.

Henry, who apparently had never seriously expected that the pact could be implemented, carried the pope off into captivity, and a few weeks later, while he was still a prisoner, Paschal conceded to the emperor the right of investiture that the German kings had claimed from the beginning of the dispute (*No.* 43). But again his action was repudiated by the church. The cardinals at Rome, the abbot of Cluny, the pope's own legate in France, all condemned the papal decision, and a few months later, after being released by Henry, Paschal revoked his concession on the ground that it had been made under duress. The dispute was finally settled under the next pope, Calixtus II (1119-24), at the Synod of Worms (1122). The terms were similar to those that had earlier been arranged with England. Bishops in Germany were to be canonically elected, and the emperor agreed to give up the practice of investing them with the ring and staff. On the other hand, he was permitted to be present at the election and to receive homage from newly elected prelates for the feudal lands of their churches (*No.* 44). Since the king could refuse to accept homage from a nominee who was unacceptable to him, he possessed in effect a power of veto over the election, and in practice secular rulers continued to have a very large say in the appointment of their bishops all through the Middle Ages.

The struggle thus ended with a compromise in which both king and pope could find some satisfaction. Neither power had been able wholly to defeat the other; royal theocracy had been defeated without papal theocracy becoming established. The strictly political issue of the pope's right to depose an emperor was not settled at all at this time but remained to be fought out in future controversies. One of the most important results of the dispute was to encourage the growth of doctrines justifying resistance by subjects to unjust rulers. This is most obviously true with regard to secular kings, but it should be noted that the pope too had been successfully opposed by the leaders of the church when his policies seemed to them unacceptable.

During the last stages of the investiture contest a new movement of thought arose that is interesting in itself and of profound significance for future theories of church and state, a movement whose earliest overt expression was Paschal's first proposal to Henry V, which seems to have embodied the pope's own preferred solution to the investitures problem. This proposal has usually been regarded as a radical departure from the ideals of Gregory VII, even as a betrayal of them. On the other hand, a recent study of Paschal's policies describes him as "a fanatical high Gregorian." [1]

It may well be that Paschal II started out from the same premises as Gregory VII and that his own policy seemed to him a logical conclusion

[1] N. Cantor, *Church, Kingship and Lay Investiture in England* (Princeton, 1958), p. 123.

derived from them; but, if for this reason he is to be called a "high Gregorian," it must be with the reservation that his conclusion was one which Gregory VII had never dreamed of and which he would certainly have viewed with dismay. The initial premise of both Gregory and Paschal—the premise indeed of the whole Gregorian reform movement—had been tersely summed up by Cardinal Humbert: "In the church the priesthood is comparable to the soul and the kingship to the body." It is not on the face of it an altogether convincing analogy. Obviously, a priest is not all soul nor a king all body. Nor were priests concerned only with souls and kings only with bodies even in principle. Ideally, priests administered corporeal charity and kings administered abstract justice. Each in his own sphere had to deal with the whole person. But if the analogy was to have any semblance of validity at all, it was essential that the priesthood constitute a spiritual élite withdrawn from material concerns as far as possible, not evidently and grossly immersed in the pursuit of worldly pleasures, wealth, and power. Gregory VII himself insisted on the detachment of the clergy from material preoccupations when he upheld the superiority of his own order and his consequent right to depose Henry IV by declaring that "[kings], far too much given to worldly affairs, think little of spiritual things; [pontiffs], dwelling eagerly upon heavenly subjects, despise the things of this world." But this line of thought, if pressed to its logical conclusion, would certainly seem to require a renunciation of temporal power and worldly wealth by the bishops. The management of material estates does not become a spiritual activity simply because bishops are set in charge of them.

Paschal came to realize this; Gregory never did so. The difference between them illustrates vividly how the overt issue of church and state that arose during the investiture contest was related to the still more fundamental problem of defining the right relationship between spiritual office and material property. For the papacy the most simple solution to that problem was one suggested by Humbert's line of argument—an assertion that since the spiritual order was intrinsically superior to the temporal, it was proper that temporal possessions and secular power should be subject to spiritual rulers. In this view, the greater the material wealth and power of the church the better; and if the argument was pressed to the point where temporal kings became mere agents of the pope, there were some who would find the conclusion palatable enough. In opposition to this world view was Paschal II's, always a minority opinion within the ecclesiastical hierarchy but never quite extinct. Its supporters upheld the higher dignity of the spiritual power as sharply as Humbert himself but maintained that the church's superiority had to be based on a real repudiation of the worldly power and wealth that secular princes sought for themselves. This attitude found its classical formulation toward the middle of the twelfth century in the writings of St. Bernard of Clairvaux.

Bernard, a younger contemporary of Paschal, was a famous ascetic and mystic and the most influential leader of the Cistercian order, a great new monastic movement of withdrawal from the world. In 1145 one of Bernard's own followers became pope, and the saint addressed to him a treatise on the conduct of the papal office which became a major source of argument for later writers on problems of church and state (*No.* 45). It was a strangely ambivalent work. Bernard rebuked the recent occupants of the papacy for their preoccupation with legal and political affairs. If this continued, he asked, how would the pope find time to pray, to teach, to meditate, to edify the church? But Bernard also extolled the Roman see as an institution and could find no language too exalted to describe the pope's eminent dignity as successor of St. Peter, vicar of Christ and head of the universal church. He asserted, moreover, in a very famous phrase, that the pope possessed "two swords," one representing spiritual power, the other material power. Bernard meant that in extreme cases the pope possessed an inherent right to use physical coercion as well as spiritual censures in the exercise of his jurisdiction. But since it was forbidden for a priest to shed blood it was necessary for the pope to summon the secular princes of Christendom to aid him in such matters and to exercise the "material sword" on his behalf. Bernard did not assert that .the whole temporal jurisdiction of princes was delegated to them by the papacy, though his phrase about the two swords was often understood in that sense in the course of later controversies.

A more explicit assertion that civil power was delegated by ecclesiastical authorities can be found in the works of another contemporary writer, Hugh of St. Victor. His key sentence, also much quoted in later controversies, declared, "The spiritual power has to institute the earthly power that it may be and to judge it if it has not been good." But he also held that "only spiritual things are committed to the clergy." Like Bernard, Hugh was a monk, a mystic, and a theologian. He was much concerned to stress the pre-eminent value of the spiritual life, but his comments on ecclesiastical power amount to only a few paragraphs in a major work which reviews the whole content of Christian theology. It is hard to extract a formal political theory from them or to be certain of Hugh's own intentions. He may have meant only that priests were qualified to judge the moral conduct of princes and that kings were "instituted" in their offices by an ecclesiastical ceremony of coronation and consecration.

It seems clear at any rate that Bernard and Hugh did not regard the pope as a worldly potentate but rather as a man of prayer, a holy high priest withdrawn from the mundane tasks of secular government. To such a pontiff they were willing to attribute the highest dignity on earth.

Paschal II and Henry V

42. Paschal's renunciation of the regalia of the church (February 1111), trans. E. F. Henderson, *Documents* (London, 1892), pp. 405-7.

Bishop Paschal, servant of the servants of God. To his beloved son Henry and his successors, forever. It is both decreed against by the institutions of the divine law, and interdicted by the sacred canons, that priests should busy themselves with secular cases, or should go to the public court except to rescue the condemned, or for the sake of others who suffer injury. Wherefore also the apostle Paul says: "If ye have secular judgments constitute as judges those who are of low degree in the church." Moreover in portions of your kingdom bishops and abbots are so occupied by secular cares that they are compelled assiduously to frequent the court, and to perform military service. Which things, indeed, are scarcely if at all carried on without plunder, sacrilege, arson. For ministers of the altar are made ministers of the king's court; inasmuch as they receive cities, duchies, margravates, monies and other things which belong to the service of the king. Whence also the custom has grown up—intolerably for the church—that elected bishops should by no means receive consecration unless they had first been invested through the hand of the king. From which cause both the wickedness of simoniacal heresy and, at times, so great an ambition has prevailed that the episcopal sees were invaded without any previous election. . . . And so, most beloved son, King Henry—now through our office, by the grace of God, emperor of the Romans—we decree that those royal appurtenances are to be given back to thee and to thy kingdom which manifestly belonged to that kingdom in the time of Charles, Louis, and of thy other predecessors. We forbid, and under sentence of anathema prohibit, that any bishop or abbot, present or future, invade these same royal appurtenances. In which are included the cities, duchies, margravates, counties, monies, toll, market, advowsons of the kingdom, rights of the judges of the hundred courts, and the courts which manifestly belonged to the king together with what pertained to them, the military posts and camps of the kingdom. Nor shall they, henceforth, unless by favour of the king, concern themselves with those royal appurtenances. But neither shall it be allowed our successors, who shall follow us in the apostolic chair, to disturb thee or thy kingdom in this matter. Furthermore, we decree that the churches, with the offerings and hereditary possessions which manifestly did not belong to the kingdom, shall remain free; as, on the day of thy coronation, in the sight of the whole church, thou didst promise that they should be. For it is fitting that the bishops, freed from secular cares, should take care of their people, and not any longer be absent from their churches. For, according to the apostle Paul, let them watch, being about to render account, as it were, for the souls of these [their people].

43. Paschal's concession of the privilege of investiture to Henry V (April 1111), trans. E. F. Henderson, *Documents*, pp. 407-8.

Bishop Paschal, servant of the servants of God, to his most beloved son in Christ, Henry, glorious king of the Germans, and, through the grace of Almighty God, august emperor of the Romans, greeting and apostolic benediction. The divine disposition has appointed that your kingdom should be singularly united with the holy Roman church. Your predecessors by reason of uprightness and greater virtue have obtained the crown of the city of Rome and the empire. To which dignity, viz.: that of the crown and the empire, the divine majesty has, most beloved son Henry, through the ministry of our priestship, brought thy person also. That prerogative, therefore, of dignity which our predecessors did grant to thy predecessors the catholic emperors, and did confirm by their charters, we also do concede to thee, beloved, and do confirm by the page of this present privilege: that, namely, thou may'st confer the investiture of staff and ring, freely, except through simony and with violence to the elected, on the bishops and abbots of thy kingdom. But after the investiture they shall receive the canonical consecration from the bishop to whom they belong. If any one, moreover, without thy consent, shall have been elected by the clergy and people, he shall be consecrated by no one unless he be invested by thee. Bishops and archbishops, indeed, shall have the right of canonically consecrating bishops or abbots invested by thee. For your predecessors have enriched the churches of their kingdom with such benefits from their royal appurtenances, that the kingdom itself should seek its chief safety in protecting the bishops and abbots; and popular dissensions, which often happen at elections, should be restrained by the royal majesty. Wherefore the attention of thy prudence and power ought the more carefully to be applied to this end: that the greatness of the Roman, and the safety of the other churches, should be preserved through still greater benefits—God granting them. . . .

The Concordat of Worms

44. Concordat of Calixtus II and Henry V (September 1122), trans. S. Z. Ehler and J. B. Morrall, *Church and State Through the Centuries* (London, 1954), pp. 48-49.

Privilege of the pope

I, Bishop Calixtus, servant of the servants of God, concede to you, beloved son Henry—by the grace of God August Emperor of the Romans —that the election of those bishops and abbots in the German kingdom who belong to the kingdom shall take place in your presence without simony and without any violence; so that if any discord occurs between the parties concerned, you may—with the counsel or judgment of the metropolitan and the co-provincials—give your assent and assistance to the party which appears to have the better case. The candidate elected may receive the "regalia" from you through the sceptre and he shall perform his lawful duties to you for them. But he who is elected in the other parts of the Empire shall, within six months, receive the "regalia" from you through the sceptre and shall perform his lawful duties for them, saving all things which are known as pertaining to the Church. If you complain to me in any of these matters and ask for help, I will furnish you the aid, if such is the duty of my office. I grant true peace to you and to all those who are or have been of your party during this discord.

Privilege of the emperor

In the name of Holy and Indivisible Trinity. I, Henry, by the grace of God August Emperor of the Romans, for the love of God and of the Holy Roman Church and of the lord Pope Calixtus and for the healing of my soul, do surrender to God, to the Holy Apostles of God, Peter and Paul, and to the Holy Roman Church all investiture through ring and staff; and do agree that in all churches throughout my kingdom and em- pire there shall be canonical elections and free consecration. I restore to the same Roman Church all the possessions and temporalities ["regalia"] which have been abstracted until the present day either in the lifetime of my father or in my own and which I hold; and I will faithfully aid in the restoration of those which I do not hold. The possessions also of all other churches and princes and of every one else, either cleric or lay- man, which had been lost in that war, I will restore, so far as I hold them, according to the counsel of the princes or according to justice; and I will faithfully aid in the restoration of those that I do not hold And I grant a true peace to the lord Pope Calixtus and to the Holy Roman Church and to all who are or have been on its side. In matters where the Holy Roman Church would seek assistance I will faithfully grant it;

and in those where she shall complain to me, I will duly grant justice to her.

Bernard of Clairvaux

45. *Treatise on Consideration* (1153), trans. by "A priest of Mount Melleray" (Dublin, 1921), pp. 11, 17-18, 56-58, 119-21.

What slavery can be more degrading and more unworthy of the Sovereign Pontiff than to be kept thus busily employed, I do not say every day, but every hour of every day, in furthering the sordid designs of greed and ambition? What leisure hast thou left for prayer? What time remains over to thee for instructing the people, for edifying the Church, for meditating on the law? True, thy palace is made to resound daily with noisy discussions relating to law, but it is not the law of the Lord, but the law of Justinian.

I have read indeed that the apostles *were brought to judgment,* but that they ever *sat in judgment* themselves I can nowhere find. The judicial office they have never yet exercised: they reserve that for the day of doom. . . . Hence it reveals a lack of good sense, or of a proper appreciation of values, to regard it as a dishonour for the apostles and their successors (who have been constituted judges over matters of greater moment) not to sit in judgment concerning the things of earth. Why should they not disdain to give judgment about our contemptible earthly possessions, who are appointed to judge even angels in heavenly places (1 Corinthians 6:3)? Consequently, it is on the sins of men, not with regard to their possessions, that thy judicial power ought to be exercised; for it is on account of the former thou hast received the keys of the kingdom of heaven, not for the sake of the latter. . . . Tell me, which power and office dost thou consider to be the greater, that of forgiving sins, or that of dividing possessions? But in truth there can be no comparison. These vile terrestrial things have their own proper judges, namely, the princes and rulers of the earth. Why then wouldst thou invade a province that belongs not to thee? Wherefore put thy sickle into another man's harvest? It is not that thou art unworthy to give judgment concerning such things, but rather this is unworthy of thee, who shouldst be occupied with matters of more consequence. . . .

Well, then, let us examine with still greater diligence who thou art, that is to say, what role thou fulfillest, according to the time, in the Church of God. Who art thou? Thou art the High Priest and the Sovereign Pontiff. Thou art the Prince of pastors and the Heir of the apostles.

By thy primacy thou art an Abel; by thy office of pilot (in Peter's barque), a Noe [Noah]; by thy patriarchate, an Abraham; by thy orders, a Melchisedech; by thy dignity, an Aaron; by thy authority, a Moses; by thy judicial power, a Samuel; by thy jurisdiction, a Peter; and by thy unction, a Christ. . . . Yea, not only of the sheep, but of the other pastors also art thou the sole supreme Shepherd. Wouldst thou know how I prove this? I prove it from the words of Christ. "If thou lovest Me," He said to Peter, "feed My sheep" (John 21:17). To which—I do not say of the other bishops, but even of the other apostles, was the entire flock entrusted so absolutely and so indiscriminately? For to what sheep did the Saviour refer? Was it to the people of this or that city? of this or that country or kingdom? "Feed My sheep"—these were His words. Who does not see plainly that, instead of designating some portion of the flock, they rather assign the whole? For there can be no exception where there is no distinction. And probably all the other apostles were present when the Lord committed all the sheep to the care of Peter alone, thus commending unity to all in one flock and one Shepherd (John 21), according to what is written, "One is My dove, My beautiful one, My perfect one" (Canticles 6:8). For where there is unity there is perfection. The other numbers imply, not perfection, but division, and the more so according as they recede from unity. Hence it is that the rest of the apostles, who understood this mystery, received each of them the charge of a particular community. Thus, for instance, James, although he "seemed to be a pillar" (Galatians 2:9) in the Church, was nevertheless content with Jerusalem alone, leaving the government of the universal Church to Peter. James is called the "brother of the Lord" (Galatians 1:19). Very appropriately, therefore, was he appointed to that see where Christ was slain, in order that he might "raise up issue to his Brother" (Matthew 22:24). Now if even the Lord's brother respected Peter's prerogative, is it likely that any other of the apostles would dispute it?

"What?" thou wilt say, "dost thou tell me to pasture these who are not sheep but dragons and scorpions?" All the more reason why thou shouldst endeavour to subdue them, not indeed with the sword, but with the word of God. For wherefore shouldst thou try again to wield that sword which thou wert commanded of old to replace in its scabbard? Nevertheless, he who would deny that the sword belongs to thee, has not, as I conceive, sufficiently weighed the words of the Lord, where He said, speaking to Peter, "Put up *thy* sword into the scabbard" (John 18:11). For it is here plainly implied that even the material sword is thine, to be drawn at thy bidding, although not by thy hand. Besides, unless this sword also appertained to thee in some sense, when the disciples said to Christ, "Lord, behold here are two swords" (Luke 22:38), He would never have answered as He did, "It is enough," but rather, "it is too much." We can therefore conclude that both swords, namely the spiritual and the material, belong to the Church, and that although only the former is to be wielded by her own hand, the two are to be employed in her service. It is for the priest to use the sword of the word, but to strike with the sword of steel belongs to the soldier, yet this must be by the authority and will of the priest and by the direct command of the emperor, as I have said elsewhere.* Do thou, therefore, take in hand at once the sword which has been given thee to strike with. Take it in hand, I say, and wound unto salvation, if not all, if not even many, at least such as thou canst.

* In a letter written to Eugenius in 1146, urging him to send help to the Christians in Palestine, the Saint says, "Now whilst Christ is enduring a second passion where He also endured His first, both swords, the material as well as the spiritual, must be unsheathed. And by whom but by thee? For the two swords are Peter's, to be drawn whenever necessary, the one by his own hand, the other by his authority."

Hugh of Saint Victor

46. *De Sacramentis Christianae Fidei* (c. 1134), ed. J. P. Migne, *PL* 176 (Paris, 1854), col. 417-18.

There are two lives, one earthly, the other heavenly, one corporeal, the other spiritual. By one the body lives from the soul, by the other the soul lives from God. Each has its own good by which it is invigorated and nourished so that it can subsist. The earthly life is nourished with earthly goods, the spiritual life with spiritual goods. To the earthly life belong all things that are earthly, to the spiritual life all goods that are spiritual. In order that justice may be served in both lives and prosperity flourish, men were first distributed on each side to acquire by zeal and labor the goods of each life according to reason and necessity. Then there were others to dispense equity by the power of the office committed to them so that no one should tread down his brother in business but justice should be kept inviolate.

Therefore, in each people distributed according to each life, powers were established. Among laymen, to whose zeal and forethought the things that are necessary for earthly life pertain, the power is earthly. Among the clergy, to whose office the goods of the spiritual life belong, the power is divine. The one power is therefore called secular, the other spiritual. . . . The earthly power has as its head the king. The spiritual power has the supreme pontiff. All things that are earthly and made for the earthly life belong to the power of the king. All things that are spir-

itual and attributed to the spiritual life belong to the power of the
supreme pontiff. The spiritual power excels the earthly or secular power
in honor and dignity in proportion as the spiritual life is more worthy
than the earthly, and the spirit than the body.

For the spiritual power has to institute the earthly power that it may
be and to judge it if it has not been good. The spiritual power itself
was instituted by God in the first place and, when it errs, can be judged
by God alone, as it is written: "The spiritual man judgeth all things;
and he himself is judged of no man" (1 Corinthians 2:15). That the
spiritual power is prior in time, so far as divine institution is concerned,
and greater in dignity is manifestly set forth in that ancient people of
the Old Testament among whom the priesthood was first instituted by
God and then the royal power was established through the priesthood
at God's command. Accordingly, the sacerdotal dignity still consecrates
the royal power in the church, both sanctifying it by benediction and
forming it by instruction. If then, as the Apostle says, he who blesses is
greater and he who is blessed less, it is established beyond all doubt that
the earthly power, which receives benediction from the spiritual, is rightfully regarded as inferior to it.

Part III

 THE AGE OF
THE LAWYERS

1. The Imperial Policy
of Frederick Barbarossa

The century from 1150 to 1250 was marked by a series of clashes between the popes and the Hohenstaufen dynasty of German emperors. The issues at stake were more overtly political than those involved in the investiture contest, and the theoretical discussions on church and state were carried on in more legalistic terms. Supporters of popes and princes were no longer content merely to ask whether the Scriptures and the Fathers had attributed a higher authority to priests or to kings. They also tried to define what precise classes of legal cases could be judged by a pope, what were the limits (if any) to his legislative authority, what legal sanctions he could use in his dealings with temporal rulers, and whether he could hear appeals from their courts. This new argumentation reflects a great growth of sophistication in the art of jurisprudence.

Around 1100 the jurist Irnerius began to lecture on the whole corpus of classical Roman law at Bologna, and subsequently a distinguished school of Roman lawyers grew up there. In the earlier Middle Ages the only law that men had known was a rude muddle of conflicting local customs, but Roman jurisprudence reintroduced the idea that a legal system could be a coherent body of ordered deductions from rational principles. The whole conception seems to have come to medieval intellectuals with the force of a revelation. On the practical level too, in an age of rapidly advancing civilization and expanding economic activity, there was a widespread popular demand for rational and equitable legal procedures. In such circumstances any ruler whose courts could provide fair and enforceable judicial decisions found his status greatly enhanced, and kings who sought to increase their powers came to rely more on the efficiency of their judges and administrators than on the sanctity of their office or the personal devotion of their vassals. Moreover, the study of Roman law provided a very exalted theory of legislative sovereignty together with a wholly nonpapal account of the origins of imperial authority (*Nos.* 47, 48). Eventually the assimilation of such principles contributed much to the emergence of sovereign, centralized states independent of papal control.

For the most part, however, this development took place only after the secularist principles of Roman law had been reinforced by the revival of Aristotelian political concepts in the second half of the thirteenth century. During the twelfth century the most obvious immediate result of the new study of Roman jurisprudence was that it stimulated the canonists to develop their own ecclesiastical law into a system of comparable scope and subtlety. This task of systematizing the law of the church was accomplished by a monk of Bologna called Gratian. In about 1140 he produced his *Decretum,* a massive compilation of texts selected from the canonical materials that had been accumulating for the past thousand years—decrees of popes, canons of councils, decisions of revered church Fathers—all organized for the first time into a comprehensive and orderly collection. The work was swiftly adopted throughout the Western world as a definitive statement of existing ecclesiastical law, and the use of such a single, universally accepted code of canons made possible an unprecedented growth of administrative unity in the church. The process was helped by Gratian's strong emphasis on the role of the pope as supreme judge and legislator in all ecclesiastical affairs and by the fact that all the great popes of the next century—Alexander III (1159-81), Innocent III (1198-1216), Gregory IX (1227-41), Innocent IV (1243-54)— were also great lawyers. New legal procedures, often borrowed from Roman law, were adopted in order to facilitate appeals to Rome, and as the appeals flowed in by thousands from every corner of Christendom the necessary apparatus of papal courts, bureaucratic administrators, and delegate judges was developed to cope with them. This great growth of administrative machinery in the twelfth century added flesh and bone and muscle to Gregory VII's abstract assertions of papal sovereignty.

Both the papal and imperial authorities were thus well equipped for a new round of controversies, the popes with their international bureaucracy and newly ordered canon law, the emperors with German armies at their backs and a growing knowledge of Roman law to provide ideological support for their claims. The specific political issue that divided empire and papacy in the twelfth century was the emperor's claim to sovereignty over Italy in general and over Rome in particular. It seemed to the popes that an emperor who established effective power in Rome itself would inevitably reassume control over papal appointments, and they were determined at all costs to prevent such a development. On the other hand, it was of the highest importance to the Hohenstaufen emperors that their imperial title should be recognized in Rome as something more than an empty dignity. The first great emperor of the dynasty, Frederick Barbarossa, aimed to control a contiguous block of lands north and south of the Alps, including the province of Lombardy with its rich towns and vast potential as a source of tax revenue. From such a base he might well have dominated all Germany and Italy—and perhaps he dreamed of a still greater empire. But his only shadow of a claim to govern Lombardy was in his capacity as Roman emperor, and if the imperial dignity was to imply any right to effective political authority in Italy, Rome itself could hardly be excluded from that authority. Pope Hadrian IV once wrote to inform the emperor that the government of Rome belonged to "St. Peter." Barbarossa replied grimly that if the imperial title conveyed no rights in Rome it conveyed no rights anywhere.

To the twelfth-century popes it seemed intolerable that the Roman church should be reduced to the status of just one more imperial bishopric, but they could hardly deny that the man they crowned in St. Peter's as emperor of the Romans was in some sense ruler of Rome. The solution they adopted was to assert that any rights which the emperor possessed in Rome were held from the pope as from an overlord, that the emperor was a vassal or official of the papacy. This claim safeguarded the principle of papal sovereignty in central Italy, and most probably that is why the popes advanced it. But it had much wider implications. A claim to be overlord of the emperor could very well imply a claim to universal temporal authority. In many of the texts of this period which mention the "temporal power" or "regal dignity" of the popes it is by no means clear whether such words refer merely to papal rule over Rome itself or to some dream of universal sovereignty, and at times, no doubt, the ambiguity was willful. Again, while the assertion that the empire was "held" from the papacy was put forward plainly enough, it is not clear whether the papacy based its claim on the historical fact that popes had crowned emperors since the days of Charlemagne or on the specific transaction recorded in the Donation of Constantine or on the general theological doctrine that the spiritual power, being intrinsically superior, had to "institute" the temporal power (as Hugh of St. Victor had put it).

At any rate, throughout the middle years of the twelfth century the popes attempted to establish in some fashion that they were overlords of the emperors. In 1133, for instance, when Lothar III visited Rome for his imperial coronation, he accepted certain disputed territories in Italy as a fief from the pope, and according to feudal custom he did homage to the pope for the lands he acquired. A little later a mosaic was erected in the Lateran palace showing the emperor kneeling at the pope's feet and performing the act of vassalage, while underneath were set the words: "After becoming liegeman of the pope, the king receives the crown from him." The most obvious meaning of the picture for future generations would be that Lothar had received the whole empire as a fief from the pope at the time of his coronation and had acknowledged the fact in the ceremony depicted.

Frederick Barbarossa, who became king in 1152, vigorously resisted such pretensions by the popes. On his first visit to Italy when Pope Hadrian rode out to meet him near Rome he refused at first to perform the customary service of acting as a squire to the pope by holding his stirrup. Frederick agreed to go through with the ceremony only after a delay of twenty-four hours during which time his own nobles assured him that it was indeed a customary and innocuous gesture. Pope and emperor then advanced toward Rome together. Near the city they were met by envoys from the Roman municipal government which styled itself the "senate" of Rome. The "senators" announced that the imperial crown lay within their gift and that they would be glad to bestow it on Frederick—on their own terms. Enraged at this insolence Frederick broke into a bitter harangue, denouncing the Romans as corrupt and degenerate and declaring that he claimed the empire by right of conquest alone (*No.* 49). The words were directed against the Roman commune, but they must have made hard hearing for the pope too.

All this maneuvering came to a climax at the imperial Diet of Besançon held in Burgundy in 1157. Pope Hadrian dispatched two legates to the council, one of them the chancellor of the Roman church, Cardinal Rolandus, and sent with them a letter to the emperor which was read out before the diet. In it Hadrian declared that the Roman church had conferred on Frederick the "emblem of the imperial crown" and added that he would be willing in the future to bestow still greater "benefits." (*No.* 50) The last word was an ambiguous one. The Latin term *beneficium* which Hadrian used could mean simply a "favor" or "benefit," but it could also have the technical sense of a fief. The emperor's chancellor, Rainald, who was translating the pope's letter into German for the assembled nobles, apparently chose to render the word in the latter sense. A tumult arose, and the papal legate did not help matters by inquiring innocently, "From whom then does he have the empire if not from our Lord the pope?" Indeed, at that point Barbarossa had to intervene to save the pope's messenger from being cut down by an indignant noble (*No.* 51).

Both pope and emperor then wrote to the German bishops giving their accounts of the incident. Hadrian complained sharply about the treatment of his legates and repeated his original terminology—"We have bestowed the benefice of the imperial crown"—without any retraction or explanation. But to his consternation the bishops wholeheartedly supported Frederick. The emperor, meanwhile, was preparing another expedition into Italy, and Hadrian decided that it would be prudent to adopt a more conciliatory tone. He therefore wrote again to Frederick, this time explaining that by *beneficium* he had meant only a "good deed," and surely no one would deny that he had done a "good deed" in crowning the emperor (*No.* 53). Frederick accepted the explanation, and this letter ended the episode.

The incident at Besançon has sometimes been regarded as a mere misunderstanding by the emperor of a phrase that the pope intended to be quite inoffensive, but this interpretation does not account for the fact that Hadrian failed to withdraw or to explain away the term *beneficium* in his letter to the German bishops even after he knew that it had given grievous offense. A second interpretation suggests that Hadrian deliberately intended to provoke a breach with the emperor since he had recently entered upon an alliance with the king of Sicily and was anxious to persuade all the cardinals of the necessity for this new diplomatic alignment. Yet a third explanation points out that for centuries the term *beneficium* had been applied to the imperial authority in papal usage without any feudal connotation. According to this interpretation Hadrian intended to assert that the imperial dignity was an office held of the pope but not that the emperor was technically a feudal vassal. Moreover, it is suggested, the pope never withdrew this assertion, for even in his final letter he still claimed to have "conferred" the imperial crown.[1] Perhaps the most likely explanation of the whole affair is that the pope put forward a claim to lordship over the emperor in deliberately ambiguous and obscure language, hoping that at best his claim would go unchallenged and stand as a precedent, or that at worst he could explain away his words without too much loss of face.

Sovereignty and Law in the Corpus Iuris Civilis

47. Imperial authority. *The Digest of Justinian* (533), trans. C. H. Monro (Cambridge, 1904), pp. xxv-xxvi, xxxiii, 22.

It was indeed a wondrous achievement when Roman jurisprudence from the time of the building of the city to that of our rule, which period well-nigh reaches to one thousand and four hundred years, had been shaken with intestine war and the Imperial legislation infected with the same mischief, to bring it nevertheless into one harmonious system, so that it should present no contradiction, no repetition and no approach to repetition, and that nowhere should two enactments appear dealing with one question. This was indeed proper for Heavenly Providence, but in no way possible to the weakness of man. We there-

---

[1] W. Ullmann, *Growth of Papal Government* (London, 1955), pp. 340-43. For other interpretations of the incident see M. Pacaut, *Alexandre III* (Paris, 1956), pp. 90-96.

fore have after our wont fixed our eyes on the aid of Immortality, and, calling on the Supreme Deity, we have desired that God should be made the originator and the guardian of the whole work, and we .have entrusted the entire task to Tribonianus, a most distinguished man, Master of the Offices, ex-quaestor of our sacred palace and ex-consul, and we have laid on him the whole service of the enterprise described, so that with other illustrious and most learned colleagues he might fulfil our desire. Besides this, our Majesty, ever investigating and scrutinizing the composition of these men, whensoever anything was found doubtful or uncertain, in reliance on the heavenly Divinity, amended it and reduced it to suitable shape. Thus all has been done by our Lord and God Jesus Christ, who vouchsafed the means of success both to us and to our servants herein.

Now whatever is divine is absolutely perfect, but the character of human law is to be constantly hurrying on, and no part of it is there which can abide for ever, as nature is ever eager to produce new forms, so that we fully anticipate that emergencies may hereafter arise which are not enclosed in the bonds of legal rules. Wherever any such case arises, let the August remedy be sought, as in truth God set the Imperial dispensation at the head of human affairs to this end, that it should be in a position, whenever a novel contingency arrives, to meet the same with amendment and arrangement, and to put it under apt form and regulations.

The Emperor is not bound by statutes. The Empress no doubt is bound, at the same time the Emperor generally gives her the same exceptional rights as he enjoys himself.

> 48. The sources of law. *The Institutes of Justinian* (529), trans. J. B. Moyle, 3rd ed. (Oxford, 1896), pp. 3-5.

Justice is the set and constant purpose which gives to every man his due. Jurisprudence is the knowledge of things divine and human, the science of the just and the unjust. . . .

The precepts of the law are these: to live honestly, to injure no one, and to give every man his due. The study of law consists of two branches, law public, and law private. The former relates to the welfare of the Roman State; the latter to the advantage of the individual citizen. Of private law then we may say that it is of threefold origin, being collected from the precepts of nature, from those of the law of nations, or from those of the civil law of Rome.

The law of nature is that which she has taught all animals; a law not peculiar to the human race, but shared by all living creatures, whether denizens of the air, the dry land, or the sea. Hence comes the union of male and female, which we call marriage; hence the procreation and rearing of children, for this is a law by the knowledge of which we see even the lower animals are distinguished. The civil law of Rome, and the law of all nations, differ from each other thus. The laws of every people governed by statutes and customs are partly peculiar to itself, partly common to all mankind. Those rules which a state enacts for its own members are peculiar to itself, and are called civil law: those rules prescribed by natural reason for all men are observed by all peoples alike, and are called the law of nations. Thus the laws of the Roman people are partly peculiar to itself, partly common to all nations; a distinction of which we shall take notice as occasion offers. . . .

Our law is partly written, partly unwritten, as among the Greeks. The written law consists of statutes, plebiscites, senatusconsults, enactments of the Emperors, edicts of the magistrates, and answers of those learned in the law. A statute is an enactment of the Roman people, which it used to make on the motion of a senatorial magistrate, as for instance a consul. A plebiscite is an enactment of the commonalty, such as was made on the motion of one of their own magistrates, as a tribune. . . . A senatusconsult is a command and ordinance of the senate, for when the Roman people had been so increased that it was difficult to assemble it together for the purpose of enacting statutes, it seemed right that the senate should be consulted instead of the people. Again, what the Emperor determines has the force of a statute, the people having conferred on him all their authority and power by the *lex regia*, which was passed concerning his office and authority. Consequently, whatever the Emperor settles by rescript, or decides in his judicial capacity, or ordains by edicts, is clearly a statute: and these are what are called constitutions.

Barbarossa and the "Roman Senate"

49. Reply of Frederick Barbarossa to the ambassadors of the city of Rome (June 1155), trans. C. C. Mierow, *The Deeds of Frederick Barbarossa by Otto of Freising and His Continuator, Rahewin* (New York, 1953), pp. 146-48.

We have heard much heretofore concerning the wisdom and the valor of the Romans, yet more concerning their wisdom. Wherefore we cannot wonder enough at finding your words insipid with swollen pride rather than seasoned with the salt of wisdom. You set forth the ancient renown of your city. You extoll to the very stars the ancient status of your sacred republic. Granted, granted! To use the words of your own writer, "There was, *there was once* virtue in this republic." "Once," I say. And O that we might truthfully and freely say "now"! Your Rome—nay, ours also—has experienced the vicissitudes of time. She could not be the only one to escape a fate ordained by the Author of all things for all that dwell beneath the orb of the moon. What shall I say? It is clear how first the strength of your nobility was transferred from this city of ours to the royal city of the East, and how for the course of many years the thirsty Greekling sucked the breasts of your delight. Then came the Frank, truly noble, in deed as in name, and forcibly possessed himself of whatever freedom was still left to you. Do you wish to know the ancient glory of your Rome? The worth of the senatorial dignity? The impregnable disposition of the camp? The virtue and the discipline of the equestrian order, its unmarred and unconquerable boldness when advancing to a conflict? Behold our state. All these things are to be found with us. All these have descended to us, together with the empire. Not in utter nakedness did the empire come to us. It came clad in its virtue. It brought its adornments with it. With us are your consuls. With us is your senate. With us is your soldiery. These very leaders of the Franks must rule you by their counsel, these very knights of the Franks must avert harm from you with the sword. You boastfully declare that by you I have been summoned, that by you I have been made first a citizen and then the prince, that from you I have received what was yours. How lacking in reason, how void of truth this novel utterance is, may be left to your own judgment and to the decision of men of wisdom! Let us ponder over the exploits of modern emperors, to see whether it was not our divine princes Charles [Charlemagne] and Otto [I] who, by their valor and not by anyone's bounty, wrested the City along with Italy from the Greeks and the Lombards and added it to the realms of the Franks. Desiderius and Berengar teach you this, your tyrants, of whom you boasted, on whom you relied as your princes. We have learned from reliable accounts that they were not only subjugated and taken captive by our Franks, but grew old and ended their lives in their servitude. Their ashes, buried among us, constitute the clearest evidence of this fact. But, you say: "You came on my invitation," I admit it; I was invited. Give me the reason why I was invited! You were being assailed by enemies and could not be freed by your own hand or by the effeminate Greeks. The power of the Franks was invoked by invitation. I would call it entreaty rather than invitation. In your misery you besought the happy, in your frailty the valiant, in your weakness the strong, in your anxiety the carefree. Invited after that fashion—if it may be called an invitation—I have come. I have made your prince my vassal and from that time until the present have transferred you to my jurisdiction. I am the lawful possessor. Let him who can, snatch the club from the hand of Hercules. . . .

The Incident at Besançon

50. Letter of Hadrian IV to the emperor (September 1157), trans.
C. C. Mierow, *op. cit.*, pp. 181-83.

Bishop Hadrian, the servant of the servants of God, to his beloved son Frederick, the illustrious emperor of the Romans, greeting and apostolic benediction.

We recollect having written, a few days since, to the Imperial Majesty, of that dreadful and accursed deed, an offense calling for atonement, committed in our time, and hitherto, we believe, never attempted in the German lands. In recalling it to Your Excellency, we cannot conceal our great amazement that even now you have permitted so pernicious a deed to go unpunished with the severity it deserves. For how our venerable brother E[skil], archbishop of Lund, while returning from the apostolic see, was taken captive in those parts by certain godless and infamous men . . . Your Most Serene Highness knows. . . . But you are reported so to have ignored and indeed been indifferent to this deed, that there is no reason why those men should be repentant at having incurred guilt, because they have long since perceived that they have secured immunity for the sacrilege which they have committed.

Of the reason for this indifference and negligence we are absolutely ignorant, because no scruple of conscience accuses our heart of having in aught offended the glory of Your Serenity. Rather have we always loved, with sincere affection, and treated with an attitude of due kindness, your person as that of our most dear and specially beloved son and most Christian prince, who, we doubt not, is by the grace of God grounded on the rock of the apostolic confession.

For you should recall, O most glorious son, before the eyes of your mind, how willingly and how gladly your mother, the Holy Roman Church, received you in another year, with what affection of heart she treated you, what great dignity and honor she bestowed upon you, and with how much pleasure she conferred the emblem of the imperial crown, zealous to cherish in her most kindly bosom the height of Your Sublimity, and doing nothing at all that she knew was in the least at variance with the royal will.

Nor do we regret that we fulfilled in all respects the ardent desires of your heart; but if Your Excellency had received still greater benefits [*beneficia*] at our hand (had that been possible), in consideration of the great increase and advantage that might through you accrue to the Church of God and to us, we would have rejoiced, not without reason.

But now, because you seem to ignore and hide so heinous a crime, which is indeed known to have been committed as an affront to the Church universal and to your empire, we both suspect and fear that perhaps your thoughts were directed toward this indifference and neglect on this account: that at the suggestion of an evil man, sowing tares, you have conceived against your most gracious mother the Holy Roman Church and against ourselves—God forbid!—some displeasure or grievance.

51. Reception of the pope's letter at the Diet of Besançon (October 1157), trans. C. C. Mierow, *op. cit.*, pp. 183-84.

When this letter had been read and carefully set forth by Chancellor Rainald in a faithful interpretation, the princes who were present were moved to great indignation, because the entire content of the letter appeared to have no little sharpness and to offer even at the very outset an occasion for future trouble. But what had particularly aroused them all was the fact that in the aforesaid letter it had been stated, among other things, that the fullness of dignity and honor had been bestowed upon the emperor by the Roman pontiff, that the emperor had received from his hand the imperial crown, and that he would not have regretted conferring even greater benefits [*beneficia*] upon him, in consideration of the great gain and advantage that might through him accrue to the Roman Church. And the hearers were led to accept the literal meaning of these words and to put credence in the aforesaid explanation because they knew that the assertion was rashly made by some Romans that hitherto our kings had possessed the imperial power over the City, and the kingdom of Italy, by gift of the popes, and that they made such representations and handed them down to posterity not only orally but also in writing and in pictures. Hence it is written concerning Emperor Lothar, over a picture of this sort in the Lateran palace:

Coming before our gates, the king vows to safeguard the City.

Then, liegeman to the Pope, by him he is granted the crown.

Since such a picture and such an inscription, reported to him by those faithful to the empire, had greatly displeased the prince when he had been near the City in a previous year [1155], he is said to have received from Pope Hadrian, after a friendly remonstrance, the assurance that both the inscription and the picture would be removed, lest so trifling a matter might afford the greatest men in the world an occasion for dispute and discord.

When all these matters were fully considered, and a great tumult and uproar arose from the princes of the realm at so insolent a message, it is

said that one of the ambassadors, as though adding sword to flame, inquired: "From whom then does he have the empire, if not from our
lord the pope?" Because of this remark, anger reached such a pitch
that one of them, namely, Otto, palatine of Bavaria (it was said),
threatened the ambassador with his sword. But Frederick, using his
authority to quell the tumult, commanded that the ambassadors, being
granted safe-conduct, be led to their quarters and that early in the
morning they should set forth on their way; he ordered also that they
were not to pause in the territories of the bishops and abbots, but to
return to the City by the direct road, turning neither to the right nor
to the left. . . .

52. Letters of the emperor to the German bishops (October 1158
and February 1158), trans. C. C. Mierow, *op. cit.*, pp. 184-86, 193.

Whereas the Divine Sovereignty, from which is derived all
power in heaven and on earth, has entrusted unto us, His anointed,
the kingdom and the empire to rule over, and has ordained that the
peace of the churches is to be maintained by the imperial arms, not
without the greatest distress of heart are we compelled to complain to
Your Benevolence that from the head of the Holy Church, on which
Christ has set the imprint of his peace and love, there seem to be
emanating causes of dissensions and evils, like a poison, by which, unless
God avert it, we fear the body of the Church will be stained, its unity
shattered, and a schism created between the temporal and spiritual
realms.

For when we were recently at the diet in Besançon and were dealing
with the honor of the empire and the security of the Church with all
due solicitude, apostolic legates arrived asserting that they bore to Our
Majesty such tidings that the honor of the empire should receive no
small increase. After we had honorably received them on the first day
of their arrival, and on the second, as is customary, had seated ourself
with our princes to hear their tidings, they, as though inspired by the
Mammon of unrighteousness, by lofty pride, by arrogant disdain, by
execrable haughtiness, presented a message in the form of a letter from
the pope, the content of which was to the effect that we ought always
to remember the fact that the lord pope had bestowed upon us the
imperial crown and would not even regret it if Our Excellency had received greater benefits [*beneficia*] from him. . . .

Moreover, because many copies of this letter were found in their
possession, and blank parchments with seals affixed that were still to be
written on at their discretion, whereby—as has been their practice
hitherto—they were endeavoring to scatter the venom of their iniquity
throughout the churches of the Teutonic realm, to denude the altars, to
carry off the vessels of the house of God, to strip crosses of their cover-

ings, we obliged them to return to the City by the way they had come, lest an opportunity be afforded them of proceeding further.

And since, through election by the princes, the kingdom and the empire are ours from God alone, Who at the time of the passion of His Son Christ subjected the world to dominion by the two swords, and since the apostle Peter taught the world this doctrine: "Fear God, honor the king" (1 Peter 2:17), whosoever says that we received the imperial crown as a benefice [pro beneficio] from the lord pope contradicts the divine ordinance and the doctrine of Peter and is guilty of a lie. But because we have hitherto striven to snatch from the hand of the Egyptians the honor and freedom of the churches, so long oppressed by the yoke of undeserved slavery, and are intent on preserving to them all their rights and dignities, we ask Your University to grieve at so great an insult to us and to the empire, hoping that your unwavering loyalty will not permit the honor of the empire, which has stood, glorious and undiminished, from the founding of the City and the establishment of the Christian religion even down to your days, to be disparaged by so unheard-of a novelty, such presumptuous arrogance, knowing that—all ambiguity aside—we would prefer to encounter the risk of death rather than to endure in our time the reproach of so great a disorder.

There are two things by which our realm should be governed, the sacred laws of the emperors, and the good customs of our predecessors and our fathers. The limits set by them on the Church we do not wish to overstep, nor can we; whatever is not in accord with them, we reject. We gladly accord to our father the reverence that is his due. The free crown of empire we ascribe solely to the divine beneficence [beneficium]. We recognize first in the election the vote of the archbishop of Mainz, then those of the other princes, according to their rank; the anointing as king we recognize as the prerogative of the archbishop of Cologne; the final anointing, as emperor, indeed pertains to the supreme pontiff. "Whatsoever is more than these cometh of evil" (Matthew 5:37).

It is not to show disrespect for our most beloved and reverend father and consecrator that we obliged the cardinals to depart from our land. But we did not wish to permit them to proceed further, to the disgrace and shame of our empire, with their letters, written or blank. We have not closed the way in and out of Italy by edict, nor do we wish in any way to close it to those going to the Roman see as pilgrims or on their own necessary business, in reasonable fashion, with testimonials from their bishops and prelates. But we intend to resist those abuses by which all the churches of our realm have been burdened and weakened, and almost all the discipline of the cloisters killed and buried. In the chief city of the world God has, through the power of the empire, exalted the Church; in the chief city of the world the Church, not through the power of God, we believe, is now destroying the empire. It began with a picture, the picture became an inscription, the inscription seeks to become an authoritative utterance. We shall not endure it, we shall not submit to it; we shall lay down the crown before we consent to have the imperial crown and ourself thus degraded. Let the pictures be destroyed, let the inscriptions be withdrawn, that they may not remain as eternal memorials of enmity between the empire and the papacy.

53. Letter of Hadrian IV to the emperor (February 1158), trans. C. C. Mierow, *op. cit.*, pp. 199-200.

Since we assumed the care of the Church Universal by God's will and pleasure, we have been careful to do honor to Your Magnificence in all matters, that your love of us and veneration for the apostolic see might daily increase. When we heard that your feelings had been roused against us by certain people, we sent to you, to ascertain your will, two of our best and most distinguished brothers, the Cardinal Priest R[oland], the chancellor, of the title of St. Mark, and B[ernard], of the title of St. Clement, who had always been solicitous in the Roman Church for the honor of Your Majesty. Hence we learned with great astonishment that they were treated otherwise than behooved the imperial dignity. For your heart was stirred to anger, it is said, by the use of a certain word, namely *beneficium*. Yet this should not have vexed the heart of even one in lowly station, to say nothing of so great a man. For although this word *beneficium* is by some interpreted in a different significance than it has by derivation, it should nevertheless have been understood in the meaning which we ourselves put upon it, and which it is known to have possessed from the beginning. For this word is formed of *bonus* [good] and *factum* [deed], and among us *beneficium* means not a fief but a good deed. In this sense it is found in the entire body of Holy Scripture, wherein we are said to be ruled and supported *ex beneficio Dei*, not as by a fief [*feudum*] but as by His benediction and His "good deed" [*bono facto*]. And indeed Your Highness clearly recognizes that we placed the emblem of imperial dignity upon your head in so good and honorable a fashion that it merits recognition by all as a good deed. Hence when certain people have tried to twist that word and the following formula, namely, "we have conferred upon you the imperial crown," from its own proper meaning to another, they have this not on the merits of the case, but of their own desire and at the instigation of those who by no means love the concord of Church and state. For by "we have conferred" [*contulimus*] we meant nothing else than when we said before "we have placed" [*imposuimus*]. As for the report that you afterward ordered the turning back of ecclesiastical persons on due visitation to the sacrosanct Roman Church, if it be so, we believe that Your Discretion, O very dear son in Christ, must realize how unseemly an act that was. . . .

2. Alexander III &
the Empire

Pope Hadrian died in 1159. A large majority of the cardinals chose as his successor Rolandus Bandinelli, a distinguished canonist who had written one of the earliest commentaries on the *Decretum* of Gratian. More important for Frederick Barbarossa, Bandinelli was that same Cardinal Rolandus who had served as a papal legate at the Diet of Besançon, of all the candidates for the papacy the one least acceptable to the emperor. Three cardinals who formed a small pro-imperial faction in the sacred college dissented from the election and named as their choice Cardinal Octavian, a friend of Barbarossa. He styled himself Victor IV, while Rolandus took the name Alexander III. The emperor decided to support the claim of Octavian, and he could do so with some appearance of legality since the papal election decree of 1059 had not specified whether unanimity was necessary for a valid election or who was to act as judge in case of dispute.

Frederick announced that he would summon a council of bishops to judge between the two popes. When Alexander refused to appear before it on the ground that the emperor had no right to convoke a church council, Frederick replied that his predecessors Constantine, Theodosius, Justinian, and Charlemagne had all done so and that he possessed the same rights that they had had. His whole handling of this episode suggests that the popes had good grounds for their fear that an increase in imperial power would threaten the independence of the papacy. The contemporary Englishman, John of Salisbury, asserted that the emperor was determined to have a pope whom he could use as a mere tool for realizing his political ambitions (*No.* 54). The emperor's council did duly meet at Pavia, and since only imperial bishops attended, it not surprisingly declared in favor of Victor. The schism which then ensued lasted nearly twenty years. Victor was recognized in imperial territory, but his rival was acknowledged as true pope everywhere else in Europe. Barbarossa was able to drive Alexander out of Italy into exile in France, but this did not settle the issues between them. The pope made himself the center of a web of international intrigue and spun out alliance after alliance directed against the emperor. Alexander's main strength in this second great contest of empire and papacy lay in the fact that the Lombard cities were just as bitterly opposed to the imperial claims in Italy as the pope was. They rebelled against the emperor over and over again and in 1176, won a decisive victory at the battle of Legnano. At that point Frederick finally decided to liquidate a policy that had proved an expensive failure. In a treaty of 1177, the Peace of Venice, he abandoned his antipope and recognized the claim of Alexander. A little later he reached an agreement with the Lombard cities which conceded to them rights of self-government in exchange for a substantial grant of taxes. Frederick did not, however, give up all his interests in Italy and in 1185 formed a marriage alliance with the royal house of Sicily which later gave his son Henry VI a claim to inherit that kingdom.

The Peace of Venice ended the conflict of empire and papacy for the time being, but it did not settle any of the underlying problems which had given rise to it. The most important immediate result of the schism was that it impressed on Alexander the need for a fresh statement of the law on papal elections, and he promulgated a new election decree in 1179. This decree gave all the cardinals an equal vote, laid down that a two-thirds majority was required for a valid election, and declared that a candidate who received that number of votes became at once and unquestionably pope (No. 55). This rule, which in essence has been followed to the present day, made it much more difficult for kings to contest the outcome of papal elections in the course of future disputes.

Throughout the struggle with Barbarossa, Alexander was dependent on the good will of secular rulers outside Germany, and he refrained from any general pronouncements on the temporal claims of the papacy that might have offended them. When Thomas Becket, the archbishop of Canterbury, became involved in his bitter quarrel with Henry II over the rights of the church in England, Alexander supported Thomas (as he could hardly avoid doing), but he urged the implacable archbishop to act in a spirit of moderation and to seek a negotiated settlement of the dispute (No. 56). In the years after the Peace of Venice Alexander devoted himself to reforming the internal organization of church government and continued to abstain from any controversial pronouncements on political theory. His one important canonical decretal dealing with ecclesiastical and secular jurisdiction was a moderate one. The pope held that there was no normal right of appeal from a secular court to an ecclesiastical one, though he added that a local custom could render such an appeal valid. Perhaps he abstained from any definitive pronouncements on the temporal role of the papacy because he realized that during the course of his pontificate the whole problem of church-state relations had become a matter of intricate and unresolved debate in the law schools of Europe. Certainly Pope Alexander proved a much more moderate pontiff than the intimates of Cardinal Rolandus might have expected.

The Council of Pavia

54. Comment of John of Salisbury on the Council of Pavia (June 1160), trans. E. F. Henderson, *Documents* (London, 1892), pp. 424-25.

. . . It seems to me to make very little difference whom the presumption of the little Pavian convention supports, unless that the election of Alexander, if any one doubted of it, is confirmed by the very testimony of the opposing party.

To pass over the rashness of one who has presumed to judge the Roman church which is reserved for the judgment of God alone, and who, when he ought to have been excommunicated—as the disgraceful treatment of the cardinals at Besançon shows—cited through a peremptory edict before his judgment seat two men, and, having already made up his mind as to the sentence, greeted one with the name of his old office and dignity, the other with the appellation of Roman pontiff, revealing to the senators and people his secret inclination: whatever has been done at Pavia is found to be contrary, as well to common fairness, as to the lawful constitutions and sanctions of the fathers. Of course the absent were condemned, and in a case which was not investigated, nay, which had no right to be investigated there, or in that way, or by such men—impudently and imprudently and iniquitously, a sentence was hurriedly given.

But perhaps one ought to say "those who absented themselves," rather than "the absent." Surely so, for those men ignore or pretend to ignore the privilege of the holy Roman church. Who has subjected the universal church to the judgment of a single church? Who has constituted the Germans judges of the nations? Who has conferred authority on these brutal and impetuous men of electing at their will a prince over the sons of men? And, indeed, their fury has often attempted this, but, God bringing it about, it has often had to blush, prostrate and confused, over its iniquity. But I know what this German is attempting. For I was at Rome, under the rule of the blessed Eugenius, when, in the first embassy sent at the beginning of his reign, his intolerable pride and incautious tongue displayed such daring impudence. For he promised that he would reform the rule of the whole world, and subject the world to Rome, and, sure of success, would conquer all things—if only the favour of the Roman pontiff would aid him in this. And this he did in order that against whomever he, the emperor, declaring war, should draw the material sword—against the same the Roman pontiff should draw the spiritual sword. He did not find any one hitherto who would consent to such iniquity, and, Moses himself opposing—*i.e.* the law of God contradicting—he raised up for himself a Balaamitic pontiff, through whom he might curse the people of God. . . .

The Decree on Papal Elections

55. The election decree of 1179, trans. S. Z. Ehler and J. B. Morrall, *Church and State Through the Centuries* (London, 1954), pp. 63-64.

Although ordinances have emanated from our predecessors which are clear enough and destined to prevent any discord, nonetheless grave splits often occurred in the Church after these ordinances, due to the audacity of wicked ambition; in order to avoid this evil, we, too, have decided to make some addition to them, by the advice of our brothers and by the approval of the holy Council.

We therefore decree that if, by any chance, full concord could not be achieved in view of constituting a Pontiff, owing to a hostile man sowing tares of discord among the Cardinals, and one-third of them would not be willing to agree with the two other thirds united and concordant, or even would presume to consecrate some other candidate, he shall be regarded as Roman Pontiff who shall be elected and received by two-thirds.

But if any one, relying on the nomination by one-third, shall usurp for himself the episcopal name—for the substance of the episcopal function he can not usurp—he himself and those who shall have received him shall be subject to excommunication and, as further punishment, shall be deprived of the holy order in such a way that the holy Eucharist and even the Viaticum shall be denied to them, except if they are actually dying, and they shall share—unless they return to their senses—the lot of Dathan and Abiron whom the earth engulfed alive.

Moreover, if any one was elected to the Apostolic office by less than two-thirds, he shall by no means be accepted—unless a greater concord is attained—and shall be subject to the aforesaid punishment if he refuses humbly to abstain. This, however, must not engender any prejudice to the canonical ordinances and to other churches, in which the opinion of the greater and sounder part should prevail, so that if any contest occurs in them, it may be decided by judgment of a superior authority. But in the Roman church it is necessary to establish a special rule because from it no recourse to a superior authority can be made.

Letters of Alexander III

56. Letters of Alexander III to Thomas Becket (1165), trans. D. C. Douglas and G. W. Greenaway, *English Historical Documents, 1042-1189* (Oxford, 1953), p. 742.

That the less cannot judge the greater, and especially him to whom he is known to be subject by right of prelacy and is held bound by the chain of obedience, is declared by laws both human and divine, and is set forth with particular clarity in the statutes of the holy fathers. Accordingly we, whose province it is to correct errors of judgment and to amend those things which, if not corrected, would leave a pernicious example to posterity, and, having pondered these matters with anxious care, and considering that through the fault of one man the Church ought not to sustain hurt or loss, we adjudge the sentence presumptuously passed against you by the bishops and barons of England on the ground that you did not obey the king's first summons—in which sentence the said bishops and barons adjudged a forfeiture of all your movables contrary both to the form of law and ecclesiastical custom, especially since you have no movables save the goods of your church—to be utterly void, and we quash the same by apostolic authority, ordering that for the future it shall have no force, and avail nothing to bring prejudice or hurt hereafter to you or your successors or to the church committed to your governance.

Since the days are evil and many things must be endured through the nature of the times, we beg you to be discreet, and we warn, advise and exhort you to show yourself wary, prudent and circumspect in all your actions for your own sake and that of the Church. Do nothing hastily or precipitately, but act with gravity and deliberation by every means at your disposal, with a view to recovering the favour and goodwill of the illustrious king of the English, so far as is consistent with the liberty of the Church and the dignity of your office. Forbear with the king until the following Easter, and study to avoid taking any measures against him or his realm until the prescribed date. For by then God will vouchsafe better days, and both you and we may safely proceed further in this matter.

57. Letter of Alexander III on appeals from secular to ecclesiastical courts (*Decretales*, 2.28.7), ed. E. Friedberg, *Corpus Iuris Canonici*, II (Leipzig, 1881), col. 412.

You ask whether, if an appeal is made to our court from a civil judge before judgment has been given or afterwards, such an appeal is valid. It is certainly valid in matters which are subject to our temporal jurisdiction. In other matters, although it may be valid by the custom of a church, we think it is not valid according to the rigor of the law.

> 57a. Letter of Alexander III to Archbishop Eberhard of Salzburg, ed. J. P. Migne, PL 200 (Paris, 1855), col. 133-34.
> (Alexander excommunicated Frederick Barbarossa but did not formally depose him. His hope for a reconciliation with the emperor was expressed in this letter of 1162.)

. . We request, advise, and exhort you in the Lord to persuade the emperor in every way and induce him to come to his senses, take heed for the health of his soul, and return to the unity of the Catholic church . . . for otherwise, unless he is first reconciled, he cannot be saved; and if he does not withdraw from the wickedness of schism and return to the bosom of mother church, even if he seems to prosper in this world, he will not be able to avoid the penalty of eternal punishment in the next. As the Gospel truly says, what shall it profit him if he gain the whole world and suffer the loss of his soul (Matth. 16.26)? Even if he abounds in all the riches and delights of this present life, they will be of no profit to him at all if, cut off from the body of Christ which is the church and from its communion he is thrust into burning hell, the infernal region where there is everlasting night without day, punishment without end, grief without remedy, and torment unceasing.

But if almighty God, through his ineffable grace, shall so inspire him that he wishes wholeheartedly to return to the bosom of mother church, there is nothing temporal in the world that we shall welcome more willingly and more graciously, and we shall take care to love him, so great and sublime a prince, with sincere charity in the Lord and honor him in every way . . . (and) we shall consign to oblivion whatever harm, attack, or injury he has directed at us, as though he had never in any way offended us or God's church.

3. The Decretists

The *Decretum* of Gratian (c. 1140) was the greatest lawbook of the twelfth century. The author chose to arrange his work according to the then fashionable "dialectical" method. That is to say, he would first state a disputed canonical problem, then adduce all the texts that could be quoted in favor of one solution, then those that favored an opposing solution, and finally he would try to show how the two sets of texts could be reconciled with one another or why one solution was to be preferred to the other. Gratian's original title for his book was *A Concord of Discordant Canons.* The *Decretum* is divided into two main sections called *Distinctiones* and *Causae*, and the *Causae* are subdivided into *Quaestiones*. (Accordingly, its texts are cited thus: *Dist.* 22 c.1 means the first chapter of the twenty-second *Distinctio*. C.15 q.6 c.3 means the third chapter of the sixth *Quaestio* in *Causa* 15.)

The very dialectical structure of the work meant that the *Decretum* raised almost as many problems as it solved, and in the half century after its publication hundreds of commentaries appeared which aimed to continue the work of harmonization that Gratian had begun or to explore additional problems that he had overlooked. The commentators on the *Decretum* are referred to as Decretists. Many of them, like Rolandus Bandinelli, are known by name, and their careers can be traced, but some of the most distinguished works remain anonymous and are cited, like papal bulls, by the first words of the Latin text. The works of these Decretists, most of them unprinted so far, contain the most sophisticated thought of the age on problems of church and state. Almost every document or episode from the first thousand years of church history that we have mentioned as having major significance is quoted or alluded to in the *Decretum:* the teachings of Ambrose and Augustine, the doctrine of Gelasius on priesthood and kingship, the deposition of the Frankish king Childeric, the coronation of Charlemagne, the letters of Gregory VII. The men who commented on these texts brought to their task a wide variety of national backgrounds and political prejudices. The three main schools of Decretist activity that grew up in the twelfth century were at Bologna, Paris, and Oxford, but men from all Western lands studied at these centers. We know, for instance, of distinguished works by canonists from Hungary, Spain, and Germany, all written at

Bologna. Hence, in studying the Decretist texts we can observe some of the best minds from every part of Christendom engaged in a systematic reflection on a thousand years of the experience of the church in the world, trying to understand it as best they could in the light of their own political experience and religious convictions.

Their intellectual activity gains added interest from the fact that it was carried on at a time when the actual political relationships between ecclesiastical and secular rulers were often tense and sometimes violent. Moreover, the canonists did not always live in academic seclusion, divorced from the great events of the day. Many of them became bishops or royal administrators; they were consulted on legal and constitutional problems; they had among their pupils future cardinals and popes. Accordingly, in the century after 1150 we find an incessant interplay between the academic theories of the canonists and the political practice of rulers in church and state, each in turn reacting on the other.

In the texts printed below we have tried to illustrate both the technique of canonistic argumentation and the main movements of Decretist thought during the second half of the twelfth century. There were many forms of commentary on Gratian's work, but the most important one was the *Summa*, which presented a general summary of the content of the *Decretum* together with detailed investigations of particular prob lems. The canonist would cite a word or phrase from Gratian's text, point out a problem inherent in it, mention all the different canons relevant to the issue (sometimes throwing in references to Roman law for good measure), and then try to work his way toward a solution. In the sphere of church-state relations the central problem that emerged in academic theory was precisely the one that we have seen underlying the real-life conflict between Barbarossa and the popes: did the emperor receive his imperial power·from the pope? If so, did this imply that a pope could depose an emperor or exercise directly the temporal jurisdiction inherent in the office that he bestowed?

A considerable body of discussion on these points grew up around Gratian's *Dist.* 22 c.1, a text from Peter Damian (though Gratian mistakenly attributed it to Pope Nicholas II) in which the author declared that Christ "conferred simultaneously on the blessed key-bearer of eternal life rights over a heavenly and an earthly empire." It seems quite clear that Damian intended only to paraphrase the familiar verse of St. Matthew, "I will give you the keys of the kingdom of heaven and whatsoever thou shalt bind on earth it shall be bound in heaven. . . ." But the canonist Rufinus, writing at Bologna in 1157 or shortly thereafter (just about the time of the Besançon episode), suggested a new interpretation of the text. The "heavenly empire," he argued, meant the clergy and all spiritual affairs, while the "earthly empire" stood for the laity and all secular affairs. It followed then that the pope possessed supreme authority over the whole world in both the spiritual and temporal

spheres. Rufinus at once added, however, a distinction between "authority" and "administration." "Authority" was the inherent right to direct
affairs, "administration" the actual exercise of power, and it was "authority" that he claimed for the pope in temporal affairs (No. 59). The
great importance of this text was that it treated the pope's right to crown
the emperor (which in fact was derived from the specific historical incident that had taken place in 800) as a part of the original "power of
the keys" conferred on Peter at the very foundation of the church.

Subsequent commentaries on Dist. 22 c.1 sought to define with more
precision the significance of the imperial coronation ceremony. The
author of the Summa Inperatoriae Maiestate (1175-78) introduced into
his discussion the symbolism of the two swords, maintaining that the
pope possessed both swords and conferred the material one on the emperor in the act of anointing him (No. 60). It should be noted that the
image of the two swords no longer had quite the same meaning for the
canonists that it had had for St. Bernard. By the early 1180's the argument in favor of the papacy had been carried to its logical conclusion,
and the Summa Et Est Sciendum argued against contemporary canonists
who were teaching that the pope could depose the emperor simply because the emperor's authority (the power of the sword) was bestowed on
him by the pope. The French author of this Summa proposed that imperial authority could not possibly be derived from the papacy because
there had been emperors before any popes existed—it came rather "from
God and the election of the people." It followed that the pope could
not directly depose secular rulers, though he might indirectly help to
bring about their depositions by excommunicating them (No. 61).

Toward 1200 each of the two main traditions of thought found an
eminent champion at Bologna. The two canonists, whose influence persisted throughout the thirteenth century, were Huguccio, an Italian, and
Alanus, an Englishman. Huguccio followed the tradition of moderate
dualism; Alanus presented an extreme theory of papal world-monarchy.
Their views were set out in detail in commentaries on Dist. 96 c.6 and
C.15 q.6 c.3. Huguccio maintained that the separation of powers was a
matter of divine ordinance, so that the pope could depose a secular king
only by co-operating with his nobles who had the right to initiate action
against a tyrannical ruler (No. 64). Alanus declared that since Christ had
been rightful lord of the world, the pope, his vicar, necessarily possessed
full sovereignty over spiritual and temporal affairs. All legitimate authority therefore came from the pope. He bestowed imperial power on the
emperor and by his own intrinsic authority could take away that power
if the emperor proved unworthy (No. 65). The only concession Alanus
made to the apparent dualism of the text he was commenting on was
an acknowledgment that the pope could not retain the "material sword"
for his own use and so dispense with the services of secular rulers altogether.

The final texts of Huguccio and Alanus presented below dealt with a different problem, not the dethronement of an emperor, but—what was still more difficult in the eyes of a canonist—the deposition of a pope. The extensive commentaries in the writings of the Decretists on this question illustrate one of their most deep-rooted convictions: their belief that no ruler, however exalted, could be permitted to exercise his power in a fashion that would injure grievously the community entrusted to his care. The twelfth-century canonists were in fact deeply concerned over an issue that has since become a central one in Western jurisprudence: the problem of reconciling a theory of legislative sovereignty with an ideal of limited government. Many texts of the *Decretum* maintained that the pope was immune from all human judgment, but just one of them suggested a possible exception. *Dist.* 40 c.6 said that a pope could never be accused "unless he is found straying from the faith." This implied that accusations could be considered in the one case of heresy. Huguccio raised various procedural barriers that would have protected the pope from accusation except in the most flagrant cases, but, in the last resort, he thought that any notorious crime of the pope that gave scandal to the whole church, and not only heresy, could constitute grounds for his deposition (*No.* 67). Alanus argued that no crime except heresy could injure the whole church so grievously as to justify the deposition of a pope (*No.* 68). The fact that respectable and orthodox canonistic opinion did allow for the deposition of a Roman pontiff in certain exceptional cases was enthusiastically exploited by secular kings in some of the later conflicts of church and state.

The Heavenly and the Earthly Empires

58. Gratian, *Dist.* 22 c.1. (c. 1140) ed. E. Friedberg, *Corpus Iuris Canonici,* I (Leipzig, 1879), col. 73.

The Roman church established the dignities of all other churches of every rank, the eminence of each patriarch, the primacy of metropolitans, the sees of bishops. But she herself was founded and built on the rock of the dawning faith by Him who conferred simultaneously on the blessed key-bearer of eternal life the rights over a heavenly and an earthly empire.

59. Rufinus, Commentary on *Dist.* 22 c.1 (1157-59), *Summa Decretorum,* ed. H. Singer (Paderborn, 1902), p. 47.

Rights over a heavenly and an earthly empire. He calls the heavenly militia, that is, the whole body of the clergy and the things that pertain to them, a heavenly empire. He calls secular men and secular things an earthly empire or kingdom. From this it seems that the supreme pontiff, who is vicar of the blessed Peter, holds rights over the earthly kingdom. But it must be noted that a "right of authority" is one thing, a "right of administration" something different. The right of authority is like that of a bishop, to whose right all the possessions of a church are said to pertain since everything is ordered by his authority. The right of administration is like that of a steward, for he has the right to administer but he lacks the authority to rule. Whatever he commands to another is enjoined not by his own authority but by that of the bishop. Hence the supreme pontiff holds rights over the earthly kingdom as regards authority in this fashion. He first by his authority confirms the emperor in his earthly kingdom by consecrating him and then, by his sole authority, imposes penance on him as on other laymen if they abuse their temporalities and, after they have done penance, absolves them. Truly the prince has the authority of ruling secular things after the pope, and the duty of administering them apart from him, for the apostle ought not to manage secular affairs nor the prince ecclesiastical ones, as is said below at *Dist.* 96 c.6 [*No.* 63].

> 60. *Summa Inperatoriae Maiestate,* Commentary on *Dist.* 22 c.1 (1175-78), ed. A. M. Stickler, "Imperator Vicarius Papae," *Mitteilungen des Instituts für Österreichische Geschichtsforschung,* LXII (1954), p. 202.

Rights over a heavenly and an earthly empire. That is, both the material sword and the spiritual sword. Against this is C.33 q.2 c.6. Solution: we say that the apostle does have the material sword and the spiritual sword but not in the same way. He has the spiritual sword as regards authority and use, the material sword only as regards authority because, when the emperor is anointed, he is given the power and exercise of the material sword by the apostle.

> 61. *Summa Et Est Sciendum,* Commentary on *Dist.* 22 c.1 (1181-85), ed. A. M. Stickler, *art. cit.,* p. 203.

Rights over a heavenly and an earthly kingdom. From this some argue that whoever uses the sword has it from the pope. Therefore the emperor receives the power of the sword from him. And this is why the pope can depose the emperor if he abuses his power, as at C.15 q.6 c 3 [*No.* 62], which he would not do had he not conferred that power on him. Nevertheless to us the contrary seems true for these reasons. There were emperors before there was any pope and they had power then, for all power is from the Lord God. Again, before he is consecrated as emperor, the emperor can use the sword by virtue of his election by the people who "transfer to him and on him all right and power" (*Digest*, 1.4.1). Again, how can the pope bestow on him the power of the sword or its exercise when he himself does not have it, and is not competent to have it or to exercise it, as at C.23 q.8 cc.29,30? And no one can confer on another more than he has himself. He has it therefore from God as at *Dist.* 96 c.11 and C.23 q.4 c.45, and from the election of the people. Now here "a heavenly and an earthly empire" is taken as meaning the clergy and the laity, all of whom the apostle can bind or loose for just cause by his decretals. But the pope is said to have deposed a king when he has excommunicated him for some contumacious behavior, and so has withdrawn his subjects from rendering obedience and service to him, for no one ought to obey an excommunicated lord, as at C.15 q.6 cc.4,5, and so this was in effect to depose the king. What then does the emperor receive from the pope when he is anointed? Confirmation of the power already received, or permission to exercise it in the capacity of an em-peror.

The Deposition of a King

62. Gratian, C.15 q.6 c.3, (c. 1140) ed. E. Friedberg, *Corpus Iuris Canonici* I (Leipzig, 1879), col. 756.

Another Roman pontiff, namely Zacharias, deposed a king of the Franks, not so much on account of his evil deeds as because he was not equal to so great an office, and set in his place Pippin, father of the emperor Charles, releasing all the Franks from the oath of fealty which they had sworn to him. And this is often done by Holy Church when it absolves fighting men from their oaths to bishops who have been deposed by apostolic authority.

63. Gratian, *Dist.* 96 c.6 (c. 1140), ed. E. Friedberg *Corpus Iuris Canonici*, I (Leipzig, 1879), col. 339.

(This passage was taken by Gratian from a letter of Pope Nicholas I, but Nicholas in turn was quoting Pope Gelasius [No. 4].)

After the coming of the Truth the emperor did not seize the rights of the pontificate nor did the pontiff usurp the title of the em-perors, for the same mediator between God and Man, the man Christ Jesus, so distinguished between the offices of both powers according to their own proper activities and separate dignities, wanting his people to be raised on high through healthful humility and not plunged into Hell through human pride, that Christian emperors would need pontiffs for attaining eternal life and pontiffs would use imperial laws in the conduct of temporal affairs. In this fashion spiritual activity would be set apart from worldly encroachments and the "soldier of God" would not be involved in secular affairs, while on the other hand he who was involved in secular affairs would not seem to preside over divine matters.

64. Huguccio, Commentary on *Dist.* 96 c.6 (1189-91), ed. G. Catalano, *Impero, Regni e Sacerdozio nel Pensiero di Uguccio da Pisa* (Milan, 1959), pp. 64-67.

After the coming of the Truth. Up until the coming of Christ the imperial and pontifical rights were not separated, for the same man was emperor and pontiff, as at *Dist.* 21 c.1. But the offices and rights of the emperor and the pontiff were separated by Christ and some things, namely temporal affairs, were assigned to the emperor, others, namely spiritual affairs, to the pontiff, and this was done for the sake of preserving humility and avoiding pride. If the emperor or the pontiff held all offices he would easily grow proud but now since each needs the other and sees that he is not fully self-sufficient he is made humble. . . . Here it can clearly be gathered that each power, the apostolic and imperial, was instituted by God and that neither is derived from the other and that the emperor does not have the sword from the apostle. The argument is stated here and below in the same Distinction at c.8, c.10, c.11 and also at *Dist.* 93 c.24 and at C.3 q.4 c.45.

There is a contrary argument at *Dist.* 22 c.1 [*No.* 58], *Dist.* 63 c.33, *Dist.* 63 c.23, c.15 q.6 c.3 [*No.* 62]. . . . All these contrary arguments seem to imply that the emperor receives the power of the sword and the imperial authority from the apostle and that the pope makes him emperor and can depose him. I believe however, that the emperor has the power of the sword and the imperial dignity from election by the princes and people, as at *Dist.* 93 c.24, for there was an emperor before there was a pope, an empire before a papacy. Again the words, "Behold, here are two swords" (Luke 22:38), were spoken to symbolize the fact that the two powers, namely the apostolic and imperial, are distinct and separate. If, therefore, it is anywhere stated or implied that the emperor has the power of the sword from the pope, I understand it as meaning the unction and confirmation which he has from the pope when he swears fidelity to him; for before this, although he is not called emperor, he is an emperor as regards dignity though not as regards unction, and before this he has the power of the sword and exercises it. When it is said that the pope can depose him I believe this to be true, but by the will and consent of the princes if he is convicted before them. Then I take it, in the last resort, if he has been convicted and admonished and will not desist or give satisfaction, he should be excommunicated and all should be removed from fealty to him as argued at C.15 q.6 c.4,5. If still he is not corrected then finally he is justly smitten with a sentence and rightly expelled by armed force, and another legitimately elected. But by whom is the sentence pronounced? By the lord pope before whom he was convicted or by his princes if the Roman pontiff has approved this.

65. Alanus, Commentary on *Dist.* 96 c.6 (c. 1202), ed. A. M. Stickler, "Alanus Anglicus als Verteidiger des monarchischen Papsttums," *Salesianum,* XXI (1959), pp. 361-63.

In the conduct of temporal affairs. It is argued here that the emperor does not have the sword from the pope. The argument occurs also at *Dist.* 63 c.30 and above at *Dist.* 93 c.24, where it is said that the army makes an emperor for itself, and also below in this same Distinction c.11, where it is said that the emperor receives power from heaven; also below at C.23 q.4 c.35, C.12 q.1 c.15. A contrary argument occurs at *Dist.* 22 c.1 [*No.* 58]. *Dist.* 63 cc.23,33 and C.15 q.6 c.3 [*No.* 62].

This indeed is certain according to everyone, that the pope has jurisdiction over the emperor in spiritual matters so that he can bind and loose him . . . but, according to Huguccio, by no means in temporal matters though the pope can judge him in temporal matters and depose him by the wish of the princes who elect him according to customary law. According to Huguccio the emperor has the sword from God alone and not from the pope except as regards coronation and confirmation, and he has full imperial jurisdiction beforehand although he is not called emperor.

But in truth, and according to the Catholic faith, he is subject to the pope in spiritual matters and also receives his sword from him, for the right of both swords belongs to the pope. This is proved by the fact that the Lord had both swords on earth and used both as is mentioned here, and he established Peter as his vicar on earth and all Peter's successors. Therefore today Innocent has by right the material sword. If you deny this you are saying that Christ established a secular prince as his vicar in this regard. Again Peter said to the Lord, "Behold, here are two swords" (Luke 22:38), so the material sword too was with Peter. Again if the emperor was not subject to the pope in temporalities he could not sin against the church in temporalities. Again the church is one body and so it shall have only one head or it will be a monster.

This opinion is not invalidated by the fact that there were emperors before there were popes, because they were only *de facto* emperors and none except those who believed in the true God had a right to the sword; nor do infidel rulers have it nowadays. Likewise it is not invalidated by the fact that Constantine conferred temporal jurisdiction on Sylvester as is said at *Dist.* 63 c.30. [In a reference to the Donation of Constantine at *Dist.* 63 c.30 Alanus commented, "From his plenitude of right the pope could take away the City and other possessions even if the emperor was unwilling."]

The emperor then has the sword from the pope. The electors indeed confer it on him, not the pope, but every bishop has his bishopric from the pope and yet the pope does not confer it but rather canonical election of the clergy does. The pope therefore is the ordinary judge of the emperor in both temporal and spiritual affairs and can depose him, as at C.15 q.6 c.3 [No. 62]. But can he depose him for any crime? I answer, rather for none, unless he is determined to persist in it, and even then perhaps not for any offence but only for those which harm the people, as for instance the continued discord of heresy. But could the pope keep the material sword for himself if he wished? I answer no, because the Lord divided the swords as is said here, and the church would be gravely disturbed by this.

What has been said of the emperor may be held true of any prince who has no superior lord. Each one has as much jurisdiction in his kingdom as the emperor has in the empire, for the division of kingdoms that has been introduced nowadays by the law of nations is approved by the pope although the ancient law of nations held that there should be one emperor in the world.

The Deposition of a Pope

66. Gratian, *Dist.* 40 c.6 (c. 1140), ed. E. Friedberg, *Corpus Iuris Canonici,* I (Leipzig, 1879), col. 146.

. . . No mortal shall presume to rebuke [the pope's] faults, for he who is to judge all is to be judged by no one, unless he is found straying from the faith. . . .

67. Huguccio Commentary on *Dist.* 40 c.6 (1189-91), ed. B. Tierney, *Foundations of the Conciliar Theory* (Cambridge, 1955), pp. 248-49.

Unless he is found straying from the faith. Behold, a pope can be condemned for heresy by his subjects! *Dist.* 21 c.7 above states the contrary. There it is said that Marcellinus was guilty of heresy but none the less his subjects did not condemn him. Some say that they did not wish to do so, but I say that they could not and should not have condemned him because he freely and humbly confessed his error, for the pope can be condemned for heresy only in the last resort when he contumaciously and persistently resists and strives to defend and uphold his error. . . . But behold, a pope invents a new heresy; some one wishes to prove that it is a heresy; the pope says it is not a heresy but the Catholic faith; is the proof against him to be accepted? I believe not. Again, he secretly adheres to a heresy already condemned. Some persons, however, know of this and wish to prove that the pope follows such a heresy. But he denies it. Ought they to be heard? I believe not; for the pope can be accused of heresy only in the last resort when there is agreement concerning the fact of heresy and the pope does not deny the fact and, being admonished, refused to come to his senses but contumaciously defends his error. . . .

Can the pope be accused of simony or any other crime? Some say no, whether it is notorious or not, because we ought not to stipulate what the canon does not stipulate. They say that the reason for the difference —why he can be accused of heresy more readily than of any other crime— is that if a pope were a heretic he would not harm only himself but the whole world, especially since the simple and foolish would easily accept that heresy, not believing it to be a heresy. But if the pope commits simony or fornication or theft or anything of the sort he seems to harm only himself, for everyone knows that no one is permitted to steal or commit fornication or simony or anything of the sort. But I believe that it is the same in any notorious crime, that the pope can be accused and condemned if, being admonished, he is not willing to desist. What then? Behold, he steals publicly, he fornicates publicly, he keeps a concubine publicly, he has intercourse with her publicly in the church, near the altar or on it, and being admonished will not desist. Shall he not be accused? Shall he not be condemned? Is it not like heresy to scandalize the church in such a fashion? Moreover contumacy is the crime of idolatry and like to heresy, as at *Dist.* 91 c.9, whence a contumacious person is called an infidel as at *Dist.* 38 c.16. And so it is the same with any notorious crime as with heresy.

68. Alanus, Commentary on *Dist.* 40 c.6 (c. 1202), ed. B. Tierney, "Pope and Council: Some New Decretist Texts," *Medieval Studies,* XIX (1957), p. 218.

If he was a public usurer might he not be accused? He can be accused of any notorious crime according to some who accept "to sin in faith" in a broad sense as meaning to sin against the teaching of the faith, just as anyone committing mortal sin is said to deny Christ, as at C.11 q.3 c.83. But, according to this view, the privilege of the pope would amount to nothing. Therefore it is to be said that, since he has no superior judge, he cannot be judged against his will except for the crime of heresy, in which case it was so decreed because of the enormity of the crime and the common danger to the church. But can anyone lay down a law for the pope, when the pope is not bound by the canons and can change them? Perhaps it is so in the case of that crime because there, as a consequence of it, a question arises whether he really is pope; for it seems that if he is a heretic he is not the head of the church. If he is suspected of any other crime and some one wishes to accuse him, lest he bring scandal on the church, although he cannot be compelled, nevertheless, having been admonished, he ought to select a judge and go to trial under him, for although he is not bound by the laws nevertheless he ought to live according to them.

(At *Dist.* 19 c. 9 Gratian referred to a Pope Anastasius [496-498] who allegedly fell into heresy by holding a doctrine contrary to the teaching if the Council of Chalcedon [451].)
68a. Alanus, Commentary on *Dist.* 19 c. 9 (c. 1202), ed. B. Tierney, *art cit.*, p. 214.

Here is an argument that, in a question of faith, a council is greater than a pope . . . which is to be held firmly. Whence it happens that in such a case a council can judge and condemn him and that he incurs an excommunication previously decreed by a council concerning a heresy, which would not happen if a pope were equal to or greater than a council in this case.

4. The Reign of
Innocent III

In 1198, at the age of thirty-seven, Lothario di Segni was elected pope and took the name of Innocent III.

His policies have evoked more discussion and less agreement among modern historians than those of any other medieval pontiff except perhaps Gregory VII. No one denies Innocent's superlative ability or his very great importance in the history of the church. He came to the Roman see at a crucial point in European diplomatic history. Barbarossa's son Henry VI, a powerful and aggressive ruler who had been both king of Sicily and German emperor, had died a few months earlier. He left a child of three to succeed him in the hereditary fief of Sicily, while two other candidates struggled for the imperial throne. The ideological situation was unsettled too, for by the end of the twelfth century there existed two quite distinct canonical theories concerning the temporal power of the papacy, either of which a new pope could take up and expound as the official doctrine of the Roman church. At the outset of his reign, therefore, Innocent had an exceptional opportunity to define for the future the proper role of the papacy in the temporal affairs of Europe both in practice and in theory.

An older point of view, reflected in the great church histories of Albert Hauck and Johannes Haller, maintains that he used this opportunity to commit the papacy to a disastrous dream of unlimited world-monarchy. According to this view Innocent betrayed his priestly office by devoting his whole pontificate to unscrupulous diplomacy and to incessant political machinations which aimed always at the exaltation of his own power—he wanted to be "lord of the world" and would stop at nothing to achieve that end. It is certainly true that Innocent was much concerned with matters of diplomacy and politics. He intervened decisively in the disputed imperial election; he claimed the right to arbitrate in the feudal disputes that arose between John of England and Philip of France; he helped to crown a king in Bulgaria and tried to depose one in Norway; he extended the boundaries of the papal states in central Italy. Nevertheless, distinguished modern scholars such as

127

Maccarrone, Mochi Onory, Kempf, and Tillman[1]: have argued that all these interventions of Innocent in the temporal sphere were inspired by the highest spiritual motives and that his theory of church and state was based on a cautious dualism, not on a theocratic doctrine attributing supreme temporal and spiritual power to the papacy.

At the beginning of his pontificate Innocent made a series of pronouncements on the authority of the papacy that at first glance read like uninhibited assertions of extreme theocratic principles. He described himself as "lower than God but higher than man." Quoting St. Bernard, but with a slight change of wording that altered the whole meaning of the phrase, he declared that Peter was given "not only the universal church but the whole world to govern." He wrote to the emperor at Constantinople that the priesthood was as superior to the kingship as the soul to the body. He congratulated the king of Armenia on appealing to the papacy in a purely temporal matter, and he informed the nobles of Tuscany that "just as the moon derives its light from the sun . . . so too the royal power derives the splendor of its dignity from the pontifical authority."

A great deal of ingenuity has been expended in attempts to prove that these phrases of Innocent do not mean what they seem to say. The real difficulty of interpretation arises from the fact that in none of his really important interventions in secular affairs did Innocent declare simply and lucidly that he was acting by virtue of a supreme temporal authority inherent in his office. On the contrary, he always found some other argument to justify his actions and frequently declared that he had no wish to usurp the jurisdiction of secular rulers. The decretal *Novit* (No. 76) provides an excellent example of this approach. It was written in 1204 in connection with a dispute that had broken out between King John of England and King Philip Augustus of France. Philip had invaded John's great fief of Normandy, and when Innocent attempted to mediate the French bishops protested that the pope had no right to interpose his judgment in a purely feudal dispute which had already been tried before their king's feudal court. Innocent replied in the decretal *Novit* that he did not wish to diminish or disturb the jurisdiction of the king of France. He had no intention of judging concerning a fief, but Philip had been denounced to him as a man who was pursuing a sinful course of conduct and the pope could certainly judge concerning sin. Moreover, the sin of which Philip was accused had led to an outbreak of war and it was the special duty of the pope to defend the peace. And, again, the case involved a breach of a solemn oath, a matter which belonged to the jurisdiction of the church. Innocent was clearly convinced

---

[1] M. Maccarrone, *Chiesa e Stato nella Dottrina di Innocenzo III* (Rome, 1940); S. Mochi Onory, *Fonti Canonistiche dell' Idea Moderna dello Stato* (Milan, 1951); F. Kempf, *Papsttum und Kaisertum bei Innocenz III* (Rome, 1954); H. Tillmann, *Papst Innocenz III* (Bonn, 1954).

of his right to decide essentially political issues like this one, but he
defended that right by every conceivable argument except the straightforward theocratic one that he was the overlord of all kings and so empowered to judge cases between them.

There is a similar pattern of argument in the decretal *Venerabilem*
(*No.* 75), in which Innocent put forward his claim to decide between
two candidates for the imperial throne, Otto of Brunswick and Philip
of Swabia, each of whom was supported by a faction of princes. Innocent
acknowledged at the outset that the right of electing an emperor did
indeed belong to the princes by law and custom and therefore disclaimed
any intention of having his legate participate in the proceedings either
as an elector or as a judge. But, he added, it was universally acknowledged that the pope had to consecrate and crown the candidate chosen
by the princes. It followed then that he had the right and duty to
examine the man elected to determine that he was fit to be crowned, and
in a disputed election it was for the pope to choose which of the candidates was the more worthy of coronation. In the course of his exposition
Innocent took over a whole body of canonical rules relating to the confirmation of episcopal elections and simply assumed that they applied
to secular elections also.

The decretal *Per Venerabilem* falls into a different category. There
was no very great issue of European politics involved in this case but
there was an important issue of principle. In 1202 Count William of
Montpellier petitioned Innocent for a papal privilege that would legitimize his bastard children. It certainly lay within the pope's competence
to legitimize them so far as the laws of the church were concerned; that
is to say, he could make them eligible to become priests. But William
wanted his children legitimized in the temporal sphere also so that they
could be his legal heirs, and this was a privilege normally granted by a
secular king. The principle involved then was whether the pope could
exercise the prerogatives of a temporal ruler outside the papal states.
The issue was complicated by the fact that a little earlier Innocent had
granted to two illegitimate children of the king of France precisely the
privilege that Count William was requesting for his sons.

Innocent refused the count's request, pointing out that the king of
France had no other superior to whom he could appeal in such a case,
whereas the count had a superior lord; namely, the king himself. But
the pope was not content to leave the matter at that. He set his decision
in the context of a general dissertation on the nature of papal power
which was subsequently incorporated into the canon law of the church.
The pope, he pointed out, was the vicar of one who had been "a priest
after the order of Melchisedech," and Melchisedech had been both priest
and king. Accordingly, Innocent maintained that he did possess very
extensive powers in temporal affairs, even though he was not choosing
to exercise them in this particular case. From an obscure passage of

Deuteronomy he extracted the conclusion that the pope could, if he chose, act as supreme judge in all cases, whether civil or criminal, spiritual or secular. Modern scholars have been uncertain whether Innocent really intended to put forward such an all-embracing claim, but thirteenth century canonists who commented on the decretal had no doubt that this was what the pope meant. Alongside this claim to supreme jurisdiction in all cases must be set the decretal *Licet* (*No.* 79), addressed to the Bishop of Vercelli, in which Innocent declared that appeals from secular courts to the papacy would not normally be entertained, but that they could be received if the secular judge was accused of negligence or bias, and especially when there was no emperor to hear an appeal.

There is evidently room for disagreement about the theoretical assumptions underlying Innocent's political activity. But the texts in the first series printed below (*Nos.* 69-74) are very difficult to understand unless we assume that Innocent did believe in a theocratic idea of papal world-monarchy. On the other hand, the various reservations and qualifications that appear in his other letters are not too difficult to explain if we consider the particular circumstances in which those letters were written. Innocent was not a recluse writing political theory locked away in his study. He intended his decretals to determine the outcome of great issues in the real world of events. By 1200 there were many grounds on which a pope could claim to intervene in political affairs. Innocent always chose the ground that was most likely to be accepted by the disputants in a particular case. It is arguable, moreover, that none of the passages in decretals like *Novit* and *Licet* in which Innocent disavowed the intention of judging certain kinds of cases were really incompatible with a claim to universal jurisdiction. Innocent did maintain (especially in *Per Venerabilem*) that the papacy was a supreme court of appeal for all the cases in Christendom. But no supreme court hears all the lawsuits that litigants may want to bring before it. The court has to define the classes of cases appropriate to its jurisdiction. They will probably include cases in which a disputed point of law is involved, or in which there is some injustice of a lower court to be rectified, or in which the parties are such that no other court can give judgment. These are exactly the kinds of cases we find mentioned in the letters of Innocent that explained how the secular jurisdiction of the Roman see would be exercised. He used phrases like "when the matter is difficult and ambiguous," or "when the judge is suspect," or "when there is no superior judge."

Innocent no doubt wrote sincerely that he did not intend to usurp the rights of others. He always saw the need for two orders of government in Christian society, a priestly one and a royal one, and he never claimed that either order could be abolished or wholly absorbed by the other. He does seem to have claimed that the pope held a unique position as head of both orders, and this because the pope alone exercised on earth the full powers of Christ, who had been both priest and king.

Historians who have come to the conclusion that Innocent sought both spiritual and temporal power have usually assumed without more ado that he should be condemned for "worldly ambition" or "cold selfishness." But there is more to it than that. Any over-all assessment of Innocent's pontificate must take into account the fact that he was not only an active statesman but also a great ecclesiastical reformer, concerned at least as much with the right ordering of the church as with the details of worldly diplomacy. As a legislator he showed a brilliant talent for translating the most advanced and humane insights of contemporary theologians into effective new law. He promulgated, for instance, decrees on marriage, on education, and on judicial procedure which had far-reaching and wholly beneficial effects on European society. Innocent's openness to new concepts, his encouragement for new ways of life in the church, his real zeal for reform, are evidenced above all by the warm support that he gave to the radical movement of apostolic poverty initiated during his pontificate by St. Francis of Assisi, a movement that later on, after Francis's death, inspired some of the most extreme and eloquent critics of the medieval papacy.

Just as Francis shaped human language into a hymn of praise to God for all his creatures, just as contemporary architects shaped material stone into cathedrals that symbolized by their very form the divine order of the universe, so too, Innocent believed, a great ruler set "below God but above men" could shape mundane human affairs in such a fashion that the ordered peace of a universal society would reflect the immanent harmony and justice of God's universe. Even if we conclude that in pursuing such an ideal he and his successors were led into grievous errors of abstract theory and practical action, we need not suppose that the vision itself sprang from selfish pride or disordered ambition. Above all it must be remembered that theocracy is a normal pattern of government. Once the royal theocracy of the eleventh century had been defeated it was almost inevitable that there would be an attempt to assert a system of papal theocracy. That too would have to be defeated before Western society could learn to live with the permanent tension between church and state that was coming to characterize it.

Some Observations on Papal Power

69. Sermon on the consecration of a pope, ed. J. P. Migne, *PL* 217 (Paris, 1855), cols. 657-58.

. . . To me is said in the person of the prophet, "I have set thee over nations and over kingdoms, to root up and to pull down, and to waste and to destroy, and to build and to plant" (Jeremias 1:10). To

me also is said in the person of the apostle, "I will give to thee the keys
of the kingdom of heaven. And whatsoever thou shalt bind upon earth
it shall be bound in heaven, etc." (Matthew 16:19) . . . thus the others
were called to a part of the care but Peter alone assumed the plenitude
of power. You see then who is this servant set over the household, truly
the vicar of Jesus Christ, successor of Peter, anointed of the lord, a God
of Pharaoh, set between God and man, lower than God but higher than
man, who judges all and is judged by no one. . . .

70. Letter to the archbishop of Ravenna (1198), ed. J. P. Migne,
PL 214 (Paris, 1855), col. 21.

Ecclesiastical liberty is nowhere better cared for than where
the Roman church has full power in both temporal and spiritual affairs. . . .

71. Letter to the prefect Acerbus and the nobles of Tuscany
(1198), ed. J. P. Migne, PL 214, col. 377.

Just as the founder of the universe established two great
lights in the firmament of heaven, a greater one to preside over the day
and a lesser to preside over the night, so too in the firmament of the
universal church, which is signified by the word heaven, he instituted
two great dignities, a greater one to preside over souls as if over day and
a lesser one to preside over bodies as if over night. These are the pontifical authority and the royal power. Now just as the moon derives its light
from the sun and is indeed lower than it in quantity and quality, in
position and in power, so too the royal power derives the splendor of its
dignity from the pontifical authority. . . .

72. Letter to the patriarch of Constantinople (1199), ed. J. P.
Migne, PL 214, col. 759.

. . . James, the brother of the Lord who "seemed to be a
pillar" (Galatians 1:19), content with Jerusalem alone . . . left to Peter
not only the universal church but the whole world to govern. . . .

73. Letter to the king of Armenia (1199), ed. J. P. Migne, PL
214, col. 813.

We give thanks with all our heart to him from whom is
every good gift and every perfect gift, who holds the hearts of princes in
his hand and from whom is all power, that you are so rooted in devotion
to the apostolic see as to have recourse to the aid of the Roman church

not only in spiritual matters but also in temporal matters and to appeal
to her strength in defence of your just rights. . . .

74. Letter to the emperor Alexius of Constantinople (1201), ed.
J. P. Migne, *PL* 216 (Paris, 1855), col. 1185 (*Decretales*, 1.33.6
Solitae).

. . . To us in the person of blessed Peter the flock of Christ
was committed when the Lord said, "Feed my sheep" (John 21:17), not
making any distinction between these sheep and those in order to show
that any one who fails to acknowledge Peter and his successors as pastors
and teachers is outside his flock. We need hardly mention, since they
are so well known, the words that Christ spoke to Peter and through
Peter to his successors, "Whatsoever you bind upon earth, etc." (Matthew
16:19), excepting nothing when he said, "Whatsoever."

Innocent and the Empire

75. The decretal *Venerabilem* (1202) (*Decretales* 1.6.34), ed.
E. Friedberg, *Corpus Iuris Canonici*, II (Leipzig, 1881), col. 79-82.

. . . Among other things certain princes urge this objection
particularly, that our venerable brother the bishop of Palestrina, legate
of the apostolic see, acted as either an elector [of the emperor] or as a
judge of the election. If as an elector, he put his sickle in a stranger's
harvest and, by intervening in the election, detracted from the dignity of
the princes; if as a judge, he seems to have proceeded incorrectly since
one of the parties was absent and should not have been judged contumacious when he had not been cited to appear. We indeed by virtue
of our office of apostolic service, owe justice to each man and, just as we
do not want our justice to be usurped by others, so too we do not want
to claim for ourselves the rights of the princes. We do indeed acknowledge, as we should, that the princes, to whom this belongs by right and
ancient custom, have the right and power to elect a king who is afterwards to be promoted emperor; and especially so since this right and
power came to them from the apostolic see which transferred the Roman
empire from the Greeks to the Germans in the person of the great
Charles. But the princes should acknowledge, and indeed they do acknowledge, that right and authority to examine the person elected as
king, who is to be promoted to the imperial dignity, belong to us who
anoint, consecrate and crown him; for it is regularly and generally observed that the examination of a person pertains to the one to whom the
laying-on of hands belongs. If the princes elected as king a sacrilegious

man or an excommunicate, a tyrant, a fool or a heretic, and that not just by a divided vote but unanimously, ought we to anoint, consecrate and crown such a man? Of course not. Therefore, replying to the objection of the princes, we maintain that our legate the bishop of Palestrina, our dearly beloved brother in Christ, did not act as either an elector . . . or as a judge when he approved King Otto and rejected Duke Philip. And so he in no way usurped the right of the princes or acted against it. Rather he exercised the office of one who declared that the king was personally worthy and the duke personally unworthy to obtain the imperial dignity, not considering so much the zeal of the electors as the merits of those elected. . . .

It is clear from law and precedent that, if the votes of the princes are divided in an election, we can favor one of the parties after due warning and a reasonable delay, especially after the unction, consecration and coronation are demanded of us, for it has often happened that both parties demanded them. For if the princes after due warning and delay cannot or will not agree, shall the apostolic see then lack an advocate and defender and be penalized for their fault? . . .

Innocent and the Kingdoms

76. The decretal *Novit* (1204), (*Decretales* 2.1.13), ed. E. Friedberg, *Corpus Iuris Canonici*, II (Leipzig, 1881), cols. 243-44.

. . . Let no one suppose that we wish to diminish or disturb the jurisdiction and power of the king when he ought not to impede or restrict our jurisdiction and power. Since we are insufficient to exercise all our own jurisdiction why should we want to usurp another's? But the Lord says in the Gospel, "If thy brother shall offend against thee, go, and rebuke him between thee and him alone. If he shall hear thee thou shalt gain thy brother. And if he will not hear thee, take with thee one or two more, that in the mouth of two or three witnesses every word may stand. And if he will not hear them, tell the church. And if he will not hear the church let him be to thee as the heathen and the publican" (Matthew 18:15); and the king of England is ready, so he asserts, to prove fully that the king of the French is offending against him and that he has proceeded according to the evangelical rule in rebuking him and, having achieved nothing, is at last telling it to the church. How then can we, who have been called to the rule of the universal church by divine providence, obey the divine command if we do not proceed as it lays down, unless perhaps [King Philip] shows sufficient reason to the contrary before us or our legate. For we do not intend to judge concerning a fief, judgement on which belongs to him—except when some special privilege or contrary custom detracts from the common law—but to decide concerning a sin, of which the judgement undoubtedly belongs to us, and we can and should exercise it against any-one. . . .

The emperor Theodosius decreed and Charles, ancestor of the present king, confirmed that "If anyone has a legal case . . . and chooses to take it before the bishop of the most holy see, without question and even if the other party objects, he is to be sent to the bishop's court with the statements of the litigants." This, however, we pass over in humility for we do not rely on human statutes but on divine law since our power is not from man but from God.

No man of sound mind is unaware that it pertains to our office to rebuke any Christian for any mortal sin and to coerce him with ecclesiastical penalties if he spurns our correction. That we can and should rebuke is evident from the pages of both the Old and New Testaments. . . . That we can and should coerce is evident from what the Lord said to the prophet who was among the priests of Anathoth, "Lo I have set thee over nations and over kingdoms to root up and to pull down and to waste, and to destroy, and to build, and to plant" (Jeremias 1:10). No one doubts that all mortal sin must be rooted up and destroyed and pulled down. Moreover, when the Lord gave the keys of the kingdom of heaven to blessed Peter, he said, "Whatsoever thou shalt bind upon earth, it shall be bound also in heaven: and whatsoever thou shalt loose on earth it shall be loosed also in heaven" (Matthew 16:19). . . . But it may be said that kings are to be treated differently from others. We, however, know that it is written in the divine law, "You shall judge the great as well as the little and there shall be no difference of persons" (cf. Deuteronomy 1:17). . . . Although we are empowered to proceed in this fashion against any criminal sin in order to recall the sinner from error to truth and from vice to virtue, this is especially so when it is a sin against peace, peace which is the bond of love. . . . Finally, when a treaty of peace was made between the kings and confirmed on both sides by oaths which, however, were not kept for the agreed period, can we not take cognizance of such a sworn oath, which certainly belongs to the judgement of the church, in order to re-establish the broken treaty of peace? . . .

77. Letter to King John of England accepting his feudal homage (April 1214), ed. T. Rymer, Foedera I (London, 1816), p. 119.

The king of kings and lord of lords, Jesus Christ, a priest for ever after the order of Melchisedech, has so established the priesthood and kingship in the church that the kingship is priestly and the priesthood is royal, as Peter in his Epistle and Moses in the Law bear witness, and he has set over all one whom he appointed to be his vicar on earth so that, just as every knee on earth and in heaven and even

under the earth is bowed to him, so all should obey his vicar and strive
that there be one fold and one shepherd. The kings of the world so
venerate this vicar for the sake of God that they do not regard themselves as reigning properly unless they take care to serve him devotedly.
Prudently heeding this, beloved son, and mercifully inspired by him
in whose hand are the hearts of kings and who sways them as he wishes,
you have decreed that your person and your kingdom should be temporally subject to the one to whom you knew them to be spiritually
subject, so that kingship and priesthood, like body and soul, should be
united in the one person of the vicar of Christ to the great advantage
and profit of both. He has deigned to bring this about who, being alpha
and omega, related the end to the beginning and revealed the beginning
in the end, so that those provinces which formerly had the holy Roman
church as their proper teacher in spiritual matters now have her as their
special lord in temporal affairs also. . . .

Innocent as Judge

78. The decretal *Per Venerabilem* (1202) (*Decretales* 4.17.13), ed.
E. Friedberg, *Corpus Iuris Canonici*, II (Leipzig, 1881), cols. 714-
16.

Your humility has requested through our venerable brother
the archbishop of Arles, who came to the apostolic see, that we deign to
adorn your sons with the title of legitimacy so that defect of birth
would not hinder their succeeding to you. That the apostolic see has
full power in the matter seems clear from the fact that, having examined
various cases, it has given dispensations to some illegitimate sons—not
only natural sons but also those born of adultery—legitimizing them for
spiritual functions so that they could be promoted to be bishops. From
this it is held to be more likely and reputed to be more credible that
it is able to legitimize children for secular functions, especially if they
acknowledge no superior among men who has the power of legitimizing
except the Roman pontiffs; for greater care and authority and worthiness
are required in spiritual affairs and so it seems that what is conceded
in greater matters is lawful also in lesser ones. . . .

Now the king [of France] acknowledges no superior in temporal affairs
and so, without injuring the right of anyone else, he could submit himself to our jurisdiction and did so. It seemed to some indeed that he
could perhaps have granted the dispensation himself, not as a father to
his sons but as a prince to his subjects. But you know that you are
subject to others and so you cannot submit yourself to us in this matter
without injuring them unless they give consent, and you are not of

such authority that you have the power of granting a dispensation yourself.

Motivated therefore by these considerations we granted to the king
the favor requested, deducing from both the Old and the New Testaments that, not only in the patrimony of the church where we wield
full power in temporal affairs, but also in other regions, we may exercise
temporal jurisdiction incidentally after having examined certain cases.
It is not that we want to prejudice the rights of anyone else or to usurp
any power that is not ours, for we are not unaware that Christ answered
in the Gospel "Render to Caesar the things that are Caesar's, and to
God the things that are God's" (Luke 20:25). Consequently, when he
was asked to divide an inheritance between two men, he said, "Who
hath appointed me judge over you?" (Luke 12:14). But in Deuteronomy
this is contained, "If thou perceive that there be among you a hard and
doubtful matter in judgement between blood and blood, cause and cause,
leprosy and leprosy: and thou see that the words of the judges within
thy gates do vary: arise and go up to the place the lord thy God shall
choose. And thou shalt come to the priests of the Levitical race, and to
the judge that shall be at that time: and thou shalt ask of them, and
they shall shew thee the truth of the judgement. And thou shalt do
whatsoever they shall say that preside in the place which the Lord shall
choose, and what thy shall teach thee according to his law; and thou
shalt follow their sentence: neither shalt thou decline to the right hand
nor to the left hand. But he that will be proud, and refuse to obey
the commandment of the priest who ministereth at that time to the
Lord, thy God, and the decree of the judge, that man shall die, and
thou shalt take away the evil from Israel." (Deuteronomy 17:8-12). Now
since the word "Deuteronomy" means a second law, it is proved from
the meaning of the word itself that what is laid down there is to be
observed also in the New Testament. For the place which the Lord
has chosen is known to be the apostolic see from this, that the Lord
founded it on himself as its corner stone, for, when Peter was fleeing
from the city, the Lord, wanting him to return to the place that he had
chosen and being asked by him, "Lord whither goest thou?" replied, "I
am going to Rome to be crucified again." Peter understood that this
was meant for him and at once returned to the place.

The priests of the Levitical race are our brothers who, according to
Levitical law, act as our coadjutors in the discharge of the priestly office.
There is indeed a priest or judge above them to whom the Lord said in
the person of Peter, "Whatsoever thou shalt bind upon earth it shall
be bound also in heaven; and whatsoever thou shalt loose on earth it
shall be loosed also in heaven" (Matthew 16:19). This is the vicar of
him who is a priest for ever according to the order of Melchisedech,
established by God as judge of the living and the death. Three kinds
of judgement are distinguished, the first between blood and blood by

which civil crimes are signified, the last between leper and leper by which ecclesiastical crimes are signified, and a middle kind, between cause and cause, which refers to both civil and ecclesiastical cases. In these matters, whenever anything difficult or ambiguous has arisen, recourse is to be had to the apostolic see, and if anyone disdains to obey its sentence out of pride he shall be condemned to death to "take away the evil from Israel," that is to say he shall be separated from the communion of the faithful, as if dead, by a sentence of excommunication. Paul too, writing to the Corinthians to explain the plenitude of power, said, "Know you not that we shall judge angels? How much more the things of this world?" (1 Corinthians 6:3.) Accordingly [the apostolic see] is accustomed to exercise the office of secular power sometimes and in some things by itself, sometimes and in some things through others.

Therefore, although we decided to grant a dispensation to the sons of the aforesaid king of the French . . . we do not assent to your petition although we embrace your person with arms of especial affection and are willing to show you special favor in any matters in which we can do so honorably and in accordance with God's will.

79. The decretal *Licet* (1206) (*Decretales* 2.2.10), ed. E. Friedberg, *Corpus Iuris Canonici*, II (Leipzig, 1879), col. 250.

If it happens that laymen of Vercelli have obtained letters from the Apostolic See on matters which pertain to secular jurisdiction we command that you adjudge them by our authority to be void and of no effect, provided that the consuls and commune will do full justice to the plaintiffs in a secular trial. However, if those who have taken their cases before the consuls feel themselves oppressed in any way, they are permitted to appeal to you for a hearing, as has been the custom, or to me if they prefer. This is especially so when the empire is vacant so that those who are oppressed in the courts of their superiors cannot appeal to a secular judge. If there is reasonable cause of suspicion against the consuls they shall be accused before mutually selected arbitrators and the grounds of suspicion investigated. If they prove just, recourse is to be had to you or to me for justice as is stated above.

5. Frederick II & the Papacy

For most of his reign Innocent III supported the claim of Otto IV to the imperial throne. By 1210, however, he had quarreled with Otto, the cause of the breach being the usual, inevitable dispute about the emperor's territorial claims in Italy. The pope then brought forward a new protégé, the young prince Frederick II, son of the emperor Henry VI and grandson of Frederick Barbarossa, whose claim to the imperial throne came to be generally recognized in Germany and Italy. It seemed at the time that Innocent had achieved his greatest diplomatic triumph. In fact, however, he had launched into European politics the most dangerous enemy that the medieval papacy ever knew.

Frederick grew up into a formidable ruler, avid for power, ruthless, amoral, brilliantly intelligent. He displayed exceptional skill as a legislator and discerning taste as a patron of the arts, but he shocked the more conventional rulers of his age by maintaining a harem of Saracen women and, what was worse, an army of Saracen mercenaries which he deployed effectively in incessant wars against the Christian cities of Italy. Since he frequently referred to the divine origin of his own power he presumably believed in some sort of God, but apart from that he was probably a sceptic in matters of religion. Frederick was king of Sicily by hereditary right so his advancement to the imperial dignity gave him a title to rule the whole of Italy—but the consolidation of Italy into a single absolutist state within which the pope might become a mere dependent bishop was the one political development above all others that the Roman see was determined to prevent. Innocent III had foreseen the danger, of course, and he had extracted from Frederick the most solemn assurances that the imperial and Sicilian crowns would never be united, that Frederick would abdicate the throne of Sicily when he was crowned emperor. Pope Innocent, an astute and mature diplomat, was no doubt entirely confident of his ability to handle a prince who was little more than a boy and who seemed entirely dependent on the pope's good will. But, as it turned out, Innocent died a year after he had finally approved the deposition of Otto IV in 1215, while Frederick lived on to harass the papacy for another thirty-five years. In 1220 Frederick managed to persuade Innocent's successor, Honorius III, a

139

mild and peace-loving pontiff, to crown him as emperor before he had relinquished control over Sicily. After that Frederick never did give up Sicily but devoted his whole life to the project of uniting all Italy under his rule. From 1220 to 1226 Frederick concerned himself primarily with the reorganization of his Sicilian kingdom and turned it into the most efficiently ordered centralized state that medieval Europe had yet seen. In 1226 he turned his attention to Lombardy, announcing his intention of reviving the imperial rights in that region, and the cities of north Italy that had fought for so long against Frederick's grandfather came together once more in a league to defend their autonomy.

Honorius died at this point. His next two successors, Gregory IX and Innocent IV, were rulers of a different stamp. Gregory was a fiery old zealot and Innocent a man of hard, inflexible will, renowned for legal craft and diplomatic cunning. These two kept up an unceasing struggle against Frederick. They condemned him for heresy, sacrilege, and immorality, for perjury and blasphemy, for not going on crusade when he had vowed to do so and then for presuming to go when he had been excommunicated—but all this could not hide the fact that their real quarrel with the emperor was a political one. A king of Sicily endowed with Frederick's unusual gifts and idiosyncrasies would have made an uncomfortable neighbor for the papacy at the best of times, but the popes could have put up with him if he had been content to stay in Sicily. What they could not permit was that any one man, whoever he might be, should rule over all Italy, north and south.

Gregory IX excommunicated Frederick in 1227, patched up a truce with him in 1230, condemned him violently again in 1236, and finally excommunicated him for a second time in 1239, in which year Gregory died. Innocent IV at the outset of his pontificate resolved on a bold new tactic to cope with the threat of physical coercion that the emperor could always use against a papacy established in Rome. While pretending to negotiate with Frederick he slipped out of Rome in disguise and rode by night to the port of Civitavecchia, where a fleet was waiting to take him to his native city of Genoa. From Genoa Innocent set out over the Alps for Lyons, and there, safe from the imperial armies, he re-established the papal curia.

His first major action after settling at Lyons was to summon a general council of the church to meet there. The council was supposed to deal with a variety of matters—plans for a new crusade to the Holy Land, the schism between the Greek and Latin churches, the recent invasion of Eastern Europe by Tartar armies—and all these matters did come under discussion when the council assembled in 1245. But everyone knew from the first that the one essential business of the meeting from the pope's point of view was the condemnation and deposition of Frederick II. The emperor was accused before the council of perjury, sacrilege, and heresy. These charges were probably well founded, but they contained not a word about the emperor's ambitions in Lombardy, the real cause of the pope's hostility to him. Frederick was defended by Thaddeus of Suessa, one of his most eminent jurists, but the result was a foregone conclusion, and at the third session of the council Innocent read out a lengthy denunciation of the emperor, concluding with a solemn sentence of deposition (*No.* 81). Frederick, of course, did not accept the papal sentence but reacted to it by launching a series of new offensives in Italy. He suffered setbacks during the following year, but he was still fighting vigorously when he died in 1250. He left a son, Conrad, to succeed him, but Conrad was defeated and killed in 1254. The real greatness of the Hohenstaufen dynasty ended with the death of Frederick.

Innocent IV, without ever winning a decisive victory, triumphed in the end by his relentless perseverance and above all by the very fact that he succeeded in outliving the emperor. His persistent hostility destroyed the Hohenstaufen dynasty and with it the medieval dream of a universal empire. Many historians have thought that in the process he also destroyed the ideals of the medieval papacy, or at any rate debased them beyond all recognition. Innocent himself became bitterly, obdurately convinced that a victory for the emperor would mean the enslavement of the Roman see, and he may well have been right in that assumption. But to contemporaries it seemed that the pope was using every spiritual resource at his command for the sole purpose of advancing his interests as a temporal ruler in Italy. Certainly Innocent used every power inherent in the papacy that was meant for the good governance of the church and the defence of Christian society—excommunication, interdict, ecclesiastial taxes, episcopal appointments, crusading privileges—for the one end of coaxing or coercing reluctant supporters all over Europe to join in the struggle against Frederick. He was lucky in that the contemporary kings of France and England, Louis IX and Henry III, were men of exceptional piety and genuine devotion to the papacy, but even they would not lend whole-hearted support to the pope's anti-imperial policies. It seemed to them that the troubles in Italy were essentially territorial disputes between temporal rulers that could and should be settled in a reasonable fashion by negotiations or arbitration. They had no sympathy with Frederick's alleged impieties but little taste for the pope's political maneuverings. It should be said on Innocent's behalf that he did not create the crisis in the political affairs of the papacy with which he had to cope, and that if he used the emergency powers of the Roman see to the utmost, it must have seemed to him that his reign was one long, desperate emergency.

In the letters exchanged between Frederick and the popes there can be found two important developments in the theory of empire and papacy. Immediately after his deposition Frederick II launched a more extreme attack on the whole hierarchy of clerical government than any of his predecessors had permitted themselves. Up until that time Frederick had always insisted that he was a most loyal and Catholic son of the church. It was he in fact who established the practice of burning heretics alive. To the emperor it no doubt seemed a painless way of demonstrating his zeal for orthodoxy in an age when a reputation for such zeal was a diplomatic asset. In his disputes with Gregory IX the emperor always expressed reverence for the papal office and insisted that he was opposed only to the personal policies of the particular pope then reigning. But when Innocent IV, supported by a council of bishops, presumed to depose him, Frederick threw discretion to the winds. In a furious letter addressed to the kings of Europe (No. 82) he inveighed bitterly against the greed for power and wealth that characterized the clergy of the time and announced his intention of initiating a radical reform of the church by confiscating all its wealth. This return to the poverty of the primitive church, he suggested, half seriously, might bring about a revival of those happy days when clerics devoted themselves to healing the sick and working miracles (an art they seemed to have quite lost in his own day) instead of meddling in politics. The letter, with its radical attack on the whole structure of ecclesiastical property rights, seems to have shocked respectable contemporary opinion. It can be read as a foreshadowing of later, more explicit theories of a laical, antisacerdotal state.

On the papal side we find a new interpretation of the Donation of Constantine. During the preceding two centuries the Donation had played surprisingly little part in all the arguments and counterarguments about the temporal power of the papacy. Gregory IX, however, drew it into the center of the discussion, relying heavily on the Donation to support both the territorial claims of the papacy in Italy and the pope's right to crown emperors (No. 80). It was a surprisingly weak argument for Gregory to have advanced. The Roman lawyers in the universities were already raising doubts, not so much about the validity of the document as about the legality of the grant it purported to record. Moreover, if all the temporal claims of the papacy rested on a supposed grant by a former emperor, it could well be argued that a contemporary emperor might revoke that grant and reduce the popes to their former relatively humble position. This, in effect, was what Frederick proposed to do in his letter of 1246.

Innocent IV's reply to the emperor's protests against his deposition set out the new papal interpretation of the Donation (No. 83). (It is not quite certain that the pope himself composed this encyclical but it certainly presents views that were current in the papal curia.) The exposition relied heavily on the theories of the canonist Alanus and on the political decretals of Innocent III. The Donation was discussed in a most involved passage that fairly clanked with the symbolism of keys and swords. It argued that the popes from the very beginning had inherited the royal as well as the priestly powers of Christ. Accordingly, when Constantine surrendered the empire to Sylvester he did not bestow temporal power on the popes for the first time but merely acknowledged a regal authority that had always been inherent in the papal office. The argument was essentially a defense against a new line of attack to which Gregory IX's injudicious use of the Donation had exposed the papacy.

Gregory IX and the Donation of Constantine

80. Letter of Gregory IX to Frederick II (October 1236), trans. S. Z. Ehler and J. P. Morrall, *Church and State Through the Centuries* (London, 1954), p. 77.

. . . Go back to the memory of your predecessors and behold, pass to the examples of the Emperors of happy memory Constantine, Charlemagne, Arcadius and Valentinian and examine more carefully those things in which the conclusion of an infallible solution is accepted without contradiction and where the reprobate assumption of a false opinion is refuted. For we by no means overlook that it is publicly obvious to the whole world that the aforesaid Constantine, who had received the exclusive monarchy over all parts of the world, decided as just—with the unanimity of all and with the full consent of the whole Senate and people, established not only in the City of Rome but in the whole Roman Empire—that as the vicar of the Prince of Apostles governed the empire of priesthood and of souls in the whole world so he should also reign over things and bodies throughout the whole world; and considering that he should rule over earthly matters by the reins of justice to whom, as it is known, God had committed on earth the charge over spiritual things, the Emperor Constantine humbled himself by his own vow and handed over the Empire to the perpetual care of the Roman Pontiff with the Imperial insignia and sceptres and the City and Duchy of Rome, which you endeavour now to disturb by distributing money in it following in this the example of him who "will drink up a river and not wonder; he trusteth that the Jordan may run into his mouth" (Job 40:18); and declaring it to be impious that the earthly Emperor should enjoy any authority where the head of all the Christian religion had been established by deposition of the Heavenly Emperor, he left Italy to the Apostolic deposition and chose for himself a new habitation in Greece. Whence later in the person of the aforesaid Charlemagne, who thought that the difficult yoke imposed by the Roman Church should be carried with pious devotion, the Apostolic See transferred the judgment-seat of the Empire to the Germans, placed it upon your predecessors and your own person—as you will admit that it happened by means of consecration and anointment, although reducing in nothing the substance of its own jurisdiction—and conceded to them the power of the sword in the subsequent coronation; you should therefore realize that you will clearly stand convicted of infringing the rights of the Apostolic See and your own faith and honour as long as you do not recognize your own creator. . . .

The Deposition of Frederick II

81. Sentence of deposition promulgated by Innocent IV in the General Council of Lyons (June 1245), trans. S. Z. Ehler and J. P. Morrall, *Church and State*, pp. 81, 86.

. . . He has committed four very grave offences, which can not be covered up by any subterfuge (we say nothing for the moment about his other crimes); he has abjured God on many occasions; he has wantonly broken the peace which had been re-established between the Church and the Empire; he has also committed sacrilege by causing to be imprisoned the Cardinals of the holy Roman Church and the prelates and clerics, regular and secular, of other churches, coming to the Council which our predecessor had summoned; he is also accused of heresy not by doubtful and flimsy but by formidable and clear proofs. . . .

We therefore, who are the vicar, though unworthy, of Jesus Christ on earth and to whom it was said in the person of blessed Peter the Apostle; "Whatsoever thou shalt bind on earth," etc., show and declare on account of the above-mentioned shameful crimes and of many others, having held careful consultation with our brethren and the holy Council, that the aforesaid prince—who has rendered himself so unworthy of all the honour and dignity of the Empire and the kingdom and who, because of his wickedness, has been rejected by God from acting as king or Emperor—is bound by his sins and cast out and deprived of all honour and dignity by God, to which we add our sentence of deprivation also. We absolve for ever all who owe him allegiance in virtue of an oath of fealty from any oath of this kind; and we strictly forbid by Apostolic authority that any one should obey him or look upon him henceforth as king or Emperor, and we decree that whoever shall in the future afford him advice, help or goodwill as if he were Emperor or king, shall fall "ipso facto" under the binding force of excommunication. But let those in the same Empire whose duty it is to look to the election of an Emperor, elect a successor freely. We shall make it our business to provide for the aforesaid kingdom of Sicily as seems best to us with the advice of our brethren.

Frederick's Reply

82. Letter of Frederick to the kings of Christendom (1246), ed.
J. Huillard-Bréholles, *Historia Diplomatica Friderici Secundi*, VI,
i (Paris, 1860), pp. 391-93.

The ancients call happy those who learn caution from the
danger of others, for a later condition is shaped on the principle of a
preceding one and, as wax receives its impression from a seal, so the
character of human life is shaped by example. Would that we had
tasted this happiness, so that the practised caution which we pass on
to you, O Christian kings and princes, from the great harm done to
our majesty had been rather bequeathed to us by injured Christian
kings and princes. But instead those who are considered clerics, grown
fat on the alms of princes, now oppress princes' sons; and the sons of
our subjects who are ordained as apostolic fathers, forgetting their
fathers' position, do not deign to show any reverence for emperor or
king. What is implied by our maltreatment is made plain by the presumption of Pope Innocent IV for, having summoned a council—a
general council he calls it—he has dared to pronounce a sentence of
deposition against us who were neither summoned nor proved guilty
of any deceit or wickedness, which sentence he could not enact without
grievous prejudice to all kings. You and all kings of particular regions
have everything to fear from the effrontery of such a prince of priests
when he sets out to depose us who have been divinely honored by the
imperial diadem and solemnly elected by the princes with the approval
of the whole church at a time when faith and religion were flourishing
among the clergy, us who also govern in splendor other noble kingdoms;
and this when it is no concern of his to inflict any punishment on us for
temporal injuries even if the cases were proved according to law. In
truth we are not the first nor shall we be the last that this abuse of
priestly power harasses and strives to cast down from the heights; but
this indeed you also do when you obey these men who feign holiness,
whose ambition hopes that "the whole Jordan will flow into their mouth"
(*cf.* Job 40:18). O if your simple credulity would care to turn itself
"from the leaven of the Scribes and Pharisees which is hypocrisy" (Luke
12:1) according to the words of the Savior, how many foul deeds of that
court you would be able to execrate, which honor and shame forbid us
to relate. The copious revenues with which they are enriched by the
impoverishment of many kingdoms, as you yourself know, make them
rage like madmen. Christians and pilgrims beg in your land so that
Patarene heretics may eat in ours. You are closing up your houses there
to build the towns of your enemies here. These poor followers of Christ

are supported and enriched by your tithes and alms, but by what compensating benefit, or what expression of gratitude even do they show themselves beholden to you? The more generously you stretch out a hand to these needy ones the more greedily they snatch not only the hand but the arm, trapping you in their snare like a little bird that is the more firmly entangled the more it struggles to escape.

We have concerned ourselves to write these things to you for the present, though not adequately expressing our intentions. We have decided to omit other matters and to convey them to you more secretly; namely the purpose for which the lavishness of these greedy men expends the riches of the poor; what we have found out concerning the election of an emperor if peace is not established at least superficially between us and the church, which peace we intend to establish through eminent mediators; what dispositions we intend to make concerning all the kingdoms in general and each in particular; what has been arranged concerning the islands of the ocean; how that court is plotting against all princes with words and deeds which could not be concealed from us who have friends and subjects there, although clandestinely; with what stratagems and armies trained for war we hope in this coming spring to oppress all those who now oppress us, even though the whole world should set itself against us.

But whatever our faithful subjects, the bearers of this letter, relate to you you may believe with certainty and hold as firmly as if St. Peter had sworn to it. Do not suppose on account of what we ask of you that the magnanimity of our majesty has been in any way bowed down by the sentence of deposition launched against us, for we have a clean conscience and so God is with us. We call him to witness that it was always our intention to persuade the clergy of every degree that they should continue to the end as they were in the early days of the church living an apostolic life and imitating the Lord's humility, and that it was our intention especially to reduce those of highest rank to this condition. Those clergy [of former days] used to see angels and were resplendent with miracles; they used to heal the sick, raise the dead and subject kings and princes to themselves by holiness, not by arms. But these, drunk with the pleasures of the world and devoted to them, set aside God, and all true religion is choked by their surfeit of riches and power. Hence, to deprive such men of the baneful wealth that burdens them to their own damnation is a work of charity. You and all princes, united with us, ought to be as diligent as you can in achieving this end so that, laying aside all superfluities and content with modest possessions, they may serve the God whom all things serve.

A Defense of the Deposition

83. The encyclical letter *Eger Cui Levia* (c. 1246), ed. E. Winkelmann, *Acta Imperii Inedita*, II (Innsbruck, 1885), pp. 696-98.

When a sick man who cannot be helped by mild remedies undergoes a surgical incision or cautery, he rages in bitterness of spirit against his doctor and, unable to endure the harsh remedies of the cure, complains that he is being cruelly murdered by the one who is performing a health giving operation. In the same way a condemned man is sometimes inflamed against his condemner . . . and mistakenly blames what he suffers, not on his own faults, but on the injustice of the judge. . . . If then Frederick, formerly emperor, strives to accuse with noisy widespread complaints the sacred judge of the universal church through whom he was declared cast down by God so that he might no longer rule or reign, it ought not to seem anything new or marvellous, for he is behaving in the same fashion as others in like case. . . .

He says to be sure that the order of justice was perverted and that he was not legitimately cited or convicted but was criminally condemned by a judge who had no power to judge him. Thus in his usual fashion he persists in reducing to nothing the primacy of apostolic dignity which Peter, the head of all the faithful, and his successors are known to have received not from man but from God, as all agree. Indeed anyone who claims to be exempt from the authority of his vicar diminishes the authority of God and does not acknowledge God, the son of God, to be inheritor and lord of all things. For we act as a general legate on earth of the king of kings who bestowed on the prince of the apostles, and in him on us, a plenitude of power to bind and loose not only everyone but everything "whatsoever," including all things in the more general neuter form lest any thing or any business should seem to be exempted. Also the teacher of the gentiles showed this plenitude to be unbounded when he said "Do you not know that we shall judge angels? How much more the things of this world" (1 Corinthians 6:3). Did he not explain that the power given over angels extended also to temporalities in order to make it understood that lesser things also are subordinated to those to whom greater ones are subject?

The eternal priesthood of Christ established under his grace in the unshakeable see of Peter is to be credited not with less power but with much more than the ancient priesthood that served for a time according to the forms of the law, and yet God said to the priesthood of those times, "See I have set thee over nations and over kingdoms to root up and to pull down, and to waste and to destroy, and to build and to plant" (Jeremias 1:10); not only "over nations" but also "over kingdoms," so that it might be known that power was committed over both. We read that many pontiffs of the Old Testament used this power, removing from the royal throne by the authority divinely committed to them not a few kings who had become unworthy to rule. It remains then that the Roman pontiff can exercise his pontifical judgment at least incidentally over any Christian of any condition whatsoever especially if no one else can or will render to him the justice that is due, and particularly by reason of sin. Thus he may decree that any sinner whose contumacy has brought him to the depths of depravity is to be held as "a publican and a stranger" and outside the body of the faithful so that, by implication at least, he is deprived of the power of any temporal rulership that he had, for such power most certainly cannot be borne outside the church, since there, where everything builds for Hell, there is no power ordained by God. Therefore they do not discern shrewdly or know how to investigate the origins of things who think that the apostolic see first received rule over the empire from the prince Constantine, for this rule is known to have been inherent in the apostolic see naturally and potentially beforehand. For our Lord Jesus Christ, the son of God, was a true king and true priest after the order of Melchisedech just as he was true man and true God, which he made manifest by now using the honor of royal majesty before men, now exercising on their behalf the dignity of the pontificate before the Father, and he established not only a pontifical but a royal monarchy in the apostolic see, committing to Peter and his successors control over both an earthly and a heavenly empire, which was adequately signified in the plurality of the keys, so that the vicar of Christ might be known to have received the power of judging over the heavens in spiritual things through the one key that we have received, over the earth in temporal things through the other.

In truth when Constantine was joined to the Catholic church through the faith of Christ he humbly resigned to the church the inordinate tyranny that he had formerly exercised outside it—and we, respectfully imitating the fathers of old, retain the insignia of the princely dress left by him as a permanent symbol and full pledge of the mystical reason for this resignation—and he received within the church from Christ's vicar, the successor of Peter, a duly ordered power of sacred rulership which thenceforward he used legitimately for the punishment of the evil and the praise of the good, and he who had formerly abused a power permitted to him afterwards exercised an authority bestowed on him. For both swords of either administration are kept in the flock of the faithful church as the assertion of the apostle shows and the divine authority agrees, whence anyone who is not within it has neither sword. Moreover neither is to be regarded as outside Peter's sphere of right, since the Lord did not say concerning the material sword "Lay it aside," but, "Return your sword to its sheath" (Matthew 26:52) meaning that you shall not yourself exercise it in future. He said expressly "your sword" and "your sheath" to indicate that there resided with his vicar, the head of the church militant, not the actual exercise of this sword, which was forbidden to him by divine command, but rather the authority by which this same exercise is made manifest in the service of the law for the punishment of the wicked and the defence of the good. For indeed the power of this material sword is implicit in the church but it is made explicit through the emperor who receives it from the church, and this power which is merely potential when enclosed in the bosom of the church becomes actual when it is transferred to the prince. This is evidently shown by the ceremony in which the supreme pontiff presents to the emperor whom he crowns a sword enclosed in a sheath. Having taken it the emperor draws the sword and by brandishing it indicates that he has received the exercise of it. It was from this sheath, namely from the plenitude of the apostolic power, that the aforesaid Frederick received the sword of his exalted principate, and in order that he might defend the peace of the church, not disturb it. . . .

6. The Decretalists

The *Decretum* of Gratian codified the law of the church as it existed in the mid-twelfth century, but new ecclesiastical law continued to be promulgated after Gratian's book appeared. This legislation was codified by command of Pope Gregory IX, and the new compilation, known as the *Decretales,* was promulgated in 1234. It contained nearly all the important "political" decretals that had been issued by the popes of the preceding century, most especially those of Innocent III. The thought and action of those popes had been much influenced by the work of the twelfth-century academic lawyers. Now, by a sort of juristic feedback, the decretals of the popes in their turn served as the starting point for a new round of canonistic speculation. A most interesting feature of the whole situation is that one of the most influential of all the Decretalists was Pope Innocent IV himself. He had lectured in canon law at Bologna as a young man, and somehow during his crowded pontificate he found time to keep on working at an academic commentary on the *Decretales.* The book, issued about 1250, was terse, shrewd, and brilliant, and it became one of the most influential of Decretalist works. Any final judgment on Innocent IV must take into account not only his controversial policies as a pope but also his distinguished achievement as a canonist.

It has been commonly held that, just as Innocent IV's diplomacy was more obviously directed to temporal ends than Innocent III's, so too in the field of political theory he abandoned all the reservations and subtleties of his predecessor and proclaimed a crude doctrine of outright theocracy. A study of Innocent IV's decretals and of his commentary on the *Decretales* does not confirm this impression. His basic theory adhered very closely to the thought and even to the words of his great predecessor. Sometimes, indeed, certain reservations were spelled out even more explicitly in the writings of Innocent IV. In commenting on the decretal *Novit,* for instance, in which Innocent III had disclaimed the intention of judging concerning a fief, Innocent IV not only accepted the doctrine of his predecessor but added a technical little commentary on procedure, making it clear that in his view any king who tried to bring a strictly feudal matter before the papal court on the pretext that sin was involved would have a very hard time proving his case (*No.* 84). He also read quite a restrictive meaning into the decretal *Licet,* in which Innocent III had laid down that appeals to the pope in secular cases could be made when the throne of the empire was vacant. Innocent IV pointed out that the ruling applied only to cases that pertained to the emperor's jurisdiction, since the empire was held from the papacy. Other kings did not hold their lands from the pope, he declared, and so the pope could not claim to succeed to their jurisdiction for that reason (though there might be other grounds on which he could base such a claim) (*No.* 85). Innocent IV went on in this same passage to list all the exceptional cases in which ecclesiastical courts could hear suits that would normally have belonged to the jurisdiction of a secular judge. These lists of exceptions are very common in the canonistic literature of the thirteenth century; they occur in all the major commentaries on the *Decretales.* Some scholars have pointed out that the "exceptions" became so numerous as to be almost all-embracing. Other scholars, who maintain that the political theory of the medieval popes was always essentially dualistic, have asserted that the very need to draw up lists of such exceptions, however long, shows that even the most extreme papalists of the mid-thirteenth century still acknowledged a separation in principle between the ecclesiastical and temporal spheres of jurisdiction. A third line of argument would maintain that some of the claims to secular jurisdiction in the lists of exceptions were compatible with a dualistic theory but that others were not.

Even in his more extreme claims on behalf of the Roman see Innocent IV adhered very closely to the thought of Innocent III. His assertion in the letter *Eger Cui Levia* (*No.* 83) that the word "whatsoever" in the famous phrase "whatsover thou shalt bind on earth . . ." meant that nothing at all was exempted from the papal jurisdiction echoes the words of Innocent III in his decretal *Solitae* (*No.* 74). His reference to 1 Corinthians 6.3 and the interpretation of it were both borrowed from *Per Venerabilem* (*No.* 78). His assertion that the papacy possessed a supreme appellate jurisdiction in all cases "whether it is a necessity of law because the judge is doubtful . . . or a necessity of fact because there is no other superior judge" (*No.* 85) was a conflation of Innocent III's claims in *Per Venerabilem* and in *Licet* (*No.* 79). Even his explanation of the Donation of Constantine, which has often been regarded as a radically new claim on behalf of the papacy, was entirely consistent with his predecessor's pattern of thought. Indeed, Innocent IV's imaginary account of how Sylvester received the empire from Constantine seems closely modeled in thought and language on the real letter in which Innocent III accepted England as a fief from King John (*No.* 77). Many difficulties of interpretation disappear if we realize that both pontiffs possessed some sense of historical development. They both taught that there had been a regal power inherent in the papacy from its very first foundation, but they conceded that this power was at first merely "potential" and that it became "actual" only over the course of the centuries as different princes acknowledged the temporal authority of the popes and submitted to it.

A problem that especially fascinated Innocent IV was that of the origin of legitimate political authority. In one passage he traced human government in the Christian world from the direct governance of God through the rule of various Old Testament figures to the universal authority of Christ and then of Christ's vicars the popes (No. 85). At another point in his work he lifted his eyes from the Christian world altogether and in a remarkable passage considered whether legitimate government could exist among infidel peoples. He discussed this question with philosophic detachment and a surprising magnanimity of spirit. Government was necessary not only for Christians, he argued, but for all "rational creatures," and all men were God's children and under his care. Therefore legitimate government could grow up among all peoples and did in fact exist among infidels (No. 86). The practical conclusion of the argument was that Christians had no inherent right to deprive infidel rulers of their authority or to despoil infidel peoples of their goods. This passage suggests that Innocent had extracted from his study of Roman jurisprudence a "natural law" theory of the state that is commonly encountered only a little later on after the assimilation of Aristotelian political ideas into Western thought.

The only Decretalist of the mid-thirteenth century whose reputation equaled that of Innocent IV was his younger contemporary, Cardinal Hostiensis. In reading his comments on church and state we seem to leave the subtleties and nuances of the two Innocents (whose freedom to theorize was limited by the responsibilities of power) to return to the hard, uncompromising theocratic line that the canonist Alanus had laid down at the beginning of the century. According to Hostiensis God had willed that two kinds of authority should exist on earth, but he had subordinated the temporal to the spiritual in every conceivable way (No. 88). The one limitation on the power of the papacy that Hostiensis recognized lay in his view that the pope ought not himself to wield the material sword of physical power to shed blood. This is the same reservation that Alanus had made, and this kind of "separation of powers" continued to be advocated even by the most ardent theocrats. Hostiensis took it for granted that the only proper function of the civil power (and the only justification for its existence) was to use the material sword of physical coercion in order to carry out tasks delegated by the church which were too sordid and brutal for the clergy themselves to perform. This is an echo, but a distorted echo, of St. Augustine, just as Hostiensis's commentary in this same passage on Innocent's phrase "the pontifical authority and the royal power" is an echo of Gelasius.

To sum up, then, we may say that by the middle of the thirteenth century there had emerged a fully developed theory of papal world-monarchy. The popes had all but committed the Roman see to the acceptance of this theory, but they still expressed themselves with an ambiguity that has made possible a variety of different interpretations of their thought.

Innocent IV

84. On *Decretales*, 2.1.13, *Novit* [*No.* 76], *Commentaria Super Libros Quinque Decretalium* (c. 1250) (Frankfurt, 1570), fol. 194.

Some say, and perhaps correctly, that these judges [sent by the pope] may decide not only whether the denunciation is legally admissible but also concerning the principal issue involved, in the following manner. The king of England may say: "The king of France holds the county of Poitiers at the peril of his soul or against his conscience, for it belongs to me, and I seek the help of your office to compel him to repent." If the king of France replies: "It does not pertain to you to decide whether I hold it legally or illegally, but this indeed I know, that I do not hold it against my conscience, and I am bound to answer before you concerning that and nothing else." And if then the king of England wishes to prove that the land was his own, the church may not consider his proofs, for it may be that it was once his but passed to the king of France by a licit judgment or in some other just fashion, or at least that the king acquired a probable right to it and so is without sin, as in the Code, 3.32.38. But if the king of England wishes to prove that [the king of France] holds against his conscience or unjustly, then his plea is to be admitted; but this is a very difficult sort of proof to establish for, as we have said, if the king of England proves that the land was once his he does not thereby prove that the other holds against his conscience or unjustly.

85. On *Decretales*, 2.2.10, *Licet* (c. 1250) [*No.* 79], *Commentaria*, fol. 197-98.

. . . This is because of a vacancy in the empire, for the pope succeeds only to the rights of the empire and so if another ruler subject to some superior other than the emperor is negligent in rendering justice or if there is no ruler in such a territory, then jurisdiction does not devolve to the pope; for there is a special bond of union between pope and emperor because the pope consecrates and examines the emperor, and the emperor is the protector of the pope and takes an oath to him and holds the empire from him, as above at *Decretales* 1.6.34 *Venerabilem* [*No.* 75]. . . . And so it is that, when the empire is vacant, the pope succeeds to a right which is held from the Roman church. . . . But what if another king or prince who has no superior is negligent? We say the same, namely that the pope succeeds to his jurisdiction as at C.15 q.6 c.3 [*No.* 62]. . . . However, the pope does not do this because the kingdom is held from him but out of the plenitude of power which he has because he is vicar of Christ as in the previous title c. *Novit* [*No.* 76]. . . . Or say that when kingdoms are vacant he could not intervene unless first there was a request in the form of a denunciation as in the above mentioned c. *Novit.* . . . This is one case when the ecclesiastical judge can intervene in a matter of secular jurisdiction, namely when the empire is vacant, though only as regards the jurisdiction that belongs to the empire, as is stated in the next chapter. A second case is when the judge neglects to do justice to widows, even rich ones. . . . A third case is at C.23 q.5 c.26 [rulers who fail to protect widows and minors to be excommunicated]. A fourth case is at C.24 q.3 c.21 [men who attack clerics or others protected by the church to be excommunicated]. A fifth case is when the judges disagree about a question because of its difficulty as below at X.4.17.13 *Per Venerabilem* [*No.* 78]. A sixth case is below at X.2.28.7 *Si duobus* [*No.* 57] [when a special custom exists]. A seventh case is in a denunciation as above in the previous title, X.2.1.13, *Novit* [*No.* 76]. An eighth case is when suspicion falls on the secular judge, as here. . . . A ninth case is by reason of relatedness because from the fact that an ecclesiastical judge has jurisdiction concerning matrimony, so also he has concerning dowry. A tenth case is as noted above at X.2.2.9 and at X.2.1.13 *Novit* [*No.* 76] in the gloss *Nota crimen* [cases of sacrilege, disturbing the peace, perjury, usury, heresy, adultery]. An eleventh case is at *Dist.* 89 c.5 and C.12 q.2 c.69 [attacks on church property]. . . . These things have been truly and usefully noted here. Someone may say, however, that the supreme pontiffs establish all this for themselves; but since a man incurs the guilt of sacrilege in speaking thus no credence is to be given to him, as in the *Digest* 11.1.11.1. If such persons are carefully attending to what they say, they really do incur the guilt of sacrilege.

To understand better the foregoing material note that in the beginning God created heaven and earth and himself ruled all things that were in them, angelic and human nature, spiritualities and temporalities, as a maker controls the things he has made, and he gave commands to the man he made and laid down penalties for transgressions as in Genesis c.2 . . . and so the world was ruled by God himself up until Noah. And in the time of Noah God began to rule his creatures through his ministers. The first was Noah. That he was ruler of the people appears from this that God committed to him the government of the ark, by which the church is signified, as in Genesis c.5. . . . We do not read that Noah was a priest but nevertheless he exercised the office of a priest immediately after the entry into the ark before he gave laws to the people. . . . Now in this vicariate there succeeded patriarchs, judges, kings and priests and others who for a time were rulers of the Jewish people, and this lasted until the coming of Christ who was our natural lord and king, of whom it is said in the psalm, "Give to the king thy judgment" (Psalm 71:2). And Jesus Christ himself established as his vicar Peter and the successors to him when he gave him the keys of the kingdom of heaven and when he said to him, "Feed my sheep" (John 21:17). Although in many things the offices and governing powers of the world are distinct, nevertheless, whenever it is necessary, recourse is to be had to the pope, whether it is a necessity of law because the judge is doubtful what sentence he ought rightfully to pronounce or a necessity of fact because there is no other superior judge or because lesser judges cannot execute their sentences or are unwilling to do justice as below at *Decretales* 4.17.13, *Per Venerabilem* [No. 78].

> 86. On *Decretales*, 3.34.8, *Quod Super*, *Commentaria* (c. 1250). fol. 429 30.

. . . I read of just and lawful jurisdiction where the sword given for vengeance is mentioned above at *Decretales* 1.33.6. But how this jurisdiction first began I do not know unless perhaps God assigned some person or persons to do justice to criminals or unless in the beginning the father of a family had complete jurisdiction over his family by the law of nature, though now he has it only in a few minor matters. . . . This at any rate is certain, that God himself exercised jurisdiction from the beginning as is noted above at *Decretales* 2.2.10, *Licet* [No. 85].

Again the people could have princes by election as they had Saul and many others. . . . I maintain, therefore, that lordship, possession and jurisdiction can belong to infidels licitly and without sin, for these things were made not only for the faithful but for every rational creature as has been said. For he makes his sun to rise on the just and the wicked and he feeds the birds of the air, Matthew c.5, c.6. Accordingly we say that it is not licit for the pope or the faithful to take away from infidels their belongings or their lordships or jurisdictions because they possess them without sin. Nevertheless we do certainly believe that the pope, who is vicar of Jesus Christ, has power not only over Christians but also over all infidels, for Christ had power over all, whence it is said in the psalm, "Give to the king thy judgment O God" (Psalm 71:2), and he would not seem to have been a careful father unless he had committed full power over all to his vicar whom he left on earth. Again he gave the keys of the kingdom of heaven to Peter and his successors and said, "Whatsoever you shall bind, etc." (Matthew 16:19). And again, elsewhere, "Feed my sheep, etc." (John 21:17). . . . But all men, faithful and infidels, are Christ's sheep by creation even though they are not of the fold of the church and thus from the foregoing it is clear that the pope has jurisdiction and power over all *de iure* though not *de facto*.

Hostiensis

87. On *Decretales*, 4.17.13, *Per Venerabilem* [*No.* 78], *Summa Domini Henrici Cardinalis Hostiensis* (1250-53) (Lyons, 1537), fol. 215-16.

Huguccio said that the emperor has power in temporal affairs from God alone and likewise the pope in spiritual affairs, and so the jurisdictions are separate. . . . Alanus and Tancred said that, although the imperial power may be held to have proceeded from God alone, nevertheless the emperor receives the exercise of the temporal sword from the church, for which reason the pope is greater and can use either sword. . . . I maintain that the jurisdictions are separate and that both proceeded from God. . . . Nevertheless, in proportion as one approaches closer to God it is greater than the other; therefore the priesthood is greater. . . . It is for this reason that a bishop is anointed on the head but a king on the arms and a bishop with chrism but a king with oil, to inform us that the bishop is a vicar of our head, i.e. Christ, and to show how great is the difference between the authority of a pontiff and the power of a prince, as in *Decretales* 1.15.1; for the difference between the priestly dignity and the royal is as great as that between sun and moon. Although these words have been expounded in different ways by the doctors you may say that, just as the moon receives its light from the sun and not the sun from the moon, so too the royal power receives authority from the priestly and not *vice versa*. Again, just as the sun illuminates the world by means of the moon when it cannot do so by itself, that is at night, so too the priestly dignity enlightens the world by means of the royal when it cannot do so by itself, that is when it is a question of inflicting a blood penalty. . . . This means also that the sacerdotal dignity is seven thousand, six hundred and forty-four and a half times greater than the royal, for we read in the fifth Book of the Almagest of Ptolemy, Proposition 18, "It is clear that the magnitude of the sun contains the magnitude of the moon seven thousand six hundred and forty-four and a half times."
. . . Therefore, although the jurisdictions are separate as regards their exercise, nevertheless the emperor holds his imperial power from the Roman church and can be called its official or vicar. The Roman church transferred the empire from the Greeks to the Romans in the person of the great Charles; and the pope confirms, anoints and crowns the em-

peror or rebukes and even deposes him, as is clear from *Decretales* 1.6.34 *Venerabilem* [*No.* 75]. Nor can the law of the emperor bind anyone except those who are subject to the laws of the Romans and the discipline of the holy Catholic church, for outside it there is no empire. . . . Nevertheless the pope ought not to interfere with what the emperor has done licitly in temporal affairs or meddle with those subject to the emperor except in special cases. . . .

Therefore, in the order of greatness, there is only one head, namely the pope. There ought to be only one as our head, one lord of spiritualities and temporalities, because "the earth and the fulness therefore" belong to Him who committed all things to Peter, as in the *Decretales* 1.33.6 and 1.6.4; and Peter had both swords. Therefore the Lord of lords said, "Behold, here are two swords" (Luke 22:38), and again, he said to Peter, not without reason, "I will give you the keys of the kingdom of Heaven" (Matthew 16:19). Note that he did not say "key" but "keys," so that there were two, one which opens and closes, binds and looses in spiritual affairs, the other which is used in temporal affairs.

88. On *Decretales* 1.33.6, *Solitae* [*No.* 74], *Commentaria in Quinque Libros Decretalium* (c. 1270) (Venice, 1581), fol. 171.

(In the decretal *Solitae* Innocent repeated his image of the sun and moon and, as in *No.* 71 above, declared that they were comparable to "the pontifical authority and the royal power.")

Royal power, that is, an executive power to inflict punishment. He used the word "power" as if to say that the pontiff's power inheres in the righteousness with which he should be imbued, but the king's in the actual force with which he should be supported, and so it seems that each needs the other and that if they are in harmony with one another all is well in the government of the holy church of God. Nevertheless the pontifical power ought to have precedence as being greater and more honorable like one that enlightens in the manner of a shining lamp, while the royal power ought to follow, as being lesser and cruder like a club for striking and beating down infidels and rebels. . . . Nowadays in many places the secular sword has become a priestly one, judging clerics and spiritual cases like laymen and temporal ones, which is against the laws . . . and the spiritual sword has become a military one, stirring up and prolonging wars for trivial reasons and doing this not only through others but through itself, which is against the laws. . . . This pestilential situation will not end until each power stays content within its own limits. . . . It would be salutary to enact a special statute on this matter.

Part IV

ARISTOTLE &
THE NATIONAL STATE

1. The Kingdoms &
the Empire

In its century-long conflict with the Hohenstaufen emperors the popes not only won the diplomatic struggle; they had the best of the war of words too. The doctrine that Christ had bestowed his own powers on St. Peter and on Peter's successors in the papacy was universally accepted; the further argument that such a divinely established authority was necessarily superior to any other power on earth seemed convincing to many; and even those who were unconvinced found it difficult to refute. During the first half of the thirteenth century, however, new ideas spread through the universities of Europe which would eventually provide a more adequate theoretical defense of the lay power than any that had been available before. And at the same time a new kind of state was emerging that could offer a more effective practical challenge to the papacy than the medieval empire had ever done.

The ideas were those of Aristotle. The great bulk of his writings were not known in the West until the end of the twelfth century. Then translations began to appear of Aristotelian works on philosophy, on the various sciences, and on ethics and politics. Their most important consequence in the sphere of political thought was to stimulate the development of a philosophical theory of the state that required no appeal to theological premises. It did not exactly refute the papal arguments but rather rendered them superfluous. The new states that were emerging in the thirteenth century were the kingdoms of national rulers, each of whom claimed to be "an emperor in his own realm" and recognized no external superior in temporal affairs. (As early as 1202 Innocent III had acknowledged that Philip Augustus was such a ruler [*No.* 78].) These kings—or their advisers—had learned much from the theories of Roman law and much from the institutional organization of the medieval church. They had built up organized bureaucracies with networks of local administrators and centralized departments for the administration of justice and finance. They were relying more and more on paid mercenary troops in place of the old feudal levies. They had begun to legislate sporadically and to tax systematically. Several of them had called into existence national representative assemblies in which the support of all classes could be mobilized for policies that the king wished to pursue.

Growing bureaucracies and mercenary armies required increased revenues, and the church possessed enormous wealth. The insistence of the king of France on his right to tax the church for reasons of state led to the first conflict in which the papacy suffered a total defeat. The church was especially vulnerable to attacks on its property rights. The theoretical justification for the accumulation of ecclesiastial endowments was plain enough. As Innocent IV had put it, the church owned all its property "so that it might come to the aid of all in need," and the canonists, when pressed to explain precisely who was the legal owner of ecclesiastical property, often answered simply "the poor." By 1300 it was all too obvious that the rich were doing very well out of it as well. Prelates and monks lived like lords, and kings commonly used ecclesiastical benefices that lay in their gift to provide substantial incomes for royal servants. Moreover, papal taxation was levied throughout Christendom for purposes often quite frankly political. For example, after the end of the Hohenstaufen dynasty in Sicily a war broke out there between the French king, supported by the papacy, and a Spanish claimant to the throne (1282). Churches in England or Germany or Scandinavia were required to pay taxes to support campaigns in Sicily, campaigns that were of deep concern to the pope in his capacity as temporal ruler of a neighboring Italian principality but that seemed quite unrelated to his role as spiritual pastor of the universal church.

Such conditions provoked a growing body of criticism directed against the excessive wealth of the church and its perpetual involvement in secular politics. The most effective protests came from the more radical followers of St. Francis of Assisi, the so-called Spiritual Franciscans, who by the end of the thirteenth century were developing Francis's ideas on apostolic poverty as a way of Christian perfection into a general attack on the wealth and external power of the organized church. The simultaneous growth of new centers of power in the national kingdoms, new theories of the state based on Aristotelian premises, and new movements of criticism within the church changed the whole climate of opinion within which problems of church and state were debated, focusing attention once again on the problem of property as a central issue of medieval political theory.

The following section of documents illustrates the claims to independence from any international authority put forward on behalf of national kingdoms during the course of the thirteenth century. In the earlier period, although there had been no universal temporal government in fact, jurists who discussed the question had always acknowledged the authority of the emperor in principle. The examples are taken from England, Spain, Sicily, and France. Of the authors, Ricardus Anglicus and Vincentius Hispanus were distinguished canonists, Marinus de Caramanico a Sicilian jurist who composed a commentary on the *Constitutions* of Frederick II, and Jean de Blanot a French lawyer in the service of Louis IX. The text of Dante is added by way of a reminder that the dream at least of a universal empire was not dead at the beginning of the fourteenth century. Dante argued that the end of man on earth was nothing less than the realization of every potentiality of the human intellect, that this end could be achieved only in a world at peace, and that peace could be assured only by the submission of all nations to a single governing power. It is the standard perennial argument for world government, and it had the same intellectual attractiveness and the same difficulties of practical implementation then as now.

The Kingdoms

89. England. Ricardus Anglicus, gloss on *Compilatio I* (c. 1200), ed. F. Gillmann, "Ricardus Anglicus als Glossator der Compilatio I," *Archiv für katholisches Kirchenrecht*, CVII (1927), p. 626.

. . . What is left for the king then when there are only two swords in the Gospel and the pope has one as at C.33 q.2 c.6, the emperor the other as at *Dist.* 96 c.10? And just as all are subject to the pope as regards the spiritual sword so they are subject to the emperor as regards the secular one as at C.7 q.1 c.41. It is established that all were subject to the Roman empire by the witness of Lucan. Moreover it is written in the Gospel, "A decree went forth from Caesar Augustus that a census of the whole world should be taken" (Luke 2:1). But how could he send forth a decree except among his own subjects as at C.2 q.1 c.7?

But, on the other hand, it is evident that many kings are not subject to the emperor, for it seems that, just as they were subdued by force, so they can return by force to their proper liberty. Again, we read of kings invincible by command of the Lord (Ecclesiastes 18:1) which we

do not read of the emperor. Again, the people of a city can confer jurisdiction and ruling authority as in *Novella* 15 c.1; much more those of a
kingdom. And the army elects an emperor, so by the same reason it can
elect a king as at *Dist.* 93 c.24. Since then both emperor and king are
anointed with the same authority, with the same consecration, with the
same chrism as at C.16 q.1 *post* c.40, why should there be a difference
in their powers?

90. Spain. Vincentius Hispanus, gloss on *Decretales*, 1.6.34
(c. 1240), ed. G. Post, *Speculum*, XXIX (1954), p. 206.

[According to Johannes Teutonicus] no kingdom can be
excluded from the empire, for it would be headless and without a
head it would be a monster as at *Dist.* 21 c.8. . . .
    Make an exception, O Johannes Teutonicus, for the Spaniards who
are exempted by the law itself and who barred the way to Charlemagne
and his peers. I, Vincentius, say that the Germans have lost the empire
by their folly. Every city contends with them for independence and
every hut usurps lordship for itself. Only the Spaniards have acquired
an empire by their valor, and they too have chosen bishops as at *Dist.*
63 c.25. [Is it not known] in France and England, in Germany and Constantinople, that the Spaniards rule blessed lady Spain, that they brought
this lordship into existence and, as lords, are expanding it by their
virtues of boldness and probity? The Spaniards then are supported by
their merits and worth; and like the Germans they do not lack a body
of prescripts and customs. Who can number your praises, O Spain?—
rich in horses, famous for food, shining with gold, slow to retreat,
prudent, the envy of all, versed in the laws and standing high on sublime
columns.

91. Sicily. Marinus de Caramanico, gloss on the *Constitutiones
Regni Siciliae* (c. 1280), ed. F. Calasso, *I Glossatori e la Teoria
della Sovranità*, 3rd ed. (Milan, 1957), pp. 179-80.

. . . This book of statutes is the principal law and it is
observed as law in our kingdom of Sicily according to Digest 1.2.2.12
and Institutes 1.2.6. Let no one urge that the Roman laws cited apply
only to the Prince, that is to the emperor of the Romans, and that to
him alone it is conceded to establish a law . . . we say the same of an
independent king who is not subject to the power of any other, that
he can establish a law . . . and such is the king of Sicily as we shall set
out below. Therefore we make bold to say that the king can make law
for the subjects of his realm and can even enact a statute contrary to the
common Roman law.

92. France. Johannes de Blanosco (Jean de Blanot) *Tractatus super Feudis et Homagiis* (1225-56), ed. J. Acher, *Nouvelle revue historique de droit français et étranger*, XXX (1906), p. 160.

. . . A baron who rebels against the king is seen to offend against the Julian Law on Majesty on this ground, that he has plotted the death of a magistrate of the Roman people (Digest 48.4.1.1.); or more truly because he is seen to have acted directly against the Prince, for the king of France is Prince in his own kingdom, for he recognizes no superior in temporal affairs.

The Empire

93. Dante, *De Monarchia* (c. 1312), trans. D. Nicholl (New York, 1954), pp. 8-9, 10-11.

Thus it is quite clear that the task proper to mankind considered as a whole is to fulfil the total capacity of the possible intellect all the time, primarily by speculation and secondarily, as a function and extension of speculation, by action. Now since what applies to the part applies also to the whole, and since the individual man becomes perfect in wisdom and prudence through sitting in quietude, so it is in the quietude or tranquillity of peace that mankind finds the best conditions for fulfilling its proper task (almost a divine task, as we learn from the statement: "Thou hast made him a little lower than the angels" [Hebrews 2.7]). Hence it is clear that universal peace is the most excellent means of securing our happiness. This is why the message from on high to the shepherds announced neither wealth, nor pleasure, nor honour, nor long life, nor health, nor strength, nor beauty, but peace. The heavenly host, indeed, proclaims: "Glory to God on high, and on earth peace to men of good will" (Luke 2:14). "Peace be with you" was also the salutation given by the Saviour of men (Matthew 10:12), because it was fitting that the supreme Saviour should utter the supreme salutation—a custom which, as everyone knows, his disciples and Paul sought to preserve in their own greetings.

This argument shows us what is the better, indeed the very best means available to mankind for fulfilling its proper role; and also what is the most direct means of reaching that goal to which all our doings are directed—universal peace. This will serve as the basis for our subsequent argument. Such is the common ground which we declared to be essential so as to have something axiomatic to which all our proofs and demonstrations can refer.

. . . If we consider a village, whose purpose is mutual help in questions of persons and goods, it is essential for one person to be supreme over all others, whether he is appointed from outside or raised to office by the consent of the others; otherwise, not only would the community fail to provide mutual sustenance, but in some cases the community itself would be utterly destroyed through some members' scheming to take control. Similarly, if we examine a city, whose purpose is to be sufficient unto itself in everything needed for the good life, we see that there must be one governing authority—and this applies not only to just but even to degenerate forms of government. If this were not so, the purpose of civil life would be frustrated and the city, as such, would cease to exist. Lastly, every kingdom (and the end of a kingdom is the same as that of a city but with a stronger bond of peace) needs to have a king to rule over and govern it; otherwise its inhabitants will not only fail to achieve their end as citizens but the kingdom itself will crumble, as is affirmed by the infallible Word: "Every kingdom divided against itself shall be laid waste" (Matthew 12:25).

If this is true of all communities and individuals who have a goal towards which they are directed, then our previous supposition is also valid. For, if it is agreed that mankind as a whole has a goal (and this we have shown to be so), then it needs one person to govern or rule over it, and the title appropriate to this person is Monarch, or Emperor.

Thus it has been demonstrated that a Monarch or Emperor is necessary for the well-being of the world.

2. Thomas Aquinas

It was the life's work of Thomas Aquinas (1225-74) to present the central concepts of Aristotle's philosophy within a framework of thought acceptable to Christian intellectuals. Modern Catholic scholars have generally considered that he succeeded brilliantly. His own contemporaries were not so sure, and on various points of metaphysics they preferred to follow other thinkers. But in the fields of ethics and politics Thomistic teaching was strikingly successful from the outset, and his principal doctrines, which were in the main those of Aristotle, were assimilated into the most widely used manuals of law and moral theology in the fourteenth century.

Thomas's work added a new philosophical dimension to the study of political theory. It provided a complete theoretical justification for a concept of the state which some lawyers had begun to discern in classical Roman jurisprudence, but which had always seemed incompatible with the presuppositions of the dominant Augustinian system of thought. For Augustine civil government existed only because men had fallen into sin. Coercive authority was necessary, he conceded, but on his theory the prince who wielded it was little more than a highly respectable hangman, a divinely appointed executioner of criminals. According to Augustine true justice was to be found only in the Christian church—and it had seemed but a small step to many medieval propagandists to argue that the ministers of the church were accordingly qualified to direct all the activities of secular rulers.

Following Aristotle, Thomas argued that civil society did not arise from a corruption of human nature but from the intrinsic quality of human beings as such. Man was not by nature a solitary creature, Thomas pointed out. He was endowed with potentialities that could be fulfilled only in day-to-day social intercourse within a community of his fellows, and when such a community existed, there was also a need for government. Each man in isolation could look after his own interests by the light of his own individual reason, but in a community there were common interests and need for a commonly acknowledged public authority to care for them. Thomas's views on the structure of this public authority were quite conventional. A good king, he thought, provided the best government, a tyrant the worst; probably the most satisfactory practical arrangement would be a monarchy so limited that it could not easily degenerate into a tyranny (*No.* 94). The real significance of the argument is this. Once the idea was accepted that man's intrinsic nature required an organized society, it became possible in principle to determine the best mode of government for that society by rational reflection on human ends and human needs without any necessary recourse to supernatural authorities. (Thomas did cite some scriptural texts in his discussion of kingship, but his argument could have stood just as well without them.) By a parallel line of argument Thomas also maintained that the right to hold private property grew out of the nature and needs of man.

Thomas's theory of the natural origin of the state was complemented by a most impressive restatement of the old doctrine of natural law. The jurists of the previous century had used the term in many different senses. Thomas gave it a precise definition within the framework of a new synthesis that dealt with every kind of law from the ultimate will of the creator to local municipal regulations. He distinguished four different types of law. First was "eternal law," the whole divine plan of the universe as perceived by God and by God alone. Next came "natural law," defined as "the rational creature's participation of the eternal law." This requires some explanation. In Aristotelian thought every being had a mode of conduct natural to itself and by fulfilling its own nature played its proper part in the over-all scheme of the universe. It was the nature of a stone to fall, Aristotle would say, or of a flame to rise; it was the nature of an acorn to grow into an oak tree. According to Thomas man also had his own proper nature, modes of activity proper to him as man. It was, for instance, natural to man to live in society. But the maintenance of any orderly society required adherence to defined rules of conduct, the fundamental one being that men had to treat their neighbors with due consideration. From this requirement some basic laws could be deduced, such as laws forbidding murder and theft. Such laws did not have to be revealed by divine inspiration. They could be worked out by rational reflection on the human situation. They were natural to man in that both the need for them and the means of devising them were rooted in man's intrinsic nature.

Thomas pointed out an obvious difference between men and all other creatures in the fulfillment of natural law. When a stone falls it is not conscious of falling, it cannot stop itself from falling. But a man is conscious of the law and, being a free agent, can choose to disobey it. Some men do choose to murder and to steal. Thomas regarded this as a distortion of nature—as though an acorn were to grow up into a dandelion instead of an oak tree—a turning away from the ends proper to man. On the other hand, when a man freely conformed his action to the law whose necessity he perceived by reason, he was contributing according to his own proper nature to the general harmony of the universe. This is what Thomas meant when he described natural law as "the rational creature's participation of the eternal law."

Natural law, then, defined a basic framework of moral principles necessary to the coherence of human societies. Thomas's third category of law, "human law," consisted of the detailed regulations that governments had to make in order to apply those principles in practice. Finally Thomas mentioned a fourth kind of law, "divine law," by which he meant those commands of God known to Christians through divine revelation. This divine law was necessary, according to Thomas, because man had a supernatural destiny, an eternal life to live in heaven as well as a temporal life on earth, and he needed divine guidance to attain that end. If the only end of man had been to work out a felicitous way of life on earth, natural law would have sufficed. The two ends were both proper to man (though to a medieval theologian it seemed that the second was more important), and Thomas insisted that they did not conflict with one another. "Divine law does not abolish natural law which arises from natural reason," he wrote.

On Thomistic premises it became possible to construct a theory of an autonomous state, functioning justly according to its own laws and independent of ecclesiastical supervision. Since Thomas was a Christian he believed that all lawful authority was subject to God, and in a Christian society he expected church and state to support one another, but he denied that the secular power was derived from the ecclesiastical and maintained that each was supreme in its own proper sphere. He did not discuss in any great detail the problems of church and state that have concerned us, and, unfortunately, the passage in which he set out his views most explicitly ends in a disconcerting ambiguity. After asserting the essential independence of the secular power he added, "Unless, perhaps, the secular power is joined to the spiritual, as in the pope, who holds the apex of both authorities, the spiritual and the secular." A possible explanation of these words is that they refer to the special position of the pope in central Italy, where he was indeed both supreme pontiff and temporal sovereign.

Society and Government

94. *On Kingship* (1260-65), trans. G. B. Phelan and I. T. Eschmann (Toronto, 1949), pp. 3-7, 23-24.

In all things which are ordered towards an end wherein this or that course may be adopted, some directive principle is needed through which the due end may be reached by the most direct route. A ship, for example, which moves in different directions according to the impulse of the changing winds, would never reach its destination were it not brought to port by the skill of the pilot. Now, man has an end to which his whole life and all his actions are ordered; for man is an intelligent agent, and it is clearly the part of an intelligent agent to act in view of an end. Men also adopt different methods in proceeding towards their proposed end, as the diversity of men's pursuits and actions clearly indicates. Consequently man needs some directive principle to guide him towards his end.

To be sure, the light of reason is placed by nature in every man, to guide him in his acts towards his end. Wherefore, if man were intended to live alone, as many animals do, he would require no other guide to his end. Each man would be a king unto himself, under God, the highest King, inasmuch as he would direct himself in his acts by the light of reason given him from on high. Yet it is natural for man, more than for any other animal, to be a social and political animal, to live in a group.

This is clearly a necessity of man's nature. For all other animals, nature has prepared food, hair as a covering, teeth, horns, claws as means of defence or at least speed in flight, while man alone was made without any natural provisions for these things. Instead of all these, man was endowed with reason, by the use of which he could procure all these things for himself by the work of his hands. Now, one man alone is not able to procure them all for himself, for one man could not sufficiently provide for life, unassisted. It is therefore natural that man should live in the society of many. . . . This point is further and most plainly evidenced by the fact that the use of speech is a prerogative proper to man. . . .

If, then, it is natural for man to live in the society of many, it is necessary that there exist among men some means by which the group may be governed. For where there are many men together and each one is looking after his own interest, the multitude would be broken up and scattered unless there were also an agency to take care of what appertains to the common-weal. In like manner, the body of a man or any other animal would disintegrate unless there were a general ruling force within the body which watches over the common good of all members. With this in mind, Solomon says: "Where there is no governor, the people shall fall" (Proverbs 11:14).

Indeed it is reasonable that this should happen, for what is proper and what is common are not identical. Things differ by what is proper to each: they are united by what they have in common. But diversity of effects is due to diversity of causes. Consequently, there must exist something which impels towards the common good of the many, over and above that which impels towards the particular good of each individual. Wherefore also in all things that are ordained towards one end, one thing is found to rule the rest. Thus in the corporeal universe, by the first body, i.e. the celestial body, the other bodies are regulated according to the order of Divine Providence, and all bodies are ruled by a rational creature. So, too, in the individual man, the soul rules the body; and among the parts of the soul, the irascible and the concupiscible parts are ruled by reason. Likewise, among the members of a body, one, such as the heart or the head, is the principal and moves all the others. Therefore in every multitude there must be some governing power.

Therefore, since the rule of one man, which is the best, is to be preferred, and since it may happen that it be changed into a tyranny, which is the worst . . . a scheme should be carefully worked out which would prevent the multitude ruled by a king from falling into the hands of a tyrant.

First, it is necessary that the man who is raised up to be king by those whom it concerns should be of such condition that it is improbable that he should become a tyrant. Wherefore Daniel, commending the providence of God with respect to the institution of the king says: "The Lord hath sought him a man according to his own heart and the Lord hath appointed him to be a prince over his people" (1 Kings 12:4). Then, once the king is established, the government of the kingdom must be so arranged that opportunity to tyrannize is removed. At the same time his power should be so tempered that he cannot easily fall into tyranny.

The Nature of Law

95. *Summa Theologica* I-II Q.91 (1269-70), trans. by "Fathers of the English Dominican Province," VII (London, 1915), pp. 9-10, 11-12, 13, 15.

. . . A law is nothing else but a dictate of practical reason emanating from the ruler who governs a perfect community. Now it is evident, granted that the world is ruled by divine providence, as was stated in the First Part, that the whole community of the universe is governed by divine reason. Wherefore the very Idea of the government of things in God the Ruler of the universe has the nature of a law. And since the divine reason's conception of things is not subject to time but is eternal, according to Proverbs 8.23, therefore it is that this kind of law must be called eternal.

. . . Law, being a rule and measure, can be in a person in two ways: in one way, as in him that rules and measures; in another way, as in that which is ruled and measured, since a thing is ruled and measured in so far as it partakes of the rule or measure. Wherefore, since all things subject to divine providence are ruled and measured by the eternal law, as was stated above, it is evident that all things partake somewhat of the eternal law, in so far as, namely, from its being imprinted on them, they derive their respective inclinations to their proper acts and ends. Now among all others the rational creature is subject to divine providence in the most excellent way, in so far as it partakes of a share of providence, by being provident both for itself and for others. Wherefore it has a share of the eternal reason, whereby it has a natural inclination to its proper act and end: and this participation of the eternal law in the rational creature is called the natural law. Hence the Psalmist after saying: "Offer up the sacrifice of justice," as though someone asked what the works of justice are, adds: "Many say, Who showeth us good things?" in answer to which question he says: "The light of Thy countenance, O Lord, is signed upon us" (Psalm 4:6); thus implying that the light of natural reason, whereby we discern what is good and what is evil, which is the function of the natural law, is nothing else than an imprint on us of the divine light. It is therefore evident that the natural law is nothing else than the rational creature's participation of the eternal law.

. . . A law is a dictate of the practical reason. Now it is to be observed that the same procedure takes place in the practical and in the speculative reason, for each proceeds from principles to conclusions, as stated above. Accordingly we conclude that just as, in the speculative reason, from naturally known indemonstrable principles we draw the conclusions of the various sciences, the knowledge of which is not imparted to us by nature, but acquired by the efforts of reason: so, too, it is from the precepts of the natural law, as from general and indemonstrable principles, that the human reason needs to proceed to the more particular determination of certain matters. These particular determinations, devised by human reason, are called human laws, provided the other essential conditions of law be observed, as stated above.

Besides the natural and the human law it was necessary for the directing of human conduct to have a divine law. . . . First, because it is by law that man is directed how to perform his proper acts in view of his last end. And indeed, if man were ordained to no other end than that which is proportionate to his natural faculty, there would be no need for man to have any further direction on the part of his reason besides the natural law and human law which is derived from it. But since man is ordained to an end of eternal happiness which is inproportionate to man's natural faculty, as stated above, therefore it was necessary that, besides the natural and the human law, man should be directed to his end by a law given by God.

Church and State

96. *Commentum in IV Libros Sententiarum* (1253-55), trans.
E. Lewis, *Medieval Political Ideas* (New York, 1954), pp. 566-67.

. . . A superior and an inferior power can be related in
either of two ways. Either the lower power is totally derived from the
higher; in this case the whole force of the lower is founded on the force
of the higher; then, absolutely and in everything, the higher power is
to be obeyed rather than the lower; . . . the power of God is related to
all created power in this way; in the same way the power of the emperor
is related to the power of a proconsul; in the same way the power of the
pope is related to all spiritual power in the church, since the diverse
grades and dignities in the church are disposed and ordained by the
pope himself, whence his power is a sort of foundation of the church,
as appears in Matthew 16:[18]. . . . Or, on the other hand, the higher
power and the lower power can be so related that both derive from one
supreme power, which subordinates one to the other as he wishes; in
that case one is not superior to the other unless in those things in which
the other has been subordinated to him by the supreme power, and the
higher is to be obeyed rather than the lower in such things only; the
powers of bishops and archbishops, which descend from the power of
the pope, are related in this way. . . .

. . . The spiritual and the secular power are both derived from the
divine power; and therefore the secular power is under the spiritual only
in so far as it has been subjected to it by God: namely, in those things
that pertain to the salvation of the soul; and therefore the spiritual power
is, in such matters, to be obeyed rather than the secular. But in those
things that pertain to civil good, the secular power is to be obeyed
rather than the spiritual, according to the saying in Matthew 22:[21],
"Render to Caesar the things that are Caesar's."

Unless, perhaps, the secular power is joined to the spiritual, as in the
pope, who holds the apex of both authorities, the spiritual and the
secular.

3. Boniface VIII & Phillip IV:
The First Dispute

The struggle between Pope Boniface VIII and King Philip the Fair of France was the first medieval conflict of church and state which can properly be described as a dispute over national sovereignty. France was indeed still far from being a centralized nation state in the modern sense, but the idea of the state was in the air and the administrative machinery to make it a reality had already begun to develop. Meanwhile the Roman see was becoming ever more explicitly committed to a doctrine of universal papal lordship whose realization in practice would have rendered the rise of national states impossible.

A dramatic clash of personalities accompanied the conflict of theories. Philip IV was a man of cold ambition. He worked behind a screen of extraordinarily efficient and ruthless royal servants, so that we know more about the motives and attitudes of his chief ministers—men like Pierre Flotte and Guillaume de Nogaret—than about Philip's own personal convictions. Many of the men who served him most prominently were trained in Roman law. They were for the most part hard, worldly minded administrators, totally unperturbed by the spiritual censures that Boniface heaped on them. Philip's own personality has always been something of a mystery. Some historians have regarded him as little more than a tool in the hands of his powerful servants, but it seems most improbable that a mere nonentity would ever have surrounded himself with such formidable counselors.

There is little mystery about the personality of Boniface VIII. He was an arrogant, very able ruler, impatient of opposition, given to hot outbursts of rage. By temperament he was a self-confident aristocrat, a member of the Gaetani family of Rome, and by conviction, it seems certain, a sincere believer in the extreme doctrine of papal sovereignty over temporal affairs that had been formulated earlier by the canonists Alanus and Hostiensis and that was being restated in his own day by the theologian Giles of Rome. Already an old man when he was elected pope after a lifetime of service in the Roman curia, he suffered from the very painful disease of "the stone." Often his savage language and bursts of bad temper may have served to mask attacks of intense physical pain, but nonetheless they made enemies for him at the papal court.

So too did the policy of unconcealed nepotism that he used to enhance the power of his own family as princes of the Roman *campagna*. Boniface cared little for the opinion of others; his coarse and careless speech laid him open to charges—certainly unproven and probably untrue—of immorality and even heresy. He said on one occasion, for instance, that he would rather be a dog than a Frenchman, and the supporters of Philip solemnly pointed out that the statement was heretical since it implied that Frenchmen had no immortal souls (*No.* 104).

There is one more point about Boniface which is important for understanding the course of his conflict with Philip. That is the unusual background of his election to the papacy. For nearly two years, from 1292 to 1294, there was a vacancy in the Roman see. The cardinals, hopelessly deadlocked, could not agree on any candidate from among themselves, and at last, in desperation, they elected a holy hermit, one Peter Murrone, who took the name Celestine V. Under Celestine the business of the curia fell into a chaos worse than the actual vacancy had caused. The pope himself, well aware of his total incapacity to fill the office that a weird mischance had thrust upon him, abdicated after a few months. Then the cardinals chose Boniface. But there was no clear precedent in the history of the church for a pope resigning his office, and an academic debate grew up around the question whether such a resignation could be licit. Several treatises considered the point, and the masters of the university of Paris debated it. The eventual consensus was that Celestine's resignation was licit and Boniface's election accordingly valid. But it was an enormous advantage to the pope's enemies that serious doubts about the question had been raised at all.

The first dispute between Boniface and Philip arose over a clear-cut issue—the right of secular kings to tax the clergy of their realms. Innocent III's Fourth Lateran Council of 1215 had decreed that clergy were not to pay tax levies to lay rulers without first consulting the pope. In practice, however, kings had imposed taxes on ecclesiastical property throughout the thirteenth century with papal acquiescence. The usual occasion for such a levy was the financing of a military campaign, and it was considered proper for the clergy to contribute to the expenses of a "just war," such as a crusade. In 1296, however, France and England were engaged in a war over feudal technicalities and commercial rivalries. The Christian king of England was taxing the English church to finance his "just war" against France, and simultaneously the Christian king of France was taxing the French church to finance his "just war" against England. Boniface, convinced of his own right to settle such international disputes as a superior judge set over all kings, found the situation intolerable. His bull *Clericis Laicos* (*No.* 97) attempted to bring both parties to heel by cutting off one of their major sources of revenue. It also denied the principle that kings (even kings supported by representative assemblies as in England) possessed an absolute authority in their own kingdoms. The heart of the bull was its specific command to the clergy to disobey their kings. There were many ways in which Boniface could have opened up negotiations with France and England about the question of clerical taxation, but he chose to pounce directly on the issue of national sovereignty by declaring that lay rulers possessed no authority over ecclesiastical persons or ecclesiastical goods within their own realms.

Philip did not at this point enter into a theoretical debate on the issue. He responded instead with a practical measure of overwhelming effectiveness. In August, 1296, he issued a royal ordinance forbidding all export from France of precious metals, precious stones, and all forms of negotiable currency. Boniface relied very heavily on revenue from the French church for financing the operations of papal government and the conduct of papal diplomacy.

On September 25 he addressed to the king an indignant letter declaring that he would suffer ruin and death rather than sacrifice any of the liberties of the church, but for all his brave words he became more and more financially embarrassed as the winter wore on, and by February of 1297 he was ready to make major concessions. He wrote to Philip again to point out that the bull *Clericis Laicos* had not been directed against France in particular but was intended to apply to all kings, and in a separate letter he conceded that in an emergency so desperate that there was no time to consult the pope the clergy might pay a tax before obtaining papal consent. Philip was still not satisfied and decided to send his chief minister, Pierre Flotte, to Italy for a personal confrontation with the pope.

Quite apart from his troubles with France the pope had two sets of enemies in Italy who at this point united against him. The powerful Colonna family of Rome, two of whose members were cardinals, had become exasperated by the favors that Boniface showered on his own Gaetani kin in the states of the church. The Spiritual Franciscans, for their part, hated Boniface as the epitome of the clerical worldliness that they despised and denounced. Celestine V had been the only pope who had ever sympathized wholeheartedly with their ideals, and they were profoundly reluctant to accept the fact of his resignation. At the beginning of May an open breach occurred between Boniface and the Colonna cardinals. The Colonnas withdrew to their fortress of Longhezza and were joined there by some of the leaders of the Spiritual Franciscans, including Jacopone da Todi, a famous preacher and poet. They then issued a manifesto declaring that the resignation of Celestine V had been illegal and Boniface's election consequently invalid, and they demanded that a general council be summoned to consider the whole question of the succession to the papacy. In two subsequent manifestoes they accused Boniface of heresy and simony and charged further that he had tricked Celestine into resigning and then had had him murdered. It was the

first public statement of the charges that were to bedevil Boniface for
the rest of his reign (*No.* 98).

On his way south to join the papal curia at Orvieto, Pierre Flotte discussed the whole situation with representatives of the Colonnas, and
when he came to negotiate with Boniface his hand was greatly strengthened by the possibility that Philip might support the cardinals' appeal
to a general council against the pope. Under that threat Boniface finally
capitulated. In the bull *Etsi de statu* (*No.* 99) he clearly conceded the
principle that the king alone, without the consent of the pope, could decide when a state of necessity existed in his own kingdom which made
it expedient to tax the clergy. Philip had won an easy victory.

Clericis Laicos

97. The bull *Clericis Laicos* (February 1296), trans. H. Bettenson,
Documents of the Christian Church (New York, 1943), pp. 159-61.

Boniface Bishop, servant of the servants of God, for the
perpetual record of the matter. That laymen have been very hostile to
the clergy antiquity relates; and it is clearly proved by the experiences
of the present time. For not content with what is their own the laity
strive for what is forbidden and loose the reins for things unlawful. Nor
do they prudently realize that power over clerks or ecclesiastical persons
or goods is forbidden them: they impose heavy burdens on the prelates
of the churches and ecclesiastical persons regular and secular, and tax
them, and impose collections: they exact and demand from the same the
half, tithe, or twentieth, or any other portion or proportion of their
revenues or goods; and in many ways they try to bring them into slavery,
and subject them to their authority. And, we regret to say, some prelates
of the churches and ecclesiastical persons, fearing where there should
be no fear, seeking a temporary peace, fearing more to offend the temporal majesty than the eternal, acquiesce in such abuses, not so much
rashly as improvidently, without obtaining authority or license from the
Apostolic See. We therefore, desirous of preventing such wicked actions,
decree, with apostolic authority and on the advice of our brethren, that
any prelates and ecclesiastical persons, religious or secular, of whatsoever
orders, condition or standing, who shall pay or promise or agree to pay
to lay persons collections or taxes for the tithe, twentieth, or hundredth
of their own rents, or goods, or those of the churches, or any other portion, proportion, or quantity of the same rents, or goods, at their own
estimate or at the actual value, under the name of aid, loan, relief, subsidy, or gift, or by any other title, manner, or pretext demanded, without the authority of the same see:

And also whatsoever emperors, kings, or princes, dukes, earls, or barons, powers, captains, or officials, or rectors, by whatsoever names they are called, of cities, castles, or any places whatsoever, wheresoever situate, and all others of whatsoever rank, eminence or state, who shall impose, exact, or receive the things aforesaid, or arrest, seize, or presume to take possession of things anywhere deposited in holy buildings, or to command them to be arrested, seized, or taken, or receive them when taken, seized, or arrested, and also all who knowingly give aid, counsel, or support, openly or secretly, in the things aforesaid, by this same should incur sentence of excommunication. Universities, too, which may have been to blame in these matters, we subject to ecclesiastical interdict.

The prelates and ecclesiastical persons above mentioned we strictly command, in virtue of their obedience, and on pain of deposition, that they in no wise acquiesce in such things without express leave of the said see, and that they pay nothing under pretext of any obligation, promise, and acknowledgment whatsoever, made in the past, or in existence before this time, and before such constitution, prohibition, or order come to their notice, and that the seculars aforesaid do not in any wise receive it; and if the clergy do pay, or the laymen receive, let them fall under sentence of excommunication by the very deed.

Moreover, let no one be absolved from the aforesaid sentences of excommunications and interdict, save at the moment of death, without authority and special leave of the Apostolic See, since it is part of our intention that such a terrible abuse of secular powers should not be carried on under any pretense whatever, any privileges whatsoever notwithstanding, in whatsoever tenors, forms or modes, or arrangement of words, conceded to emperors, kings and the others aforesaid; and we will that aid be given by no one, and by no persons in any respect in contravention of these provisions.

Let it then be lawful to none at all to infringe this page of our constitution, prohibition, or order, or to gainsay it by any rash attempt; and if anyone presume to attempt this, let him know that he will incur the indignation of Almighty God, and of his blessed apostles Peter and Paul.

The Colonna Cardinals

98. Third manifesto of the Colonna cardinals against Boniface (June 1297), ed. H. Denifle, *Archiv für Literatur- und Kirchengeschichte*, V (Leipzig, 1889), pp. 519-24.

James of S. Maria in Via Lata and Peter of S. Eustachio, by the mercy of God cardinal deacons, to the venerable chancellor and the

venerable college of masters and scholars of the university of Paris, greetings and sincere love in the Lord.

Hear the voice of our prayer, we beseech you, O cultivators of justice,
masters and disciples of the truth, that you, together with the kings and
princes and peoples of the world, may weigh accurately in the balance
of your judgement with the truth accompanying your decision the justice
of our cause or rather that of the spouse of Christ and the iniquity of
Benedict Gaetani, no bishop of the universal church but a tyrant, who
holds the Roman church that he has occupied only by an iniquitous
act. . . . By evil advice and false arguments he and his accomplices per-
suaded our lord pope Celestine V of happy memory to renounce the
apostolic office, though this was contrary to the rules and statutes of
divine, human and canon law and a cause of scandal and error to the
whole world. Then, when Celestine had resigned the papacy *de facto*—
for he could not do so *de iure* since it is clear to all who are willing to
investigate the matter carefully that the Roman pope cannot resign or
give up the papacy or be released from it except by God alone—he did
not fear to put himself *de facto* since he could not do it *de iure* in the
place of the same lord Celestine who was still alive, and this under the
eyes of ourselves and the other cardinals then present who were deceived
by the suddenness of such an unheard-of act. . . . Conscious of the evil
origin of his dignity and fearing the truth he savagely pursued the above-
mentioned holy man [Celestine] who sought in every way to escape his
tyranny, and when he had finally captured him cruelly imprisoned him
at the castle of Fumone in the Campagna, which is not far from Anagni,
and there caused him to die miserably. . . .

Who could be silent about such things with a clear conscience, when
we saw the state of the church and the honor due to prelates constantly
diminished. For he summoned to appear personally prelates from the
most remote parts of the world whom he believed to be wealthy, not
only to extort money from them but to strip them altogether, and this
on pain of deprivation which they incurred automatically if they did
not obey, and without even a pretended reason let alone a true one. As
soon as he heard that churches were vacant he reserved the appointments
to the judgement of his own disordered will, forbidding the electors to
exercise their right of election and, what is more revolting, he did this
in the case of many cathedral churches while their prelates were still
alive. . . . It was as though, conscious of his evil conduct and always
fearful of falling from his dignity, he wanted to institute prelates everywhere throughout the world by his own hand so that, when the question
of his illegal entry was raised, they would not dare to speak against him,
being afraid for their own positions. . . . And so in his time the church
has become corrupt. No one receives any favor without handing over
a gift.

Again, even a true pontiff is accustomed and even bound to seek the advice of the cardinals and to obtain their consent in certain arduous affairs, especially in alienating the goods of the church, but this pseudo-pontiff does not deign to seek their counsel or await their consent. Rather if we or any of our brothers put forward any word that is contrary to his own opinion, he attacks the speaker with scathing words and, boasting that he rules over kings and kingdoms even in temporal affairs, he does not fear to assert that he can do anything of his own will by virtue of his plenitude of power, although no legitimate papal authority inheres in him. . . .

Consider then with faithful discernment God and his holy church so that, when the illegitimate usurper has been deposed and cast out, a true and legitimate pastor may rule truly, legitimately and canonically over the church his mother, the bride of Christ, redeemed by the blood of her spouse. Lest the sacraments of the church be further profaned, let all the acts of the same Benedict be suspended since he has been justly denounced by us, and let care be taken that a universal council be swiftly assembled which, laying aside all error, will declare the truth concerning the iniquity, nullity and injustice of the process he has presumed to institute against us. And meanwhile let no one obey or heed, especially in matters touching the safety of the soul, this man who does not possess the authority of a supreme pontiff although *de facto* he rashly holds the place of one.

The Capitulation of the Pope

99. The bull *Etsi De Statu* (July 1297), ed. G. Digard, M. Faucon, and A. Thomas, *Les Registres de Boniface VIII*, I (Paris, 1884), col. 941-42.

. . . Recently, discharging the duty of our pastoral office, we enacted a decree by apostolic authority in favor of the churches and of ecclesiastical liberty, laying down that prelates and ecclesiastical persons of any state, rank or dignity should not pay taxes to emperors, kings, princes or other rulers without the authority of the apostolic see, whether under the name of an aid, loan or gift or any other name; and that emperors, kings, princes or other rulers should not presume to demand, exact or receive them from the same prelates and ecclesiastical persons. . . .

We add to this our declaration that if some dangerous emergency should threaten the aforesaid king [Philip] or his successors in connection with the general or particular defence of the realm, the above mentioned decree shall by no means extend to such a case of necessity. Rather the same king and his successors may demand and receive from the said

prelates and ecclesiastical persons a subsidy or contribution for such defence and the said prelates and persons can and must pay it to the oft-
mentioned king and his successors whether under the name of a quota
or some other name, even when the Roman pontiff has not been consulted, and this notwithstanding the above mentioned decree and notwithstanding any kind of privilege or exemption obtained from the
apostolic see, in whatever form of words it is drawn up. And the declaration of a state of necessity may be left to the consciences of the aforesaid
king and his successors. . . .

4. Boniface VIII & Philip IV:
The Second Dispute

In 1300 Boniface declared a year of Jubilee to celebrate the centennial of the church. By that time his fortunes were beginning to revive after the humiliation of 1297. His health improved, his diplomacy went well, and he was encouraged by the unexpectedly vast numbers of pilgrims, tens of thousands of ordinary folk from all over Europe, who flocked into Rome to pray at the tombs of the apostles and to win the special papal indulgences that were offered during the Jubilee celebrations. When news began to reach him of new encroachments by Philip on the privileges of the French church Boniface again adopted a reproachful tone in his letters to the king. Philip seems to have been entirely confident of his own position and to have wilfully provoked another crisis in order to assert once and for all his mastery over his own kingdom. In 1301 he ordered the arrest of a French prelate, Bernard Saisset, bishop of Pamiers, on charges of blasphemy, heresy, and treason. Saisset was taken to Paris as a captive, put on trial in the king's own presence, declared guilty, and thrown into prison. Now, a fundamental principle of canon law required that a bishop be tried only by the pope. At the urging of the archbishop of Narbonne, Philip sent an account of his proceedings to Boniface with a demand that the pope approve his condemnation of Saisset. To have done so would have amounted to a recognition of the king's unlimited power over the French episcopate.

Perhaps Philip expected another quick capitulation by the pope. He set out the alleged offenses of Bernard Saisset at length and spiced them with the additional charge that the accused bishop had maintained "that our very holy father Boniface is the devil incarnate." Saisset was an old acquaintance of the pope, and Boniface knew very well that the man had an unruly tongue and might well have been indiscreet in referring to both the pope and the king. But he did not allow himself to be deflected from the central issue of the case—and from the papal point of view this was not the question of whether the bishop happened to be guilty or not, but rather the gross presumption of the king in daring to lay hands on him at all. A sudden shower of papal bulls descended on France, demanding the release of Saisset, revoking all papal privileges that had recently been granted to Philip, and commanding all the bishops of France to attend a council in Rome a year later in November 1302. The declared purpose of the council was to consider the whole state of religion in the kingdom of France. Philip subsequently forbade his bishops to attend it, and the issue became an important test of strength between pope and king.

Together with all the peremptory bulls, Boniface sent to Philip a long personal letter which had been carefully considered and approved by the College of Cardinals. It began with the words *Ausculta fili*, "Listen, son . . . ," and, continuing in the tone of a rebuke from a superior to an erring subordinate, it accused Philip of subverting the whole state of the church in France by his abuse of clerical patronage (*No.* 100). The letter was apparently not intended to assert new political claims for the papacy, but it contained the words, "Let no one persuade you that you have no superior or that you are not subject to the head of the ecclesiastical hierarchy, for he is a fool who so thinks. . . ." Boniface did not explain any further the nature of this "subjection," but Philip seized on the words as the basis for a propaganda campaign against the pope. The papal letter itself was burned, and royal agents put into circulation in Paris a crude forgery which attributed to Boniface the flat assertion, "You are subject to us in spiritualities and in temporalities." They also circulated a still cruder forgery purporting to be Philip's reply, which began with the words, "Let your great fatuity know that in temporalities we are subject to no-one. . . ." (*No.* 101).

Boniface had set out to defend the French church against the king. Philip's ingenious maneuver ensured that in Paris the central issue would seem to be the defense of the French state against the pope. In April of 1302 a great assembly of clergy, nobles, and people met at Paris in the cathedral of Notre Dame. It was the first meeting in French history of a representative Estates-General—the institution was called into existence specifically to mobilize national opinion for Philip's antipapal policy. Pierre Flotte addressed the assembly and apparently told it that the pope had claimed feudal lordship over France. In truth, he declared, France was held from no one but God alone, as all right-thinking people knew, and anyone who declared the contrary must be accounted a heretic. The nobles and the commons then each addressed a letter to the cardinals in Rome, refusing to acknowledge Boniface as pope and demanding the support of the cardinals against him. The clergy, deeply embarrassed, wrote to Boniface, addressing him as pope but explaining that they were much perturbed at his "unheard-of statements" and asking to be excused from attendance at the council in Rome.

When messengers bearing these letters arrived at Rome in June 1302, Boniface received them in a full consistory of cardinals and delivered an address explaining further his own position. He was particularly incensed at the suggestion that he had claimed to be feudal overlord of France. A man like himself, skilled in the law for forty years, he said, could not possibly have uttered such a fatuity. But, he went on, his predecessors had deposed kings of France in the past, and he would do the same in the future if it became necessary. Boniface really was claiming a kind of lordship over Philip, as over all kings, but it was not a technically feudal relationship that he was trying to establish. The whole incident is rather reminiscent of the affair at Besançon a century and a half before, except that this time the king quite certainly made a willful misrepresentation of the pope's ambiguous language.

The position of Philip was temporarily weakened in the summer of 1302 by a major defeat of his armies in Flanders at the battle of Courtrai, in the course of which Pierre Flotte was killed. The king adopted for the moment a more conciliatory tone toward the pope, but he used the excuse of a national emergency to forbid his bishops to attend Boniface's council. The pope still insisted that they must come to Rome. When the council finally met as planned at the beginning of November less than half of the French bishops appeared—36 out of 78—and none came from the north of France. Boniface could have taken little comfort from such a response to his repeated commands. Moreover, the council took no effective steps toward the reform of the church in France which Boniface had originally announced as the whole purpose of the meeting.

Immediately after this abortive council Boniface promulgated the bull *Unam Sanctam,* probably the most famous of all the documents on church and state that has come down to us from the Middle Ages (*No.* 103). The bull made no reference to the political crises of the preceding years. It presented rather a series of general theological propositions about the nature of the church and the position of the pope within it. From its first words, "There is one Holy Catholic and Apostolic Church," the document treated above all the divinely willed unity of the Christian church and the role of the Roman see as guardian of that unity. Philip and his supporters regarded the bull as a dangerous novelty, an unprecedented attempt at a usurpation of temporal power by the papacy. In fact, however, a close reading of the text will show that it was almost entirely a patchwork of extracts from earlier sources. Apart from scriptural quotations it contained, for instance, passages from St. Bernard, Hugh of St. Victor, and Thomas Aquinas. The only phrases of the bull that constituted a formal, dogmatic definition were those of the final pronouncement: "We declare, state, define and pronounce that it is altogether necessary to salvation for every human creature to be subject to the Roman Pontiff." The words are resounding enough, but they seem to refer quite clearly to the pope's spiritual supremacy and have no obvious relevance to the problems of church and state. They were in fact borrowed from a treatise of Thomas Aquinas called *On the Errors of the Schismatic Greeks.* Again, in an earlier part of the bull, rather irrelevantly it might seem, Boniface rebuked the Greeks for failing to acknowledge the authority of Peter. This intense preoccupation with the inner unity of the church—which after all no one had denied in principle—seems strange in a letter written at the climax of a political controversy that really turned on the nature of the pope's temporal claims. An explanation may be found in the circumstances of the bull's preparation just a few days after the pope's disappointing council in Rome. In drafting *Unam Sanctam* Boniface was of course wholly preoccupied with the French crisis, but for the moment perhaps the disloyalty of the absent bishops stood uppermost in his mind rather than the misdeeds of the erring king. The pope may well have realized that the direct conflict in the commands that he and Philip had issued to the French prelates had in fact raised the issue of the unity of the church in a particularly serious fashion. If bishops, when pressed to choose, would obey their king rather than their pope in an ecclesiastical matter, the church could hardly remain a truly international body with its own autonomous center of government and discipline. It would become a cluster of national churches, each looking to its king for leadership in times of crisis. Developments of this kind did indeed take place during the next two centuries. *Unam Sanctam* may be read as an early protest against such tendencies in the ecclesiastical polity of Europe.

The fact that so much of the bull was concerned with the theological question of church unity has led some modern commentators to argue that it had virtually no significant political content at all. However, in his discussion on the unity of the church Boniface did deal very thoroughly with the subordination of the temporal jurisdiction to the spiritual as one aspect of that unity. The old imagery that had been used to assert papal supremacy in the past emerged for the first time in an official pronouncement stripped of all its ambiguity. Boniface's view that to deny the pope's rule over temporal affairs was to imitate the heresy of the Manicheans—who believed that all the material world was a creation of the Devil, not of God—provides an eccentric climax to a whole tradition of thought that can be traced back at least to Cardinal Humbert. Again, while it is possible to argue about the meaning St. Bernard attached to the allegory of the two swords, in *Unam Sanctam* the symbolism was used quite explicitly to prove that "temporal authority should be subjected to spiritual." It is the same with the words of Hugh of St. Victor, "The spiritual power has to establish the earthly power." Whatever they may have signified in the twelfth century, by Boniface's day they had certainly acquired the meaning that the power of kings was delegated to them by the papacy, and they were clearly used in that sense in *Unam Sanctam*. Boniface's views on the nature of papal authority were perhaps no different from those of several of his predecessors, but he expressed them more plainly than any previous pope had done.

After *Unam Sanctam* there was never any hope of a compromise between Boniface and Philip. The king did not reply by theological counterarguments. He resolved on an attack of extraordinary brutality on Boniface personally. In March of 1303 his new minister, Guillaume de Nogaret, denounced Boniface before a council of French bishops and nobles as a usurper, a heretic, and a notorious criminal and demanded that a general council be assembled to judge and depose the pope. The charges were repeated in much greater detail at another assembly held in June (*No.* 104), but by then Nogaret had left Paris for Italy in an attempt to settle the whole issue by physical force. During the summer Boniface departed from Rome for his native city of Anagni and there prepared a decree of excommunication against Philip. A few days before the sentence was due to be promulgated the little town was seized by an army of several hundred mercenaries led by Nogaret and Sciarra Colonna (a brother of Cardinal Peter Colonna). After an afternoon's fighting they broke into the papal chambers and found the old pope waiting for them arrayed in pontifical robes and holding a crucifix in his hands. They insulted him and perhaps struck him as well. It is not clear whether Nogaret hoped to compel Boniface to renounce the papacy there and then or whether he intended to carry him off to France to stand trial before a council. Sciarra Colonna wanted to kill him on the spot (*No.* 105). The two leaders fell into a quarrel about their next move and continued arguing through the following day. They hesitated too long. By the third day the whole district was roused against the invaders. Nogaret had lost any chance there might have been of snatching away the pope and was lucky to escape alive. Boniface returned to Rome, but he never recovered from the shock of the outrage and died a few weeks later.

The next pope, Benedict XI, promptly excommunicated Nogaret but sought to reach an understanding with Philip. This pope, however, lived for only a few months after his election. The king's final triumph came in the reign of Benedict's successor, Clement V (1305-14). Clement was himself a Frenchman, and throughout his reign he was subjected to incessant threats and harassment by Philip. At the beginning of his pontificate he renounced the principle of *Clericis Laicos* and promulgated a bull *Meruit* declaring that *Unam Sanctam* was not to be interpreted as asserting any new claim by the papacy to lordship over France (*No.* 106). Finally, in 1311, after years of persistent pressure from Philip, Clement released Nogaret from the sentence of excommunication he had incurred for his part in the Anagni affair and publicly commended Philip for the piety and zeal he had shown in his dealings with Boniface (*No.* 107).

The problem of sovereignty had two aspects. There was first the issue of "external sovereignty"—whether a king was bound to recognize the jurisdiction of any lord outside his own kingdom. Boniface VIII asserted that kings were so bound, but Philip was able to rally all the influential opinion of France behind his indignant denial of the pope's claim. The other issue was that of "internal sovereignty"—whether the king was really master in his own kingdom or whether the clergy formed a people apart, a kind of state within a state exempt from royal jurisdiction and royal taxation. On this question Philip was able to exact from Boniface himself an admission that whenever the king so willed reason of state took precedence over clerical privilege.

Boniface VIII's defeat marks the end of the road that Innocent III had marked out for the papacy a century earlier. Innocent's dream of a universal society of ordered peace may command our respect. Perhaps it never became a reality because in reaching out for worldly power the popes were going against the intrinsic nature of the religion that they claimed to represent. Certainly the combination of an exalted theory of papal overlordship with a persistent practice of using the spiritual authority of the popes to serve local political ends sapped the prestige of the Roman see to a degree that made possible the victory of Philip the Fair.

The Reopening of the Quarrel

100. The bull *Ausculta Fili* (December 1301), ed. G. Digard, M. Faucon, and A. Thomas, *Les Registres de Boniface VIII*, III (Paris, 1921), col. 328-32.

Listen, beloved son, to the precepts of a father and pay heed to the teaching of a master who holds the place on earth of Him who alone is lord and master; take into your heart the warning of holy mother church and be sure to act on it with good effect so that with a contrite heart you may reverently return to God from whom, as is known, you have turned away through negligence or evil counsel and conform yourself to His will and ours. . . . You have entered the ark of the true Noah outside of which no one is saved, that is to say the Catholic church, the "one dove," the immaculate bride of the one Christ, in which the primacy is known to belong to Christ's vicar, the successor of Peter, who, having received the keys of the kingdom of heaven, is acknowledged to have been established by God as judge of the living and the dead; and it belongs to him, sitting in the seat of judgement, to abolish all evil by his sentence. The Roman pontiff is indeed the head of this bride who descended from heaven, made ready by God like a bride adorned for her husband; nor does she have several heads like a monster for she is without stain or wrinkle or anything unseemly.

Moved by our conscience and urgent necessity we will explain to you more clearly, O son, why we are writing these things to you. For, although our merits are insufficient, God has set us over kings and king-

doms, and has imposed on us the yoke of apostolic service to root up
and to pull down, to waste and to destroy, to build and to plant in his
name and according to his teaching (*cf.* Jeremias 1:10) . . . wherefore,
dearest son, let no one persuade you that you have no superior or that
you are not subject to the head of the ecclesiastical hierarchy, for he is a
fool who so thinks, and whoever affirms it pertinaciously is convicted as an
unbeliever and is outside the fold of the good shepherd.

. . . It is quite clear and a matter of established law that the Roman
pontiff has supreme and effective power over ecclesiastical dignities,
offices and benefices, canonries and prebends whether they become vacant
at the Roman curia or elsewhere and that the bestowal of churches or
of dignities, offices, benefices and canonries does not and cannot belong
to you, nor can anyone acquire any right in them from your bestowal
except by the authority and consent, tacit or expressed, of the apostolic
see. One who receives this authority [from the pope] and then denies
that he has received it deserves to be deprived of it for ingratitude as
does one who abuses a power conceded or permitted to him, and anyone who persuades you to the contrary speaks against the truth. Notwithstanding all this you irreverently over-step the bounds and limits
appointed for you and rashly and unjustly impede the same see and do
not permit its collations, canonically made, to be executed, but oppose
them even when they are known to have preceded your collations, however made. . . .

You drag before your tribunal prelates and other clerics of your kingdom, both regular and secular, in personal actions or cases involving
rights or properties that are not held from you as fiefs; you cause them
to be detained and inquests to be held although no power over clerics
or ecclesiastical persons is conceded to laymen. Moreover you do not
permit prelates and ecclesiastical persons to use freely the spiritual sword
that is theirs against those who injure and molest them. . . . You de-
vour unjustly and without moderation the revenues and incomes of the
vacant cathedral churches of your realm which you and your servants
call regalia, so that churches whose guardianship was entrusted to kings
in the first place for their protection now undergo the evil of disastrous
depredations and are exposed to dangerous abuses.

. . . Having deliberated fully with our brothers concerning these
things we have summoned to our presence by letters patent the archbishops, bishops . . . abbots and cathedral chapters of your realm, together
with masters of theology and of canon and civil law, and other ecclesiastical
persons of the said realm and we have commanded them to present themselves in our sight next year on the first of November . . . that we may
consider the more carefully and ordain the more profitably what shall
seem fitting for the reform of the above-mentioned matters and for your
guidance and peace and health and for the good government and prosperity of that realm.

101. The forgeries of 1302, ed. P. Dupuy, *Histoire du différend d'entre le pape Boniface VIII et Philippe le Bel* (Paris, 1655), p. 44.

(Philip's supporters circulated these forged letters in Paris, claiming that the first had been sent by Boniface to Philip, the second by Philip to Boniface.)

Boniface, bishop, servant of the servants of God to Philip, king of the French. Fear God and keep his commandments. We want you to know that you are subject to us in spiritualities and temporalities. The collation of benefices and prebends does not belong to you at all and if you have the custody of any vacant churches you are to keep their revenues for those who succeed to them. If you have conferred any such benefices we declare the collations null and void and we revoke any that you have made *de facto*. Given at the Lateran on the fifth of December in the seventh year of our pontificate.

Philip, by the grace of God king of the French, to Boniface who acts as though he were pope, little or no greeting. Let your great fatuity know that in temporalities we are subject to no-one; that the collation of vacant churches and prebends belongs to us by royal right and that their revenues are ours; that the collations we have made in the past or shall make in the future are valid and that we shall strongly defend their holders against anyone. All who think otherwise we hold for fools and madmen. Given at Paris.

102. Address of Boniface to the ambassadors of the French Estates (June 1302), ed. P. Dupuy, *op. cit.*, pp. 77-79.

We hope that this Peter Flotte, this Achitophel, will be punished temporally and spiritually and we pray that God will reserve the punishing of him for us as is just. For this Peter falsified our letter to the king, our letter which was not written in haste but only after repeated deliberations of the whole college and with the counsel and consent of our brothers. . . . He falsified it or made up falsehoods about it, for we do not know for certain that he tampered with our letter since that letter has been concealed from the barons and prelates, and he attributed to us a command that the king should recognize that he held his kingdom from us. We have been expert in the law for forty years and we know very well that there are two powers ordained by God. Who can or should believe then that we entertain or will entertain such a fatuous and foolish opinion? We declare that we do not wish to usurp the jurisdiction of the king in any way, and so our brother the cardinal of Porto has said. But the king cannot deny that, like all the faithful, he is subject to us by reason of sin. . . . Our predecessors deposed three kings of France; they can read it in their chronicles and we in ours, and one case is to be found in the Decretum; and although we are not worthy to tread in the footsteps of our predecessors, if the king committed the same crimes as they committed or greater ones we would depose him like a servant with grief and great sorrow. . . . As for our summons to the prelates, we answer to you who have come on their behalf that we do not suspend the summons. Rather we confirm, strengthen and renew it. . . .

Unam Sanctam

103. The bull *Unam Sanctam* (November 1302), ed. E. Friedberg, *Corpus Iuris Canonici*, II (Leipzig, 1881), col. 1245-46.

That there is one holy, Catholic and apostolic church we are bound to believe and to hold, our faith urging us, and this we do firmly believe and simply confess; and that outside this church there is no salvation or remission of sins, as her spouse proclaims in the Canticles, "One is my dove, my perfect one. She is the only one of her mother, the chosen of her that bore her" (Canticles 6:8); which represents one mystical body whose head is Christ, while the head of Christ is God. In this church there is one Lord, one faith, one baptism. At the time of the Flood there was one ark, symbolizing the one church. It was finished in one cubit and had one helmsman and captain, namely Noah, and we read that all things on earth outside of it were destroyed. This church we venerate and this alone, the Lord saying through his prophet, "Deliver, O God, my soul from the sword, my only one from the power of the dog" (Psalm 21:21). He prayed for the soul, that is himself, the head, and at the same time for the body, which he called the one church on account of the promised unity of faith, sacraments and charity of the church. This is that seamless garment of the Lord which was not cut but fell by lot. Therefore there is one body and one head of this one and only church, not two heads as though it were a monster, namely Christ and Christ's vicar, Peter and Peter's successor, for the Lord said to this Peter, "Feed my sheep" (John 21:17). He said "My sheep" in general, not these or those, whence he is understood to have committed them all to Peter. Hence, if the Greeks or any others say that they were not committed to Peter and his successors, they necessarily admit that they are not of Christ's flock, for the Lord says in John that there is one sheepfold and one shepherd.

We are taught by the words of the Gospel that in this church and in her power there are two swords, a spiritual one and a temporal one. For when the apostles said "Here are two swords" (Luke 22:38), meaning in the church since it was the apostles who spoke, the Lord did not reply that it was too many but enough. Certainly anyone who denies that the temporal sword is in the power of Peter has not paid heed to the words of the Lord when he said, "Put up thy sword into its sheath" (Matthew 26:52). Both then are in the power of the church, the material sword and the spiritual. But the one is exercised for the church, the other by the church, the one by the hand of the priest, the other by the hand of kings and soldiers, though at the will and suffrance of the priest. One sword ought to be under the other and the temporal authority subject to the spiritual power. For, while the apostle says, "There is no power but from God and those that are ordained of God" (Romans 13:1), they would not be ordained unless one sword was under the other and, being inferior, was led by the other to the highest things. For, according to the blessed Dionysius, it is the law of divinity for the lowest to be led to the highest through intermediaries. In the order of the universe all things are not kept in order in the same fashion and immediately but the lowest are ordered by the intermediate and inferiors by superiors. But that the spiritual power excels any earthly one in dignity and nobility we ought the more openly to confess in proportion as spiritual things excel temporal ones. Moreover we clearly perceive this from the giving of tithes, from benediction and sanctification, from the acceptance of this power and from the very government of things. For, the truth bearing witness, the spiritual power has to institute the earthly power and to judge it if it has not been good. So is verified the prophecy of Jeremias [1.10] concerning the church and the power of the church, "Lo, I have set thee this day over the nations and over kingdoms" etc.

Therefore, if the earthly power errs, it shall be judged by the spiritual power, if a lesser spiritual power errs it shall be judged by its superior, but if the supreme spiritual power errs it can be judged only by God not by man, as the apostle witnesses, "The spiritual man judgeth all things and he himself is judged of no man" (1 Corinthians 2:15). Although this authority was given to a man and is exercised by a man it is not human but rather divine, being given to Peter at God's mouth, and confirmed to him and to his successors in him, the rock whom the Lord acknowledged when he said to Peter himself "Whatsoever thou shalt bind" etc. (Matthew 16:19). Whoever therefore resists this power so ordained by God resists the ordinance of God unless, like the Manicheans, he imagines that there are two beginnings, which we judge to be false and heretical, as Moses witnesses, for not "in the beginnings" but "in the beginning" God created heaven and earth (Genesis 1:1). Therefore we declare, state, define and pronounce that it is altogether necessary to salvation for every human creature to be subject to the Roman Pontiff.

The Attack on Boniface

104. Charges against Boniface presented by Guillaume de Plaisans before a royal council in Paris (June 1303), ed. P. Dupuy, *op. cit.*, pp. 102-6.

He does not believe in the immortality or incorruptibility of the rational soul but believes that the rational soul undergoes corruption with the body. He does not believe in an eternal life to come . . . and he was not ashamed to declare that he would rather be a dog or an ass or any brute animal than a Frenchman, which he would not have said if he believed that a Frenchman had an immortal soul. . . . He does not faithfully believe that, through the words instituted by Christ, spoken by a faithful and properly ordained priest in the manner prescribed by the church over a Host, it becomes the true body of Christ. . . . He is reported to say that fornication is not a sin any more than rubbing the hands together is. . . . He has often said that he would ruin himself and the whole world and the whole church to lay low the king and the French people if he could not do it otherwise. . . . He has had silver images of himself erected in churches to perpetuate his damnable memory, so leading men into idolatry. . . . He has a private demon whose advice he takes in all matters. . . . He has publicly preached that the Roman pope cannot commit simony, which is heresy. . . . He is guilty of the crime of sodomy. . . . He has caused many clerics to be murdered in his presence, rejoicing in their deaths. . . . He has compelled certain priests to reveal mens' confessions and then, without the consent of those who confessed, has made them public to their shame and confusion. . . . He does not fast on fast days or in Lent. . . . He has depressed and debased the rank and status of the cardinals. . . . He is openly called a simonist or rather the fount and origin of simony. . . . He is publicly accused of treating inhumanly his predecessor Celestine, a man of holy memory and holy life, being aware perhaps that he could not resign and that accordingly he (Boniface) could not legitimately enter upon his see—imprisoning him in a dungeon and causing him to die there swiftly and secretly, and this is notorious throughout the whole world. . . . He does not seek the salvation of souls but their perdition.

105. An eyewitness account of "the outrage at Anagni." Letter of William Hundleby to the bishop of Lincoln (September 1303), trans. H. G. J. Beck, *Catholic Historical Review*, XXXII (1947), pp. 200-5.

Behold, Reverend Father, at dawn of the vigil of the Nativity of the Blessed Mary just past, suddenly and unexpectedly there came upon Anagni a great force of armed men of the party of the King of France and of the two deposed Colonna cardinals. Arriving at the gates of Anagni and finding them open, they entered the town and at once made an assault upon the palace of the Pope and upon that of the Marquis, the Pope's nephew. . . .

After a time, however, the Marquis, nephew of the Pope, realizing that defense was no longer possible, surrendered to Sciarra and the captain, so that they spared his own life and those of his son and companions. In this fashion were the Marquis and one of his sons taken and thrown into prison, while another son escaped by means of a hidden passage. When the Pope heard this reported, he himself wept bitterly, yet not even the Pope was in a position to hold out longer. Sciarra and his forces broke through the doors and windows of the papal palace at a number of points, and set fire to them at others, till at last the angered soldiery forced their way to the Pope. Many of them heaped insults upon his head and threatened him violently, but to them all the Pope answered not so much as a word. And when they pressed him as to whether he would resign the Papacy, firmly did he refuse—indeed he preferred to lose his head—as he said in his vernacular: "E le col, e le capel" which means: "Here is my neck and here my head." Therewith he proclaimed in the presence of them all that as long as life was in him, he would not give up the Papacy. Sciarra, indeed, was quite ready to kill him, but he was held back by the others so that no bodily injury was done the Pope. Cardinal Peter of Spain was with the Pope all through the struggle, though the rest of his retinue had slipped away. Sciarra and the captain appointed guards to keep the Pope in custody after some of the papal doormen had fled and others had been slain. Thus [were] the Pope and his nephew taken in Anagni on the said vigil of the Blessed Mary at about the hour of vespers and it is believed that the Lord Pope put in a bad night.

The soldiers, on first breaking in, had pillaged the Pope, his chamber and his treasury of utensils and clothing, fixtures, gold and silver and everything found therein so that the Pope had been made as poor as Job upon receiving word of his misfortune. Moreover, the Pope witnessed all and saw how the wretches divided his garments and carted away his furniture, both large items and small, deciding who would take this and who that, and yet he said no more than: "The Lord gave and the Lord taketh away, etc." And anyone who was in a position to seize or to lay hold upon something, took and seized it and carried it off, while no one then paid any more attention to the person of the Pope than he did to Godfrey Ceco of Lincoln or to Peter Stall. . . .

Epilogue

106. Clement V, decree of February 1306, ed. E. Friedberg, *Corpus Iuris Canonici*, II (Leipzig, 1879), col. 1300.

The full and sincere affection that our son Philip, illustrious king of the French, bears toward us and the Roman church has merited—and the outstanding merits of his forefathers, together with the sincerity and purity of the devotion of the people of his kingdom have also merited—that we show benevolent favor to both king and kingdom. Hence it is that we do not wish or intend that anything prejudicial to that king or kingdom should arise from the declaration of our predecessor of happy memory Pope Boniface VIII, which began with the words "Unam sanctam"; nor that the aforementioned king, kingdom and people should be any more subject to the Roman church on account of it than they were before. But everything is understood to be in the same state as it was before the said definition, both as regards the church and as regards the aforementioned king, kingdom and people.

107. Clement V, decree of April 1311, *Regestum Clementi Papae V* (Rome, 1887), p. 414.

. . . Finally, having inquired diligently into the matter we find that the said assertors, objectors and denouncers [of Boniface] . . . and the said king . . . were not impelled by any preconceived malice but were actuated by an estimable, just and sincere zeal . . . and by apostolic authority we pronounce and with the council of our brothers we decree and by these presents declare that they were and are guiltless of malicious accusation and that they acted out of an estimable, just and sincere zeal and from the fervor of their Catholic faith.

5. The Growth of
Political Thought

There was a new richness of texture in the greater works of political theory, inspired by the conflict of Boniface VIII and Philip the Fair, a complexity of argumentation in which many earlier strands of theological, philosophical, and juristic thought were woven together into fresh patterns. Often enough the original spinners of individual threads might have been startled at the finished designs to which they had unwittingly contributed. We can only guess what St. Bernard or Hugh of St. Victor (let alone Aristotle!) might have thought of the uses to which their texts were put by contending philosophers like Giles of Rome and John of Paris. The violence of the struggle between pope and king was reflected in writings that set out their rival claims more explicitly and in more extreme terms than ever before. But some of the most distinguished works of the period were produced by writers of the middle way, who achieved a new sophistication and precision in their attempts to defend the integrity of the state and the integrity of the church and to define with due discrimination the proper sphere of action of each.

The most systematic and thoroughgoing defense of papal theocracy came from Giles of Rome. His treatise *De Ecclesiastica Potestate* formulated the ideology that lay behind Boniface VIII's pronouncements just as Cardinal Humbert's work had provided the theoretical basis for the decrees of Gregory VII. Giles, moreover, started from exactly the same premise as Humbert—the intrinsic superiority of spiritual being to material being. The originality of his work lay in his application of this old doctrine to a very personal conception of *dominium*, a term which might be translated as "rightful lordship." Giles himself used the word to mean both political authority and property ownership.

In the first book of his treatise Giles discussed the pope's *dominium* in the former sense. He argued that the pope could be identified with the "spiritual man" referred to by the apostle Paul in 1 Corinthians 2:15, "The spiritual man judgeth all things; and he himself is judged of no man," and that such a spiritual ruler was necessarily the lord of all temporal kings. He maintained, indeed, that this conclusion was implicit in the whole order of the universe. The practical outcome of the argument was an assertion that all legitimate political authority was derived from the pope and subject to his control (*No.* 108).

In his second book Giles dealt with *dominium* as property ownership. It would have been difficult in the days of Boniface VIII to defend the vast possessions of the church on the purely pragmatic ground that they were essential for its spiritual mission or charitable activities. Giles of Rome preferred to deploy again his favorite philosophical argument about the intrinsic superiority of spiritual being. For more moderate thinkers an obvious difficulty about this approach was to set any reasonable limits to its application.. If the ownership of material property by the church was to be justified by the argument that in principle temporal goods ought to be subject to spiritual power, then why should not all temporal goods be so subject? Far from seeking to evade this conclusion, Giles enthusiastically accepted all its implications and maintained that the pope was indeed the ultimate owner of all the material goods in the world. His first statement of this position had an audacious simplicity about it. Souls were governed by the pope, he pointed out; bodies were subject to souls; temporal goods existed to serve the needs of the body; therefore all temporal goods were subject to the pope. Giles' second argument on the same point was more complicated. Dominion over the whole universe belonged to God; therefore men who were alien to God could not exercise any rightful dominion; but all men were sinners and could be reconciled to God only through the church; therefore they could only acquire the right to own property justly from the church— which implied that the church had a general lordship over all earthly goods. Giles added that he did not intend to dispossess existing owners of the rights they actually possessed. It was only a kind of eminent domain that he claimed for the church (*No.* 109).

His third book dealt with the distinction between immediate control and ultimate lordship in the sphere of political authority. Giles here considered Alexander III's view that "according to the rigor of the law" there was no appeal from a secular court to an ecclesiastical one (*No.* 57), which seemed opposed to his own theory of papal authority. Giles asserted, however, that temporal rulers and temporal courts had been established not because of any defect in the spiritual power but because it was inconsistent with the dignity and excellence of that power to concern itself with mundane affairs as a matter of normal routine. Where any kind of spiritual issue was involved the pope did exercise jurisdiction in temporal affairs and could judge any case whatsoever if he chose to exercise his plenitude of power. In the ordinary course of events, however, it would be appropriate for him to leave temporal cases to temporal rulers, and the saying of Alexander III was to be understood as meaning nothing more than this (*No.* 110). Giles's utmost concession to the secular power was this acknowledgment that on the whole it was fitting for the pope to allow existing rulers to retain their jurisdiction so long as he saw no particular reason for depriving them of it.

The work of Giles of Rome has been much admired by historians of political philosophy for its formidable combination of complexity of thought with coherence of argument. Equally striking, however, was its total failure to convince the contemporary critics of the papacy against whom it was directed. No king ever acknowledged that all temporal power was held from the pope; no representative assembly of towns and nobles ever accepted such a view; no hierarchy of bishops in any country urged it on their ruler; no synod of clergy endorsed it. The idea of a superiority inherent in the papacy because of its total commitment to spiritual values had become too far removed from the reality of the bureaucratic, worldly minded Roman curia to carry any conviction. Giles of Rome had described a platonic vision that was becoming ever more remote from the real world of affairs.

The extreme vulnerability of his whole system of thought to plain, common-sense criticism is strikingly exposed in the *Disputatio inter Clericum et Militem*, written before Giles's own work but concerned with the same basic premise about the superiority of the spiritual order to the temporal. It was cast in the form of a lively dialogue between a cleric and a knight who disclaimed all pretension to sophisticated learning. The cleric threw up one by one the arguments in favor of papal theocracy; the knight shot them down with well-aimed texts of Scripture. It was the kind of argument that any French noble or merchant could understand and relish, and the work enjoyed a very wide circulation at the time of the dispute between Philip and Boniface (*No.* 111).

Although the author of the *Disputatio* upheld the right of Philip to tax the church, he set out primarily to defend lay power and lay property against clerical encroachments. Pierre Dubois presented a much more radical thesis on the royal side in his *De Recuperatione Terrae Sanctae*. Dubois proposed the wholesale expropriation of ecclesiastical estates as a part of a general reorganization of Europe under the hegemony of the French monarchy. According to his plan the king of France was to bribe the German electors to make him emperor, his brother was to seize Constantinople, and the pope was to reside in France and become in effect a sort of chaplain to the French royal house. The pope would be required to hand over the temporal possessions of the Roman church to the king of France, who could then appoint a French prince to govern in Italy and himself assume the overlordship of England, Aragon, and Majorca as successor to the feudal jurisdiction of the papacy (*No.* 112). All this was fantasy, as much so as Giles of Rome's vision of a universal papal monarchy, but Pierre Dubois typified in his radical anticlericalism and chauvinistic French patriotism some of the new forces that were stirring to life in the age of Boniface VIII.

Perhaps the greatest of all the works of political theory written at this time is the *De Potestate Regia et Papale* of the French Dominican friar John of Paris. Giles of Rome was subtle and logical but perverse in his extremism; the author of the *Disputatio* was sensible but unsubtle; Pierre Dubois was a dreamer of dreams—or nightmares. John of Paris, more than any of them, brought to his task all the qualities needed for a dispassionate analysis of church-state relations in an age of crisis and conflict: a spirit of moderation, a full cargo of theological, philosophical and juristic learning, and a great talent for lucid and orderly exposition.

His book had two major themes: the right relationship of spiritual to temporal power and the right relationship of rulers to their subjects in church and state. A preliminary discussion on church property introduced both themes. There were two major errors current in his day, John maintained: the error of those who taught that it was not licit for the church to hold any property, and the error of those who believed that all temporal possessions were subject to the spiritual power. (He called this second view the error of Herod who, when he heard of the birth of the Savior, believed that Christ was to be an earthly king— a hard blow this at Giles of Rome). The truth, according to John, lay between these two extremes. The church did lawfully hold property, but not because spiritual rulers had an intrinsic right to dominate all temporal goods; it was rather that the church had licitly received endowments from princes and other laymen who had the power to make such gifts from their own possessions. Moreover, John asserted, ownership of these endowments of the church was vested in the whole Christian people. The pope was not lord over them but rather an administrator or steward who acted on behalf of the community. As for laymen, they had the right to possess their own goods as individuals. The pope had no normal rights of administration over such goods, and the function of the temporal ruler in regard to them was merely to act as judge when disputes arose (*No.* 113).

Closely following Aquinas, John argued that civil government had its origin in man's own nature, while the priesthood was instituted to guide men to their supernatural end in the world to come. Of these two powers the priesthood was indeed greater in dignity, but this did not at all imply that secular power was subordinate to ecclesiastical within its own proper sphere or that the royal dignity was derived from the priestly (*No.* 115). There remained then the problem of explaining what kind of power a pope could licitly exercise over a prince or a prince over a pope in a Christian society. John's conclusion was that the only authority the pope could exercise was that of spiritual censure, though he might use this power in such a way as to encourage the people to depose an unworthy ruler. So too, the prince might use his power of physical coercion to assist the cardinals in deposing an evil pope. But the pope had no authority to depose a prince directly, nor the prince to depose a pope (*No.* 115).

The idea that a king's authority might be subject to constitutional restraints was well established by this time; an important feature of John's work is his application of the same idea to the government of the church. Like all men of his time he adhered to the conventional view that all legitimate authority came from God, but, he pointed out, God left to human choice the designation of particular individuals who were to bear authority. John not only maintained that the prince in the state and the pope in the church existed to promote the welfare of the whole community in their different ways, but also that they were in a real sense responsible to the community. The withdrawal of consent by the people could be just as effective in deposing an evil ruler as the giving of consent was in establishing a good one. The pope, for instance, was steward of all the goods of the church and defender of the church's faith, but if he misappropriated the goods of the church or betrayed the faith of the church he was liable to rebuke and in the last resort to deposition by a general council or by the cardinals acting on behalf of all the people. John did not regard the authority inherent in the community as a merely latent power to be called on only at a time of desperate emergency. He maintained that the best form of government for both church and state would be one in which all the people regularly participated through duly chosen representatives, for, he said, "all the people love and preserve such a government" (*No.* 114).

From the beginning of the discussions on church and state, writers who rejected both royal theocracy and papal theocracy had been concerned especially with the problem of avoiding tyranny. According to Pope Gelasius, Christ had instituted a separation of powers in the first place in order to promote a "healthful humility" in rulers. The actual course of the various controversies greatly encouraged the growth of constitutional ideas. Papal writers had to stress the principle of canonical election in the church to counter the practice of lay investiture. Imperialists, when faced with the claim that the emperor's power was bestowed by the pope, often fell back on the Roman law argument that such power was derived from the community. Moreover, popes had repeatedly called on subjects to oppose their rulers in the name of a "higher law," and secular princes had appealed against popes to general councils representing the whole church. John of Paris was the first writer on political theory who combined in a mature and harmonious synthesis the ancient principle that the two powers should be distinct, with all the constitutionalist elements of thought that had grown up around that idea. One of the most important of all the results of the conflict between Boniface VIII and Philip the Fair was that it stimulated such a lucid and impressive defense of the doctrines of dualism and constitutionalism which in the political sphere, were the most valuable legacy of the Middle Ages to the modern world.

Giles of Rome

108. On the supremacy of spiritual power. *De Ecclesiastica Potestate* (1301), ed. R. Scholz (Weimar, 1929), pp. 11-13, 15.

Hugh of St. Victor, in his book *De Sacramentis Fidei Christianae*, Part II, c.4 declares that the spiritual power has to institute the earthly power and to judge it if it has not been good. Thus is verified the prophecy of Jeremias concerning the church and the power of the church, "Lo, I have set thee this day over the nations and over the kingdoms, to root up and to pull down, and to waste, and to destroy, and to build, and to plant" (Jeremias 1:10).

. . . We can clearly prove from the order of the universe that the church is set above nations and kingdoms, for, according to Dionysius in his *De Angelica Ierarchia*, it is the law of divinity that the lowest are led to the highest through intermediaries. The order of the universe requires this therefore, that the lowest be led to the highest by intermediaries . . . and this is made plain at *Romans* 13 from the words of the Apostle who, having said that there is no power except from God, immediately added "And those that are, are ordained of God." If then there are two swords, one spiritual the other temporal, as can be gathered from the words of the Gospel, "Behold, here are two swords'" (Luke 22:38), where the Lord at once added "It is enough" because these two swords suffice for the church, it follows that these two swords, these two powers and authorities, are from God, since, as we have said, there is no power except from God. But, therefore, they must be rightly ordered since, as we observed, what is from God must be ordered. Now they would not be so ordered unless one sword were led by the other and unless one were under the other since, as Dionysius said, the law of divinity which God gave to all created things requires this. . . . Therefore the temporal sword as being inferior is led by the spiritual sword as being superior and the one is set below the other as an inferior below a superior.

It may be said that kings and princes ought to be subject spiritually but not temporally. . . . But those who speak thus have not grasped the force of the argument. For if kings and princes were only spiritually subject to the church, one sword would not be below the other nor temporalities below spiritualities; there would be no order in the powers, the lowest would not be led to the highest through intermediaries. If, therefore, they are ordered the temporal sword must be below the spiritual, kingdoms below the vicar of Christ, and *de iure*, although some act in a contrary fashion *de facto*, the vicar of Christ must have dominion over temporal affairs.

The royal power ought to recognise the priestly as a superior dignity by which, at God's command, it is instituted. And if it is said that not all royal power is instituted by the priesthood we say that there is no royal power not instituted by the priesthood which is not either un-righteous, in which case it is more a band of robbers than a power, or united with the priesthood, or subsequently confirmed by the priesthood. For in the law of nature, where there were many kingdoms of the gentiles, nearly all those kingdoms were founded by invasion and usurpation. . . . But according to Augustine, *De Civitate Dei*, king-doms without justice are great bands of robbers. Hence such rulers are not kings although they are called kings, but rather thieves and robbers.

109. On dominion of property. *Ibid.* (1301), pp. 48-50, 74-75.

We intend to explain in this chapter that all temporal things are placed under the dominion and power of the church. . . . The power of the supreme pontiff governs souls. Souls ought rightly to govern bodies or they will be badly ordered as regards the part which does not obey the soul or mind or reason. But temporal things serve our bodies. It follows then that the priestly power which governs souls also rules over bodies and temporal things.

Because some may not be satisfied with authorities we wish to adduce reasons to prove that no one can justly hold dominion over anything unless he is reborn through the church. . . . For since you ought to be under God and under Christ you are unjust if you are not under him, and, because you are unjustly withdrawn from Christ your lord, all things are justly withdrawn from your lordship. For a man who will not be subject to his lord cannot justly have lordship of anything. If a knight were unwilling to be under the king it would be fitting that the knight's subjects should not be under him. Thus if a knight unjustly withdraws from his lord he is justly deprived of all his own lordship. But anyone who is not reborn through the church [in baptism] is not under Christ's lordship; therefore he is rightly deprived of all his own lordship, so that he cannot justly be lord of anything. . . .
It follows then that you should acknowledge that your heritage and all your lordship and every right of possession are yours more from the church and through the church and because you are a son of the church than from your carnal father or through him or because you are his son. . . .

It should be noticed, however, that, although we say that the church is mother and mistress of all possessions and all temporalities, we do not thereby deprive the faithful of their lordships and possessions for, as will be explained below, the church and the faithful each have a kind of lordship; but the church has a universal and superior lordship, the faithful a particular and inferior one.

110. On the exercise of spiritual power. *Ibid.* (1301), pp. 143-45.

. . . If the church has primacy over all temporal things as we have said above . . . how can we hold true what is found in the canons of the church, namely that it is not in accordance with the rigor of the law to appeal from a civil judge to the pope, as is said at *Decretales* 2.28.7 [*No.* 57]. . . .

It is not on account of any defect of power in the spiritual sword that it may not judge concerning temporalities; rather it was on account of its excellence that a material sword was added to it. Because the spiritual sword is so exalted and such exalted things are committed to it, in order that it might attend to them more freely, the second sword was added, but this in no way diminished the jurisdiction and plenitude of power of the spiritual sword; rather it was done because it is fitting that what is appointed for great things should not concern itself directly with petty ones unless some cause arises. And so the plenitude of power is in the spiritual sword and, when it is expedient it may judge concerning temporalities. If then there is an appeal from a civil judge to the pope, although it may not be in accordance with the law on separation of courts it will be in accordance with the law on plentitude of power.

Disputatio inter Clericum et Militem

111. *Disputatio inter Clericum et Militem* (1296-98), trans. E. Lewis, *Medieval Political Ideas*, II (New York, 1954), 567-73.

THE CLERK opened the discussion in the following words: I marvel, good Sir, in how few days the times are changed, justice is buried, laws are overturned, and rights are trampled under foot.

KNIGHT: Those are big words, and I am a layman, and though I learned a few letters as a boy I never got deep enough to understand words so high. And therefore, reverend Clerk, you must use a plainer style if you want to talk with me.

CLERK: In my time I have seen the church held in great honour among all kings, princes, and nobles; but now I see it wretched. The church has been made a prey for you all; many things are exacted from us, none given to us; if we do not give up our property it is stolen from us; our rights are trampled under foot; our liberties are violated.

KNIGHT: It is hard for me to believe that the king, whose council is composed of clerics, is acting unjustly toward you or that your right is perishing.

CLERK: But indeed we are enduring countless injuries, against all right.

KNIGHT: I should like to know what you call "right."

CLERK: By "right" I mean the decrees of the fathers and the statutes of the Roman pontiffs.

KNIGHT: What they decree, if they decree concerning temporals, may be rights for you; but not for us. For no one can make decrees about things over which he certainly has no lordship. Thus the king of the French cannot make decrees in regard to the Empire, nor the Empire in regard to the kingdom of France. And even as earthly princes cannot decree anything in regard to spirituals, over which they have received no power, so neither can you decree anything in regard to their temporals, over which you have no authority. Thus whatever you have decreed about temporals, over which you have not received power from God, is a waste of time. So I had to laugh recently when I heard that Lord Boniface VIII had just decreed that he is and ought to be over all governments and kingdoms, and thus he can easily acquire a right for himself over anything whatever, since all he has to do is to write and everything will be his as soon as he has written; and thus everything will belong to you, when to decree is nothing more than to wish to have for one's self. Therefore to wish will be the same as to have a right; therefore one need only write, "I wish this to be mine," when he wants to have my castle, or my country-house, or my field, or my money and treasure. You can't help seeing, wise Clerk, to what absurdity this argument brings you.

CLERK: You argue cleverly enough, Lord Knight, and slyly produce these arguments against us. . . . But if you want to be a Christian and a true Catholic, you will not deny that Christ is Lord of all things. . . . And who will doubt the validity of the decrees of Him Who, it is certain, is Lord of all things?

KNIGHT: I certainly do not resist divine authority or lordship, since I am and wish to be a Christian. And therefore, if you will show me by various Scriptures that supreme pontiffs are lords over all temporals, then kings and princes must certainly be subject to supreme pontiffs in temporals as well as in spirituals.

CLERK: That can easily be shown from what has been said. For our faith holds that the apostle Peter was instituted plenary vicar of Jesus Christ for himself and his successors. If, therefore, you do not deny that Christ, Who is Lord of heaven and earth, can decree in regard to your temporals, you cannot without blushing deny the same authority to the plenary vicar of Christ.

KNIGHT: I have heard holy and most devout men distinguish two periods in Christ, one of humility and the other of authority: of humility up to His passion, of authority after His resurrection, when He said, "All power is given to me in heaven and on earth" (Matthew 28:18). Now Peter was constituted vicar of Christ for the state of humility, not for the state of glory and majesty. For he was not made vicar of Christ for those things that Christ does now in glory, but to imitate those things that Christ did when He was humble on earth, because those are necessary to us Therefore He committed to His vicar that power which He exercised as mortal man, not that which He received when glorified. And I shall prove this to you by the testimony of those same Scriptures which you quote. For Christ Himself said to Pilate, "My kingdom is not of this world" (John 18:36), and that He did not come to be ministered unto, but to minister (Matthew 20:28). This testimony is plain enough to confound anyone who resists it and to break a neck, however stiff. And this likewise: "A certain man from the crowd said to Jesus, 'Master, say to my brother that he should divide the inheritance with me,' and He said to him, 'O man, who made Me a judge and divider over you?'" (Luke 12:13,14). Therefore you hear clearly that Christ was constituted neither judge nor divider in temporals. . . .

CLERK: Do you deny, O Knight, that the church has cognizance of sins?

KNIGHT: Far be it from me; for that would be to deny penance and confession.

CLERK: Any injustice is sin, and he who has cognizance of sin has cognizance of the just and unjust. Since, therefore, justice and injustice are characteristics of temporal affairs, it follows that the church should be judge in temporal cases.

KNIGHT: That argument is a sophistry, and its emptiness and weakness ought to be refuted by a similar argument. Hanging robbers and other condemned criminals is a matter of the just and unjust, and of sin too. Therefore by reason of sin the pope ought also to judge concerning blood. But that argument is a feather blown into the air by a light reason. . . . And I will show you where, according to Paul, your cognizance ought to begin, because the prince by his own right has cognizance of the just and the unjust; and let everyone heed his decision, that it may be maintained, and obey him as it is commanded (Deuteronomy 17:10,11). If, however, anyone, swelling with pride, does not obey his command, and if the prince whose was the office of judging does not have power to resist or coerce him, then your jurisdiction begins; because then your admonition comes into play, as the apostle Paul says in the Epistle to Titus, 3:1: "Admonish them to be subject and submissive to princes and powers." And in the Epistle to the Romans, [13:1]: "Let every soul be subject to the higher powers.". . .

CLERK: Ought not temporals to serve spirituals? Therefore temporals ought to be subject to spirituals, and the spiritual power ought to rule the temporal power.

KNIGHT: Truly temporals ought to serve spirituals in the proper way, since they are considered necessary to minister to those who maintain the worship of God. For every people holds this principle as if innate and instinctive, and nature itself has decreed this by natural right: that whatever is necessary should be provided for those who minister to the Creator and celebrate divine things. . . . When you argue further that the supreme pontiff is superior in all things, you run into a bad joke. For if, when the pope is created, he is created lord of all things, by like reason to create a bishop will be to create the lord of his territory, and my priest will be lord of my castle, and of me too. . . . Therefore stop talking this nonsense which everybody laughs at and which has been settled by so many texts of Scripture and logical proofs. For we say that in the Old Law priests were not adored by kings, but kings and princes were adored by priests and prophets, and they were summoned to the kings and commanded to do what pleased the kings, and when they were occasionally at fault in the public administration of temporals they were reproved, as is told in the third book of Kings [1 Kings], chapters 1 and 4. . . .

CLERK: What do kings and princes have to do with the administration of our temporals? Let them have their own, and leave ours to us.

KNIGHT: It is our interest in every way. Is it not our interest to worry over the safety of our souls above all things? Is it not our interest to carry out the due rites for our dead fathers, and also to demand such rites? And were not your temporals given you by our fathers, and plentifully provided, for this purpose: that you might entirely expend them in divine worship? But certainly you do nothing with them but apply to your own needs all that with which you ought to fill the bellies of the poor through benefactions and works of charity. Is it not necessary that through holy works of this sort the dead may be freed and the living saved? When you spend these endowments as if they were your own and consume them extravagantly in defiance of the givers' intention and also, in a sense, waste them by misuse, do you not wrong the living and the dead, and damnably steal from them? Should not the wage be taken away from the soldier who refuses to earn it? . . .

Pierre Dubois

112. *De Recuperatione Terrae Sanctae* (1305-07) trans. W. I. Brandt (New York, 1956), pp. 167-79, 171-74.

When wars have been brought to an end by the means here suggested; when, in return for a guaranteed annual pension, the government, possession, and distractions of the pope's temporalities have been entrusted in perpetuity to the lord king of the French, to be governed by his brothers and sons as he shall see fit to provide, when the poisonous plots of the Romans and Lombards have ceased—then it is highly probable that the lord pope will be able to enjoy a long and healthful life in his native land, the kingdom of the French, with leisure to devote his sole attention to the governance of souls, and he may thereby avoid the inclement atmosphere of Rome, to which he has been unaccustomed from birth. This would be of inestimable and lasting benefit to all the friends, neighbors, and kindred of the lord pope, and especially to the whole kingdom of the French, since the ultramontane clergy would not have the income of fat benefices belonging to the cismontane churches— as they have had in the past—for building castles for themselves and their kin by defrauding the churches even at the expense of divine offices, nor would they control these fat benefices. The highest prelacy in the Church would no longer be withheld from the French, as has long been the custom because of the craft and natural cunning of the Romans. The latter, eager in their pride to trample on the humility of the French, have presumed to attempt what has elsewhere never been heard of, namely, to lay claim to temporal dominion over the kingdom of the French and its supreme prince, damnably inciting that kingdom of greatest peace and concord to perpetual sedition. The presumptuous beginning of this storm has happily been calmed, because the king of peace imparts the greatest harmony to his deputies.

If the lord pope should remain long in the kingdom of the French, he will probably create so many cardinals from that kingdom that the papacy will remain with us and escape altogether the grasping hands of the Romans. The reason for this will be so evident that for the future they will be careful to avoid snatching at others' rights lest a worse fate befall them. . . .

Lord Charles [of Valois], when the wars of Christians obedient to the lord pope have been brought to a close, can, by the grace of God, easily seize the empire of Constantinople. [Under the proposed arrangement] he would have warriors for this, which he probably would not have otherwise.

For all these matters to occur thus favorably is and will be of more interest to our lord high king of the French, his children, brothers, and his whole posterity, than can be written. If the above suggestions be successfully carried out, he will be able to ally all kings and princes obedient to the Roman Church with himself and his brother, who, in view of the opportunity to conquer the empire of the Greeks without disorder in the kingdom of the French, cannot fail to begin the war and prosecute it to the death.

It will be a source of much honor and profit to the lord king of the.

French if he can procure the kingdom and empire of Germany for his brother and nephews in perpetuity. It would be well to come to an agreement on this matter with the present king [of Germany] before he can hear of the new plan for peace. The lord king, as is said to have been agreed elsewhere, would then have for himself and his heirs the whole territory situated on this side of the Rhine at Cologne, or at all events the direct overlordship and control of the countries of Provence and Savoy, together with all the rights which an emperor would have in Lombardy and in the cities and territories of Genoa and Venice. In this way the lord king would have free access to Lombardy. This agreement ought to be made secretly between the king of the French and the king of Germany, with the pope's approval and confirmation, so that when it has been so agreed and confirmed, the empire will be confirmed to the king of Germany and his posterity. Gifts could be made to the electors, at least to the lay electors, to gain their consent, since it would be in many ways to their advantage that the customary wars of the Empire and its subjects cease.

Then if the pope, in return for a perpetual annual pension, would turn over to the lord king the whole patrimony of the Church and temporal jurisdiction over its vassals, among whom are many kings, it could be stipulated and agreed that the lord king would appoint as Roman senator one of his brothers or sons. This individual, in the absence of the king himself, would be the supreme judicial authority in the patrimony. Appeals from his decisions could be submitted to the lord pope, who, after reviewing the procedure in cases where he was authorized to interfere, might reverse, confirm, or otherwise modify them.

If the Lombards, Genoese, and Venetians should be unwilling to render obedience to the king and to pay him the tribute and dues formerly owed by them to the emperors, they would at once be shut off from intercourse with all Catholics obedient to the lord pope and who observed the new plan and statute of peace. Trade in all commodities would also be forbidden them. The lord king might freely enter Lombardy by way of Savoy; the senator, the emperor, and the king of Sicily would come from other directions. Thoroughly subdued, [the recalcitrants] would be sent into perpetual exile. Because of the new inviolable statute of peace [established by] the allies their wonted arrogance could not endure, but would necessarily fall, as well as that of the Romans, Tuscans, Campanians, Apulians, Calabrians, Sicilians, and all other kingdoms and provinces obedient to the pope.

By this means the kings of England, Aragon, and Majorca would be obedient to the lord king just as they now are required to obey the pope in temporal matters, and a compact could be made with the prospective king of Granada that he, too, should obey the lord king.

John of Paris

113. On property. *Tractatus de Potestate Regia et Papali* (1302-03), ed. J. Leclercq, *Jean de Paris et l'ecclésiologie du XIIIe siècle* (Paris, 1942), pp. 173-75, 188-89.

. . . As regards the power of ecclesiastical pontiffs, the truth occupies a middle ground between two errors. The error of the Waldensians was to deny to the successors of the apostles, that is the pope and the prelates of the church, any rightful lordship over temporal things and to maintain that it is illicit for them to have any temporal riches. Hence they say that the church of God and the successors of the apostles and true prelates of the church lasted only until the time of Sylvester and that, when the church received the emperor Constantine's donation, the Roman church had its beginning and, according to them, this is not at present the church of God. Rather, they say, the church of God has ceased to exist except in so far as it is continued or restored in themselves. . . . The other error is that of Herod who, when he heard that Christ was born, believed him to be an earthly king. From this seems to be derived the opinion of certain moderns who, in rejecting the first error, go so far in the opposite direction as to assert that the lord pope, since he stands in place of Christ, has dominion over the temporal goods of princes and barons and jurisdiction and cognizance concerning them. . . .

Between such contrary opinions, the first of which everyone regards as erroneous, I think that the truth establishes a middle ground, namely that it is not improper for the prelates of the church to have lordship and jurisdiction over temporalities, and this is against the first error; but that nevertheless this is not owed to them by reason of their status or in their capacity as vicars of Christ and successors of the apostles. Rather it can be fitting for them to have such things by concession or permission of princes if they have bestowed any such things out of devotion, or if the prelates have received them from another source.

. . . The lord pope as head and supreme member of the universal church is the general and universal administrator of all the goods of the churches both spiritual and temporal. He is not indeed the owner of them; rather the community of the universal church is the only lord and owner of all ecclesiastical goods in general and particular churches and congregations of the things pertaining to them. . . . And just as a monastery can act to depose an abbot or a particular church a bishop if it is clear that they have squandered the goods of the monastery or church and, betraying their trust, have used them for private ends instead of for the common good, so too it is clear that if a pope were to use the goods of the churches faithlessly and not for the common good, which he is bound to watch over as supreme bishop, he might be deposed provided that, after admonition, he would not mend his ways.

. . . From the foregoing material it is clear what relation the pope has to the goods of laymen, for still less is he the owner of lay property; rather, he is not even an administrator of such goods except in some ultimate necessity of the church, and even then he is not an administrator but a declarer of right. To prove this it should be considered that the external goods of laymen are not conferred on the community like ecclesiastical goods but are acquired by individual persons through their own skill, labor and industry; and individual persons, as individuals, have right and power over them and true lordship, and each one can order, dispose, administer, retain or alienate his own property at will without injuring anyone else, since he is the owner. . . . And therefore neither prince nor pope has lordship or rights of administration over such goods. But because it sometimes happens that the common peace is disturbed on account of such external possessions when someone seizes what belongs to another, or sometimes when men love their own possessions too much and will not contribute in proportion as the necessity and utility of their fatherland require, a prince is established by the people to preside as judge in such cases and to determine what is just and unjust. . . .

114. On the origin and nature of government in church and state. *Ibid.* (1302-03), pp. 176-78, 199, 236.

First it should be known that kingship, properly understood, can be defined as the rule of one man over a perfect multitude so ordered as to promote the public good. . . . Such a government is based on natural law and the law of nations. For, since man is naturally a civil or political creature as is said in Book I of the *Politics*—and the Philosopher proves this from food, clothing and defense in which a solitary man is not self-sufficient as also from speech which is addressed to another, these things being necessary only for men—it is essential for a man to live in a multitude and in such a multitude as is self-sufficient for life. The community of a household or village is not of this sort, but the community of a city or kingdom is, for in a household or village there is not found everything necessary for food, clothing and defense through a whole life as there is in a city or kingdom. But every multitude scatters and disintegrates as each man pursues his own ends unless it is ordered to the common good by some one man who has charge of this common good. . . .

Next it must be borne in mind that man is not ordered only to such a good as can be acquired by nature, which is to live virtuously, but is further ordered to a supernatural end which is eternal life, and the whole multitude of men living virtuously is ordered to this. Therefore it is necessary that there be some one man to direct the multitude to this end. If indeed this end could be attained by the power of human nature, it would necessarily pertain to the office of the human king to direct men to this end, for we call a human king him to whom is committed the highest duty of government in human affairs. But since man does not come to eternal life by human power but by divine . . . this kind of rule pertains to a king who is not only man but also God, namely Jesus Christ . . . and because Christ was to withdraw his corporal presence from the church it was necessary for him to institute others as ministers who would administer the sacraments to men, and these are called priests. . . . Hence priesthood may be defined in this fashion. Priesthood is a spiritual power of administering sacraments to the faithful conferred by Christ on ministers of the church.

The royal power both existed and was exercised before the papal, and there were kings in France before there were Christians. Therefore neither the royal power nor its exercise is from the pope but from God and from the people who elect a king by choosing either a person or a royal house. . . . It would seem that the power of inferior pontiffs and ministers is derived from the pope more than the royal power, for ecclesiastical prelates are more immediately dependent on the pope than secular princes. But the power of prelates is not from God through the pope but immediately from God and from the people who elect or consent.

. . . Although a form of government in which one man simply rules according to virtue is better than any other simple government, as the Philosopher proves in Book III of the *Politics,* nevertheless if it is mixed with aristocracy and democracy it is better than a simple form in that, in a mixed constitution, all have some part in the government. Through this the peace of the people is maintained and all of them love such a government and preserve it.

> 115. On the relationship of spiritual to secular power. *Ibid.*
> (1302-03), pp. 183-84, 214, 225.

From the foregoing material it is easy to see which is first in dignity, the kingship or the priesthood. . . . A kingdom is ordered to this end, that an assembled multitude may live virtuously, as has been said, and it is further ordered to a higher end which is the enjoyment of God; and responsibility for this end belongs to Christ, whose ministers and vicars are the priests. Therefore the priestly power is of greater dignity than the secular and this is commonly conceded. See *Dist.* 96 c.10, "As gold is more precious than lead so the priestly order is higher than the royal power." And in the *Decretales* 1.33.6 it is said that as the sun excels the moon so spiritualities excel temporalities. And Hugh of St. Victor in his *De Sacramentis*, Book II, Part II, c.4 declares, "In proportion as the spiritual life is of greater dignity than the earthly and the spirit than the body, so the spiritual power excels the secular or earthly power in honor and dignity." And likewise Bernard to Pope Eugenius, Book I, "Which seems to you the greater dignity, the power of forgiving sins or of dividing estates? But there is no comparison." It is as if he would say, "The spiritual power is greater; therefore it excels in dignity."

But if the priest is greater in himself than the prince and is greater in dignity, it does not follow that he is greater in all respects. For the lesser secular power is not related to the greater spiritual power as having its origin from it or being derived from it as the power of a proconsul is related to that of the emperor, which is greater in all respects since the power of the former is derived from the latter. The relationship is rather like that of a head of a household to a general of armies, since one is not derived from the other but both from a superior power. And so the secular power is greater than the spiritual in some things, namely in temporal affairs, and in such affairs it is not subject to the spiritual power in any way because it does not have its origin from it but rather both have their origin immediately from the one supreme power, namely the divine. Accordingly the inferior power is not subject to the superior in all things but only in those where the supreme power has subordinated it to the greater. A teacher of literature or an instructor in morals directs the members of a household to a nobler end, namely the knowledge of truth, than a doctor who is concerned with a lower end, namely the health of bodies, but who would say therefore the doctor should be subjected to the teacher in preparing his medicines? For this is not fitting, since the head of the household who established both in his house did not subordinate the lesser to the greater in this respect. Therefore the priest is greater than the prince in spiritual affairs and, on the other hand, the prince is greater in temporal affairs. . . .

Concerning the ecclesiastical power of censure or correction it should be known that, directly, it is only spiritual, for it can impose no penalty in the external court but a spiritual one, except conditionally and incidentally. For though the ecclesiastical judge has to lead men back to God and draw them away from sin and correct them, he has to do this only in the way laid down for him by God, which is to say by cutting them off from the sacraments and from the company of the faithful and by similar measures which are proper to ecclesiastical censure. I said "conditionally" in reference to one who is willing to repent and accept a pecuniary penalty, for the ecclesiastical judge cannot impose any corporal or pecuniary penalty for a crime as a secular judge can, except only on one who is willing to accept it. . . . I said "incidentally" because if a prince was a heretic and incorrigible and contemptuous of ecclesiastical censures, the pope might so move the people that he would be deprived of his secular dignity and deposed by the people. The pope might do this in the case of an ecclesiastical crime, of which cognizance belonged to him, by excommunicating all who obeyed such a man as a lord, and thus the people would depose him, and the pope "incidentally." So too, if the pope on the other hand behaved criminally and brought scandal on the church and was incorrigible, the prince might indirectly excommunicate him and "incidentally" bring about his deposition by warning him personally or through the cardinals. And if the pope were unwilling to yield the emperor might so move the people as to compel him to resign or be deposed by the people, for the emperor could, by taking securities or imposing corporal penalties, prevent each and everyone from obeying him or serving him as pope. So each can act toward the other, for both pope and emperor have jurisdiction universally and everywhere, but the one has spiritual jurisdiction, the other temporal.

As for the argument that corporeal beings are ruled by spiritual beings and depend on them as on a cause, I answer that an argument so constructed fails on many grounds. Firstly because it assumes that royal power is corporeal and not spiritual and that it has charge of bodies and not of souls which is false, as is said above, since it is ordained, not for any common good of the citizens whatsoever, but for that which consists in living according to virtue. Accordingly the Philosopher says in the *Ethics* that the intention of a legislator is to make men good and to lead them to virtue, and in the *Politics* that a legislator is more estimable than a doctor since the legislator has charge of souls, the doctor of bodies.

MEDIEVAL ACADEMY REPRINTS FOR TEACHING